Digging Up the Dead

# DIGGING
## UP THE
# DEAD

### A HISTORY *of*
### NOTABLE AMERICAN
### REBURIALS

✠

## MICHAEL KAMMEN

University of Chicago Press | Chicago and London

The University of Chicago Press, Chicago 60637
The University of Chicago Press, Ltd., London
© 2010 by Michael Kammen
All rights reserved. Published 2010
Paperback edition 2011
Printed in the United States of America

20  19  18  17  16  15  14  13  12  11      2  3  4  5  6

ISBN-13: 978-0-226-42329-6 (cloth)
ISBN-13: 978-0-226-42330-2 (paper)
ISBN-10: 0-226-42329-8 (cloth)
ISBN-10: 0-226-42330-1 (paper)

Library of Congress Cataloging-in-Publication Data

Kammen, Michael G.
  Digging up the dead : a history of notable American
reburials / Michael Kammen.
      p. cm.
  Includes bibliographical references and index.
  ISBN-13: 978-0-226-42329-6 (cloth : alk. paper)
  ISBN-10: 0-226-42329-8 (cloth : alk. paper)
  1. Exhumation—United States—History.
2. Exhumation—Political aspects—United States.
3. Burial—United States—History. 4. Funeral rites and
ceremonies—United States—History.  I. Title.
GT3203.K365 2009
393'.10973—dc22
                    2009023515

For Carol
*with enduring love*
*because her dedications*
*are the ones that have really mattered*

Good friend for Jesus sake forebeare
To dig the dust enclosed heare;
Blest be the man that spares these stones
And curst be he that moves my bones

✠

Shakespeare's gravestone


At one point we got on the theme of immortality,
in which she believed without being sure
of its precise form. "There is no death," she said.
"No, my dear lady, but there are funerals."

✠

Peter de Vries, *Comfort Me with Apples* (1956)

# CONTENTS

For quite some time now, anthropologists and archaeologists have examined mortuary practices as an intriguing aspect of their professional inquiries. Historians have begun to do so more recently, most notably American Civil War specialists and a smaller but intensely engaged cluster of scholars who write about Eastern Europe after the collapse of Communism in 1989. What follows here is largely an inquiry into conflicted moments of historical aberration or rehabilitation in mortuary practice—the exhumation and reinterment of significant individuals, for a broad array of reasons. I have tried to trace patterns and make sense of what happens when someone, more often a family or an entire constellation of devoted followers, feels dissatisfied with where and how a person deemed worthy of note has been buried. In 1983 a U.S. congressman remarked at a hearing before the Subcommittee on Cemeteries and Burial Benefits that "the quality of a civilization is revealed in the way it reveres its dead." If that is valid, though perhaps not standing alone as the sole criterion of civilized life, how did it happen that many distinguished Americans have been buried but soon forgotten, or else it was belatedly noticed that their graves are sadly neglected? That is one key *problématique* of this inquiry.

Another complication contributing to the problem—rather a major issue as it turns out—is that during the colonial period and well into the nineteenth century, there were customarily few special markers or monuments to commemorate the careers and exact locations of figures as eminent as Roger Williams and the Revolutionary firebrand Sam Adams. As late as 1849 a poet and story writer as prominent as Edgar Allan Poe was initially buried in an unmarked grave. Is it any wonder that admirers of such individuals would eventually feel obliged to remedy these shameful situations?

Therefore I shall attempt to discern what those responsible for reburials believed they were achieving. Were they always and unambiguously seeking to do justice to the dearly departed? Were their dutiful deeds more beneficial to themselves than to the deceased? Did they recognize or acknowledge a difference between the two motives—or perhaps see any symbiotic relationship between them? To what extent was exhumation and reinterment an act of devotional fantasy, sometimes even a delusion? One criterion of postmodernism involves accepting what is called the "constructedness" of the past. Are reburials quite literally about the physical *re*constructedness of the past—a form of historical revisionism, setting the record straight in some sense? How often do aspects of American history and biography come to be understood differently by contemporaries because of a reburial? The answer to that is, quite often.

And then we have whole communities competing for the honor of burying or reburying a personage whose presence would lend luster to their new or improved cemetery. When exhumation did occur followed by reburial at a different venue, there was often anxiety over the nagging question "Did we get the *right* remains?" That was true of Daniel Boone in 1845, of Charles Thomson (secretary to the Continental Congress) in 1838, and of numerous Europeans as well, such as the German poet and philosopher Johann Friedrich von Schiller, who was disinterred several times during the nineteenth and twentieth centuries. Sometimes a coffin was opened just to satisfy curious or anxious survivors that it was actually occupied, as happened more than once with Abraham Lincoln. In 1886 Henry Adams wrote to John Hay, Lincoln's onetime secretary, expressing his personal "historical indifference to everything but facts, and my delight at studying what is hopefully debased and degraded," even shocking in terms of moral content and sense. He had the strange saga of President Lincoln's several reburials very much in mind.

The reader will encounter much that is bizarre, indeed shocking, in the pages that follow. To cite only one example: when Dr. Joseph Warren was killed at the Battle of Bunker Hill in June 1775 and became the first martyr of the Patriot cause in the American Revolution, British officers contemplated cutting off his head and mutilating the body of such a "traitor to the Crown." As Jean-Pierre Vernant has observed, the mutilation of an enemy's corpse is the inverse of the "beautiful death" so prized and lauded by the ancient Greeks. He was invoking the disfigurement of Hector's body at the hands of Achilles, an act that could rob the dead hero of his individuality and make proper memorialization all but impossible. Discussions of the "beautiful death" became commonplace during the American Civil War, when so many young men left their families behind with considerable uncertainty whether they would return intact, or even alive.

When Northerners and Southerners both wanted possession of the same famous figure, it is noteworthy that the South normally prevailed. Although the intensity of feeling about such matters cannot be measured in anything like precise terms, I have a sense that "ownership" of renowned men—like President James Monroe—mattered somewhat more in the South. Not always, to be sure, but often. The Lost Cause syndrome is only partially responsible. This pattern appears in conflicts over the most appropriate venue for Revolutionary War generals of northern provenance who either died in the South or else fought their most famous battle there, like General Nathanael Greene. Nostalgia appears to be a somewhat more distinctive quality in southern culture. Perhaps that comes as no surprise.

✣

I am deeply indebted to an array of friends and colleagues who provided counsel and suggestions and read all or part of the work-in-progress. I thank especially Paul S. Boyer, Holly A. Case, James A. Hijiya, Isabel Hull, Walter LaFeber, David W. Maxey, Robert R. Morgan, and Richard Polenberg. Although I have never met Robert E. Cray Jr., I owe him particular appreciation for his exhaustively researched essays on several important episodes from the period of the early American republic.

Several staff members of the Cornell University Library system have once again provided indispensable assistance, especially Gabriela Castro Gessner and the ever-patient and resourceful Susette Newberry. At the University of Chicago Press I owe a very special debt to history editor Robert P. Devens, editorial associate Anne Summers Goldberg, and my meticulous manuscript editor, Ruth Goring. Their help with this project has extended above and beyond the call of duty. Most of all, Carol Kammen has not only read every word, as always, but listened patiently to an excessive number of lugubrious tales. I am deeply grateful to everyone cited above but hold none responsible for information insufficiently dug up or inadequate insights.

*MK, April 2009*

# *Introduction*

In pride, in reas'ning pride, our error lies,
All quit their sphere, and rush into the skies!
Pride still is aiming at the blessed abodes,
Men would be Angels, Angels would be Gods.

✠ Alexander Pope, *An Essay on Man*, epistle 1

*J*efferson Davis, president of the Confederate States of America from February 1861 until its collapse in April 1865, died in New Orleans on December 6, 1889, at the age of eighty-one. Five days later, following a frenzy of local and regional arrangements, Confederate veterans and many others packed an immense procession that accompanied the body to Metairie Cemetery for what turned out to be temporary burial in a vault guarded round the clock, awaiting a decision about the erstwhile CSA president's permanent interment (fig. 1). Bells tolled from every church tower in New Orleans to accompany the long and solemn parade to Metairie. The issue of his final resting place, however, had actually begun on the very day that Davis died and swiftly became what we now call a "hot button issue." Although his reputation revived during the 1880s, he had been reviled by white Southerners after the Confederacy fell and he fled from Richmond only to be apprehended by Federal troops in Georgia. During his lingering last illness he wisely said to his wife, Varina, "You must take the responsibility of deciding this question, I cannot—I foresee [that] a great deal of feeling about it will arise when I am dead."[1]

Davis understood the delicate situation all too well. Southern press coverage of his death signaled swelling admiration and pride in the former leader—utterly inconceivable less than a generation earlier, at the time of unbearable defeat. Six Southern cities each hoped to "host" the body into eternity, above all Montgomery, Alabama, where Davis had reluctantly assumed the presidency, and they all intensively lobbied the quickly created Jefferson Davis Memorial Association (JDMA). The decision belonged entirely to Varina and her children, however, and they waited more than eighteen months before choosing a prime site at Hollywood Cemetery in Richmond, capital of the Confederacy, where the Davises had lived for four years and where a great many honored Southern dead already lay buried. The civic leaders of New Orleans, feeling bitter disappointment at surrendering a prized symbol of states' rights and resistance to Northern aggression, decided to build a monu-

*Figure 1.* Jefferson Davis's funeral procession by horse-drawn wagon in New Orleans, December 6, 1889. Division of Prints and Photographs, Library of Congress.

mental memorial to Davis that would equal in scale the ones already erected to Abraham Lincoln in Springfield (see fig. 18, p. 96) and just recently conceived for Ulysses S. Grant in New York City. Their ambition, however, wildly exceeded their collective or potential purse.[2]

Necessary fund-raising and the complexity of related preparations meant that the Richmond reburial would finally be scheduled for May 31, 1893. On May 27 Davis's coffin was removed from the Metairie vault and opened to make certain that the JDMA really had the right body, which then was placed in a brand-new hand-carved coffin and loaded onto a specially designed railroad car with oversized glass windows. A mournfully decorated locomotive hauled the ensemble of passenger cars. Each step in this meticulously planned event was taken, as the press reported, with "every possible mark of *respect.*" That word will recur in many episodes in the chapters that follow. Relocation and reburial (or "translation" of a body, to use the traditional, Latin-derived word) are invariably all about the resurgence of the reputation of and hence respect for someone whose lamp and visage had dimmed in some way.[3]

As the leading authority on Davis's demise has observed, "Southerners grew increasingly anxious as the departure date neared for what was expected to be one of the most elaborate and ceremonious funeral processions in American history." Intensifying the precedent and coverage of Davis's death in December 1889, newspapers across the South and quite a few in the North reported every step in lavish detail. Many sent their top reporters to accompany the special train on its mournful but politicized mission to the Old Dominion's distinctively honorific grave.[4]

The train coursed along at a top speed of sixty-two miles per hour, slipping smoothly across and then sloping eastward down the Piedmont like a child's coiled Slinky, pausing at major state capitals so that the coffin could be viewed for a few hours by dignitaries and large throngs of worshipful citizens. In Atlanta, the delegations from Texas, Louisiana, and Mississippi failed to adjust from Central Time, which had only recently been regularized, so thirty members of the honor entourage accompanying the cortège were unhappily left behind when the train departed at 8:00 p.m. Eastern Time. The embarrassed laggards caught up in Greensboro, North Carolina, on a regular train. Even though Southern pride was displayed with Confederate flags through-out the journey, talk of the bygone secession was already giving way to sentiments favoring national reconciliation. Although that seems to have been most true in progressive Atlanta, capital of the New South, it was manifest elsewhere as well. As early as 1886 one former Southern general had referred to the "circle of a new nationality." Others soon echoed that refrain.[5]

Massive crowds in Richmond attended services followed by the huge procession to Hollywood Cemetery for final interment; there a specially brick-lined, extra-deep grave waited on a spacious hillside, a site of unusual beauty overlooking the James River (fig. 2). Jefferson Davis rolled to his ultimate resting place on a bed of roses: en route to the cemetery the caisson carrying the coffin rumbled over a continu-ous carpet of flowers, strewn by young women and girls in white who preceded the line of march. Mourners insisted upon their loyalty to the Union—their support for reconciliation and American nationalism—even as they displayed the Stars and Bars alongside Old Glory. Yet in this instance state pride seems to have been an even stronger emotion than sectional pride, because certain rebel states still rankled with re-sentment that they had not been chosen for the final entombment—despite elaborate offers and schemes to build a very special monument in Davis's honor at local expense.[6]

The JDMA recognized that a major monument, inevitably to be erected in Richmond, should be a gift from all of the former Confeder-ate states rather than a local memorial from Virginia and for Richmond. The committee hoped to raise a million dollars so that the monument "should be a grand thing indeed," with a "shaft so high that the birds could not fly over it." It might even dwarf the Washington Monument. Despite earnest desires to undertake "the patriotic and pious work" of building an "everlasting memorial," reality and inertia set in soon after the funeral.[7] The ambitious goal of erecting a temple in Davis's honor soon faded. Finally, on June 3, 1907, the Jefferson Davis Monument would be dedicated: an eight-foot bronze statue standing on a five-foot pedestal with a sixty-foot column adjacent. Its installation did not gen-erate a great deal of apparent interest.[8]

Davis's moment of glory, verging upon sanctification, had peaked between the time of his Southern farewell tour in 1886 and his Rich-

*Figure 2.* The tomb of Jefferson Davis, Hollywood Cemetery, Richmond, Virginia (c. 1905). Division of Prints and Photographs, Library of Congress.

mond reinterment seven years later. With that the South seems to have spent its capacity for intense retrospection about the failed leader. The Lost Cause may very well have lived on, but its former president very gradually receded from view. A lingering apotheosis of sorts occurred in 1916, when Gutzon Borglum began carving Davis's visage on Stone Mountain, not far from Atlanta, alongside those of Robert E. Lee and Thomas "Stonewall" Jackson. After that, however, while Lee and Jackson remained as iconic immortals, Davis's profile began to dim, becoming spectral in public memory.[9]

✝

Historically considered, reburial has come to mean a figurative form of resurrection—primarily the resurrection of reputation, at least for a while. It has also meant, with the passage of time, renewed honor and frequently some form of reconciliation, or at least movement in the direction of reconciliation—familial, sectional, and above all national. That will be true of many of the episodes to be considered in the six segments of this book. While there have been some significant differences in the particular dynamics of individual situations, there have also been numerous similarities between "translations" and reinterments in America and elsewhere. The complexity of repatriation, a revived reverence for reputation, and the resolution of differences are constant themes that supply this book with much of its focus, which I call the cultural politics of exhumation.

This project is primarily about *pride*, as the opening epigraph from Alexander Pope is meant to suggest—different levels and layers of pride. National pride, for example, in the case of John Paul Jones's reburial at the Naval Academy in 1905–6. Sectional pride when we witness the instances of President James Monroe and the fiery abolitionist John Brown. State pride in battles over the decomposed bones of Revolutionary War General Nathanael Greene (Georgia versus Rhode Island) and the renowned scout Daniel Boone (Kentucky versus Missouri).

Regional pride is at stake in the burials of Revolutionary rifleman Daniel Morgan and bank robber Jesse James; local pride with the likes of Edgar Allan Poe (Baltimore, where he lived and died, versus Philadelphia, where he wrote his most famous works) and Frank Lloyd Wright (Taliesin East versus Taliesin West as burial sites); and family pride coupled with patriotic pride in the Revolutionary War cases of Dr. Joseph Warren and General Richard Montgomery (both killed in battle in 1775) and the much later contretemps involving F. Scott Fitzgerald and the Catholic Church. Finally, we also encounter ethnic and racial pride in the exhumation stories of Sioux Chief Sitting Bull and later Matthew Henson, an African American who assisted Admiral Richard Peary in first setting foot on the North Pole in 1909.

When groups of people, cities, privately owned cemeteries, or states contested where the remains of a celebrity should most properly repose, *pride of place* was often at stake. And when small bands of men came in the middle of the night to covertly dig up a body and steal it away, *pride of possession* became the prize. Matters of pride often caused but also resulted from intense rivalries—between regions, states, and families. Then add the commercial competition of newly established cemeteries seeking to become tourist attractions as well as profitable investments. People must buy burial plots, and often they like to be interred where celebrities have already been situated. I have in mind such sites as Mount Auburn Cemetery in Cambridge, Massachusetts, Green-Wood Cemetery in Brooklyn, and Laurel Hill in Philadelphia, a new cemetery in 1840 that crassly vied for the skeletons of not one but two Revolutionary leaders who had earlier been buried privately in family plots.

Readers should not be surprised to encounter a particularly lugubrious manifestation of pride that recurs with notable frequency in these pages: people handling or even taking personal possession of skulls belonging to figures they greatly admired, even revered in some instances. The historical origins of this practice can be traced back to medieval and early modern times, when the skull served as a reminder of life's earthly transience. Skulls also had religious significance, of course, because the contemplation of death as a spiritual exercise was recommended by the Jesuits and would be enhanced by the use of a skull, especially apparent to us in iconographic symbolism that survives. Paintings often depicted saints at prayer with a skull nearby. One thinks of Francis of Assisi, hermit saints (most notably Jerome), and Mary Magdalene as a penitent. Skulls were also used in a more secular context to symbolize Melancholy, one of the four temperaments.

In our nineteenth-century American episodes, however, religious or even spiritual reasons for contemplating skulls seem less significant or meaningful than physically holding the skull of a famous individual as the ultimate act of possessive connectedness to the deceased—most certainly an expression of secular admiration and pride, as we shall see with figures as different as Daniel Boone and Edgar Allan Poe. The latter-day disciple could boast, "I once held in my hands the very skull of . . ." (though the honor was not always voiced in quite those words). In the case of evangelist George Whitefield, however, actually displaying a skull at the vault of his tomb (see fig. 36 on p. 171) does hark back to premodern sentiments about holy relics, whereas holding up a skull for a kind of photo op in 1904, as with James Smithson (see fig. 23 on p. 111), had more to do with declaring that "we've really found our man and here's proof positive." The skull resists decay longer than any other part of the body. Quite often it was the sole surviving puzzle piece still intact and deemed recognizable—sometimes because of teeth or, as with the skull of Jesse James, a bullet hole.

One might very well say that this project is written in a major key—call it Pride, public and collective—yet the work intermittently modulates to a minor key, the somewhat secularized version of veneration for sacred relics among the Christian societies of medieval Europe and early modern times. For illustrative episodes of the latter, we will consider the burial and subsequently the ritualized uses of evangelist Whitefield in the Congregational Church of Newburyport, Massachusetts (formerly Presbyterian); of John Paul Jones in a new and elaborately decorated chapel at the Naval Academy in Annapolis; and of Augustus Lord Howe in several rebuilt incarnations of St. Peter's Church in Albany. If the body of a venerated person can serve in some sense to consecrate a secular site, an already consecrated site can effectively elevate the status of a civil figure's mortal remains.

The narratives here differ in time, by place, and by circumstance. The preponderant majority, however, are American, and they manifest certain clear patterns, never identical, because (as it is said) history does not repeat itself even though historians often do. Although I will touch upon different cultures, different eras, even different countries, most of the episodes that I explore clearly involve the desire to enhance respect for someone deceased, the variability of reputations, and the complexity of restitution or repatriation. Intensely felt sentiments of pride emerge on multiple levels. And they reveal that the symbolic significance of possessing "sacred relics," even in secular settings, has incalculable potency—yet often provides pleasure as well.

The compelling need to do the right thing with dead bodies has proved to be more than merely symbolic, though that significance has been notably present on many occasions as well. Moving the remains of deceased figures has mattered in social, cultural, and political ways—often in varied combinations. Moreover, we are contemplating a phenomenon at least as old as recorded history in the Western world. Two examples from antiquity should suffice. They provide precedents, of a sort, but also suggest contrasts with our modern narratives.

Herodotus tells us that after countless defeats by the Tegeans during the reign of Croesus, the Lacedaemonians consulted the oracle at Delphi, who advised that in order to prevail they must relocate the bones of Orestes, the son of Agamemnon. With a mix of luck and savvy they found a ten-foot coffin, "opened the grave, and collecting the bones, returned with them to Sparta. From henceforth, whenever the Spartans and the Tegeans made trial of each other's skill in arms, the Spartans always had greatly the advantage; and by the time to which we are come now they were masters of most of the Peloponnese."[10]

A second illustration, also situated in classical Greece, comes to us from Plutarch and bears a striking resemblance to the narrative of Orestes' efficacious exhumation. Early in the fifth century, when Cimon led Athenian forces against Persia, he successfully conquered the strategic island of Scyros. He then learned that

> the Athenians had once been given an oracle commanding them to bring back the bones of Theseus to Athens and pay them the honours due to a hero; but they did not know where he was buried, since the people of Scyros would neither admit that the story was true nor allow any search to be made. Cimon, however, attacked the task with great enthusiasm and after some difficulty discovered the sacred spot. He had the bones placed on board his trireme and brought them back with great pomp and ceremony to the hero's native land, almost four hundred years after he had left it. This affair did more than any other achievement of Cimon's to endear him to the people.[11]

Although the consultation of oracles had long since ceased to be normative in nineteenth-century America, despite a certain predilection for séances in some Victorian circles, necromancy or supernatural guidance would have come very handy when the grave sites of venerated heroes were unknown or uncertain, as I shall note. Evident among these stories is a vocation that is more valuable than an oracle or a spiritualist in calling attention to neglected burial sites. As it happened, journalists took the initiative in launching the quests to move John Paul Jones and D. H. Lawrence from France to rebury them in America, more than a generation apart. Church sextons have also played particularly useful roles.

Although quite a few of our incidents are more instructive or amusing than tragic, and reveal far more about human nature than they do about *nature morte*, one rather likely musical accompaniment might be Chopin's Piano Sonata No. 2 in B-flat Minor with its *marche funèbre*. Processions and audiences have heard it played time and time again during reinterments. At the end, however, when we come to comparisons between the United States and other cultures, we might very well bear in mind that the expression "whistling past the graveyard" is an idiomatic American usage meaning the effort to remain cheerful in a dire situation. I cannot claim that Americans whistled more than Europeans when they reburied people, but I do submit that a great many of the occasions we will visit were more celebratory than sad.

— ONE —

# *A Short History of Reburial*

## PATTERNS OF
## CHANGE
## OVER TIME

Let's talk of graves, of worms and epitaphs.

✠ King Richard II in Shakespeare,
*The Tragedy of King Richard the Second*, 3.2.145

*D*uring the 1780s, the very decade when the new American nation had its genesis, a highly unusual tomb was being planned to rebury the French philosopher and social critic Jean-Jacques Rousseau (1712–78) on an island in a small lake at Ermenonville, near Senlis. Designed and completed between 1780 and 1788, it aroused considerable interest because it indicated a radically new view of mortality—or more precisely, the circumstances surrounding what happens after death and the appropriate response for survivors. The cypress, a tree traditionally associated with mourning, disappeared, supplanted by a grove of poplars. Rousseau's tomb would be a *garden* rather than being situated in a formally bounded urban or ecclesiastical burial ground. As historian George Mosse has written, "Here men and women could contemplate nature and virtue in an atmosphere of sentimentality but not pathos. The tranquility and happiness of the living were to be retained even in death."[1]

The emerging Enlightenment view of death as tranquil sleep, a condition of repose, gradually began to replace the long-standing grim notion of dying as not merely inevitable but very likely harsh or cruel, resulting from war or disease, for example. Thomas Hobbes's seventeenth-century notion of life as nasty, brutish, and short eventually gave way to perceptions that anticipate or more nearly approximate our own. During the Jacobin phase of the French Revolution, death even underwent democratization: it was decided that all citizens, irrespective of social rank or wealth, should be buried modestly, reflected in the basic similarity of new tombs. In such practices we can perceive the origins of military cemeteries ever since the nineteenth century: row upon parallel row of identical graves. Thereafter, the state took upon itself the responsibility to regulate burials, as it has ever since in European nation-states.[2]

It is not sufficiently understood, however, that during the seventeenth and eighteenth centuries only an estimated 5–7 percent of the dead escaped the fate of a common trench. Dreading exactly that, Madame Pompadour, the influential mistress of King Louis XV, stipulated in her will that she be buried in a lead coffin near the central cross of her favorite churchyard. But even she was exhumed, reburied, and dug up once again later, and her remains were ultimately lost. As we shall see, such mishaps were not at all unusual. Yet another basic aspect of early modern interment that is significant but too little appreciated: the normative absence of individualized markers. Nonconformists in Great Britain were given a burial ground in London during the 1660s, very close to the house that became John Wesley's. The apocalyptic artist William Blake was buried there in 1827, but his precise location went unmarked and hence forgotten.

In the United States a movement developed in the 1840s to honor Boston's Revolutionary leader Sam Adams with a heroic monument, but no one knew quite where his bones reposed in the Old Granary Burying Ground.[3] That brings us to what might seem at first glance an observable discrepancy. Anyone who has walked the Freedom Trail in Boston will have noticed interesting gravestones in the King's Chapel Burying Ground or in Copp's Hill Burying Ground, where members of the Mather family were buried. Several splendidly illustrated books have been compiled about unusual and attractive individualized gravestones dating from the colonial period, especially in New England.[4] But these actually represent a rather small minority of the burials in seventeenth- and eighteenth-century America. Most early settlers were placed in unmarked graves, often hastily and under difficult circumstances. Wooden grave rails consisting of one or two horizontal markers between vertical posts were more common than tombstones, and they disintegrated fairly quickly with the passage of time.[5]

We should also bear in mind the complex legacy of Calvinism, especially in New England. John Calvin himself had unsuccessfully insisted that his own grave *not* be marked so that followers would not treat his remains as relics, a practice that seemed all too redolent of superstitious Catholicism. Some Calvinists even wanted the customary funeral liturgy abolished. Religious dissenters from the Church of England in the colonies decided to secularize burials by refusing to consecrate burial grounds as sacred space. The imperative not to do so by Calvinists in Old England and New meant that commemoration of individual lives and mundane worldly accomplishments had scant place in New England graveyards. Hence the astonishing (to us) paucity of particularized place markers at discrete burial sites.

For an illustration of this practice carried to an unusual extreme in early America, consider the case of Baron Von Steuben, the successful drillmaster and tactician of George Washington's army who retired to upstate New York, where he speculated in undeveloped real estate like several other Revolutionary War generals to be encountered in the next chapter. When he died suddenly in 1794, it was found that his will specified that he be wrapped in his military cloak and buried in a plain coffin in a "retired spot" on his estate. He had instructed two devoted aides that "they never acquaint any person with the place wherein I shall be buried." He had often insisted that he wanted no stone to mark his heavily wooded grave, perhaps near a beloved hemlock tree.[6]

Several decades later, however, commissioners of a nearby town, close to Oneida, decided to create a wagon road whose line ran directly across the grave and actually disturbed the coffin. One former Von Steuben aide, still living, removed the body farther into the woods and gave fifty acres to a Baptist society under a covenant with the provision that five acres should be fenced in and forever remain uncleared. Disregarding Von Steuben's wishes about the absence of a marker, however, in 1824 he placed a modest monument above the grave. When it began to crumble, local and New York German-Americans erected a new and grander one in 1872. The site has since become part of a New York state park dedicated to the general's memory.[7]

A widespread desire to ensure the perpetuity of graves dates only from the 1790s and early 1800s, and then the pattern spread rather slowly. The related practice of visiting graves to pay respects on the anniversary of death or some other occasion (to tidy up the site and leave flowers) also emerged gradually and became customary only as late as the 1840s. That explains a problematic issue that we shall encounter with some frequency when exhumation and reburial were desired: grave sites of prominent individuals that had become shamefully overgrown, neglected, unkempt, and difficult to locate with certainty.[8]

The changing nature of American Protestantism provides us with *some* help in understanding what might appear to be a kind of disconnect in many of the nineteenth-century episodes that will be found in the chapters that follow. Most of the reinterments seem to have been, fundamentally, *secular* commemorative events. Except for an obligatory invocation, a hymn or an anthem, and closing prayers or a benediction by clergy, I find little trace of the traditional religious views so firmly held by most Americans during the first two-thirds of the nineteenth century—visionary and optimistic notions about God's judgment and humankind's ultimate fate. There was little effort to literally sacralize these reburials, even though the phrase "sacred relics" was commonly voiced. The remains of deceased heroes were more like trophies to be secured—honored, to be sure, but not with the rituals and spiritual discourse seemingly appropriate for the Christian expectation of bodily resurrection on Judgment Day.

From recent scholarship we know a good deal about the eschatology of Americans before the Civil War; and those beliefs persisted even as they clearly evolved during the later nineteenth century, especially because biblical criticism and later Darwinism gradually made literalism and naive optimism less pervasively accepted. Nevertheless, notions of heaven and hell did not simply disappear, and many assumptions characteristic of evangelical Protestantism lingered on, albeit somewhat diluted, despite doubts during the so-called late Victorian crisis of faith.

Antebellum Americans shared a very comforting vision of eternal life, especially once orthodox Calvinism became democratized during and after the 1820s. Democratization diminished the notion of selective predestination and meant that anyone could become one of God's elect by accepting Jesus Christ as personal savior. Heaven was not envisioned as some ethereal entity or state of the soul. Rather, as recent studies have shown, heaven was a very material place, hovering just above the cloud cover, in which individual bodies and souls would be joined and perfected. In 1857 Sarah Gould compiled numerous writings about heaven in a book titled *The Guardian Angels, or Friends in Heaven*, published in Boston. "We believe Paradise to be our fatherland; our parents and patriarchs; why should we not [make] haste and fly to see our home and greet our parents?" she asked. Heaven was regarded as a real place of immense beauty, and the very point of living was to achieve heaven. As one minister proclaimed: "No night in heaven! Then no sad partings are experienced there;—no funeral processions move, no death-knell is heard, *no graves are opened.*"[9]

Countless sermons and tracts reveal the expectation that resurrected persons would exist not merely in spirit but in full possession of whole, perfected bodies. And because identifiable bodies would be preserved, the notion of "heavenly recognition" seemed virtually self-evident to those who subscribed to this notion of life beyond death. Families would be reunited, perhaps even entire communities. More often than not, the authors of these tracts held strongly materialistic ideas about bodily resurrection.[10]

True enough, in thinking about it they could not ignore the biblical pronouncement that "flesh and blood cannot inherit the kingdom of heaven, nor does the perishable inherit the imperishable" (1 Corinthians 15:50). Yet they were willing to risk intellectual or theological inconsistency and leave unresolved puzzles to God's providence. They had clear if ambiguous reassurance from 1 Corinthians (15:51–52): "for the trumpet will sound, and the dead will be raised imperishable, and we shall be changed." Those unresolved puzzles never ceased to be sources of concern, however, especially among the most devout. As Lyman Beecher, the prominent Calvinist preacher, candidly wondered in 1820: "What happens when we die?" A man with greater faith and assurance than many, he was hardly alone in asking.[11]

Because Calvinism was in transition precisely when the new garden-type cemeteries emerged during the 1830s and 40s, inconsistencies abounded. Some people resisted any thought of reburial because they wanted the body to remain intact in its original place of rest "so that it could be identified." But New England medical societies, concerned about the health effects of the interment of countless bodies in tightly crowded urban centers, began urging in the 1820s the benefits of rural burial, accepting the logic of bodily decay, and answering those who insisted that the dead would rise up on Judgment Day. During the 1820s and 30s, Boston-area Unitarians and Universalists offered strong support for the natural process of earthen burial rather than putrefaction in sealed vaults. Representative figures like the Reverend William Ware (1797–1852) could reject traditional Calvinism but still have it both ways with facile words. Death, he declared, "we regard as not so much as even a temporary, momentary extinction of being, but simply as the appointed manner in which we shall pass from one stage of existence to another—from earth to heaven."[12]

As midcentury approached, eschatological thinking made only modest rhetorical adjustments to the reality of new, naturalistic cemeteries. At Spring Grove Cemetery in Cincinnati, John McLean insisted in 1849 that "we should view the grave as the opening portal of heaven." At the dedication of the Ever Green Cemetery in Gettysburg, Pennsylvania, in 1855, Methodist minister J. H. C. Dosh declared that "we do not idolize the departed, nor would we cling too devotedly to their mortal remains; 'knowing that these *vile* bodies shall be changed,' and shall come forth from their graves glorious and immortal bodies."[13]

If these are, indeed, representative sentiments, then we must wonder what families, friends, and admirers were thinking when they exhumed incomplete skeletons in the cases that follow. Quite often the bones being sought were intermingled with others because burials had been commonly crowded together, wooden coffins disintegrated, and in smaller churchyards when space ran out, burials occurred on top of one another. Perhaps there really is no problem then. If at the time of resurrection God is going to make bodies whole again and reunite them with souls, why make such a fuss over the temporal location and condition of human remains?

The answer certainly appears to be that exhuming and relocating remains, when it occurred, had rather little connection with the prevailing Protestant eschatology and everything to do with the needs of the living. Reburial was all about possession and memorialization: matters of reputation, memory, sentiments concerning the most suitable venue, pride of ownership, plus the commercial development of privately owned cemeteries, and eventually even tourism.

When we reach chapters 3 and 4, we will confront the question of change: what happens when fewer people regard heaven as a physical place serenely hovering above the clouds where husband and wife will recognize one another and parents embrace sons and daughters lost to life in infancy or childhood? Once upon a time people could sincerely sing or recite, "O death, where is thy victory? O death, where is thy sting?" because they genuinely believed in life everlasting (First Corinthians 15:55). Perhaps the sting of death became more painful and less readily scorned once traditional belief systems were undermined by science, secularism, and skepticism. In any case, whether we look to the Age of Faith or later to an Age of Anxiety, the imperative of exhumation seems to have been unclearly linked—one might even say oddly *unrelated*—to religious values, whether strongly held or intensely desired.

This puzzling situation requires from us a kind of twofold suspension of belief: first, suspending our presumption of some rational and necessary consistency between putative eschatology and public behavior, and second, recognizing that there must have been a partial abeyance or willful avoidance of the culture's belief in the ultimate reconstitution of bodily remains on Judgment Day. Reburials occurred *despite* the discovery of incomplete or even fragmentary remains. Whatever was found when exhumation took place was clearly regarded as fundamentally symbolic, even though the living scarcely acknowledged that in so many words. The reality, however, is that in many instances (Nathanael Greene, Daniel Morgan, John Paul Jones, James Wilson, Daniel Boone, Edgar Allan Poe, and others) reburial was quite literally a civic occasion, and therefore a secular rather than an ecclesiastical event. Principal speakers devoted their eulogies or remarks to the individual's historic importance, not his divine destiny.

✠

Changing attitudes about death, urban health, and especially the democratization of interment, did not all reach or affect the United States immediately. For that matter, such concerns were not even addressed or observed consistently throughout Europe during the later eighteenth and nineteenth centuries. Wealth and rank in bourgeois societies would result in all sorts of elaborate, honorific initial burials and fancy vaults, and mourning in antebellum America became an almost formulaic phenomenon in a "culture of melancholy" with a distinctive iconography that is all too familiar today from art museums and the historic house museums of famous Americans.[14] The notion that a person was entitled not only to a proper resting place but to the right *kind* of resting place emerged not long after the new nation did.[15]

It needs to be noted that the word and concept of *cemetery* as we understand it only surfaced in the early nineteenth century and came from Europe, almost certainly from France. Before that there were private graveyards, church burying grounds, and areas simply called burying yards. Individualized markers were unusual, as I have noted, even for people of some distinction. What is known today as the very extensive

Congressional Cemetery in southeast Washington, DC, did not receive that designation until the 1830s. From the time of its creation by private citizens in 1807 it was called the Washington Parish Burial Ground. Private, enterprise-driven cemeteries emerged gradually as a commercial phenomenon during the second quarter of the nineteenth century.[16]

✠

The history of death in America has been examined from multiple perspectives, most notably, perhaps, through scrutiny of the highly commercialized funeral industry and the social pressures it can exert and through accounts of the terrible carnage caused by the savage Civil War of 1861–65.[17] Anthropologists and historians have looked at mortuary rituals and at the history of cemeteries, especially the rural cemetery movement that visibly began in 1831 with the creation of Mount Auburn Cemetery in a suburb of Boston.[18] We also have insightful studies of monuments and memorials, along with analyses of American gravestones and what they can tell us about the changing symbolism associated with death and its aftermath.[19]

What has been largely overlooked in this intriguing body of literature is the disparate and sometimes arcane yet significant story of exhumations and reburials—episodes tucked away in various antiquarian and memorial volumes and tracts, and occasionally in the coda to a biographical chronicle, often written by a descendant, disciple, or devoted hagiographer. My curiosity and interest in bringing these sagas together within some sort of meaningful framework have been heightened by the recent and ongoing surge of serious scholarship devoted to all of the politically motivated repatriations and reburials that took place in Central and Eastern Europe—most notably in Hungary, Poland, and Romania—following the fall of Communism in 1989, a subject that I will save for comparative purposes in the final chapter.

The reasons for digging up dead bodies for reburial in the United States have been less often ideological yet no less partisan than in Europe.[20] Some of the most dramatic and controversial American cases have essentially been driven by patriotism (especially arising from Revolutionary War history; see chapter 2) or by strong sectional sentiments, particularly involving deaths during and after the Civil War era, followed by intense nationalism at the turn of the nineteenth and start of the twentieth century (chapter 3). Adding to the rich diversity of American motives have been phases of hero worship and ancestor worship, as well as the determined desire of survivors to bring a loved one home and honor that person properly because the initial burial had been inappropriate or the grave had been disgraced by obscurity and neglect (chapter 4 especially). The commercial desire to attract tourists and reasons rooted in local pride have also provided ongoing stimuli in the competition to possess or repossess the bodies of famous figures.

Still other remains were moved when descendants belatedly recalled the explicit wishes of the deceased—in the case of painter John Trumbull, for example, to be buried close to his own art at Yale College in New Haven, Connecticut. Religious motives and racial discrimination provide yet another constellation of causes, with the repatriation and reburial of prominent Native Americans revealing motives that involve both ethnicity and religion (chapter 5). Above all, perhaps, and pertinent to most of these chapters, are the vicissitudes of individual reputations, which in many instances fluctuated in volatile ways and ultimately required the restitution of a proper grave and monument, at the very least, and more often complete exhumation and reburial in a place somewhat distant from the original site.

Because our primary concern is with figures whose careers have been historically significant—most often quite famous (though occasionally infamous, like the outlaw Jesse James)—I shall *not* highlight the mass reburials of large numbers of lesser known people fallen in battle or (with one important exception) those where entire cemeteries had to be relocated in the name of "progress," such as the construction of a new highway or a major building on what had become prime real estate.[21]

Moving multiple bodies, especially anonymous ones, has often prompted striking cases of political conflict, and I will touch upon a few representative instances, most notably Confederate soldiers who died in the North during the Civil War; but that is not my principal focus, which is the process of digging up prominent individuals in order to "do them justice" and, in some instances, also to open a coffin to be certain that the "right" remains are still actually within. Sometimes, once the identification was successfully made, reburial took place at or near the original site; but more often the body was moved to a far more appropriate venue for interment. I will also leave to others treatment of the exhumation of bodies to check DNA in order to determine issues of lineage, whether racial, criminal, quasi-political, or otherwise important for proving innocence or probing some mysterious or enigmatic connection.[22]

While my story (actually consisting of *many* stories) is primarily American, with some parallels and comparisons to other cultures, it is important to acknowledge at the outset what is universal and so fundamental that it transcends even cross-cultural differences and similarities. As Robert Pogue Harrison has wisely observed, "Humans bury not simply to achieve closure and effect a separation from the dead but also and above all to humanize the ground on which they build their worlds and found their histories. . . . [Humanity] is a way of being mortal and relating to the dead. To be human means above all to bury. Vico suggests as much when he reminds us that '*humanitas* in Latin comes first and properly from *humando*, burying.'"[23]

Why do I find these frequently bizarre and macabre episodes so intriguing? In part because of a fairly distinctive change in practices that piques the historian's interest in patterns of sociocultural ebb and flow. Reburials became increasingly common during but especially *after* the second quarter of the nineteenth century, a little-noticed trend. Although I will consider them in a more topical manner than a strictly chronological one, when they are plotted along a time line we find comparatively few between 1800 and 1835, many more between 1845 and 1909, something of a surge during the 1930s, and then fewer after that. During the period from 1845 until 1909, the initiative came primarily from politicians or local boosters, more often than from family—a pattern that was reversed in the twentieth century, when survivors and descendants were more likely to supply the initiative.

Most important, however, I am intrigued because the ways in which Americans have honored (and sometimes dishonored) their dead are marked by substantive and symbolic details that tell us much about the values and culture of the living. And, as I have indicated, comparisons with the relocation of bodies for political reasons in Europe are revealing because we have not had as many ideologically motivated murders that later required honorific redress, even though nationalism, sectionalism, and political partisanship have at times quite clearly served as essential stimuli for reburials in the United States.[24]

After the national capital became permanently established at Washington, DC, in 1800, a problem arose when members of Congress from northern states died during the winter season. Moving bodies to New England in severe weather on poor roads was difficult enough, but also the ground in their home states was usually frozen too firmly to permit interment. So in 1807 what later came to be known as the Congressional Cemetery was established in southeast Washington near the Anacostia River; here temporary burials could take place until climatic conditions in summer permitted the removal of coffins for proper burial on "native ground." Some families chose to leave their statesmen permanently in Washington, however: currently nineteen senators and seventy-one representatives remain there. Eventually six thousand individuals who had not been members of Congress also received burial rights in this very first national cemetery. They range from mayors of Washington, craftsmen and architects of the U.S. Capitol, and veterans of the Revolutionary and other early wars to Indian chiefs and foreign diplomats. What began as a 4.5-acre square grew by annexation to its present size, 32.5 acres, in 1875. But even to this day, the section initially devoted to temporary burial is still set aside as a memorial to those who were initially laid to rest in the city planned by Pierre L'Enfant.[25]

If we inquire about other national cemeteries involving reburials, real and envisioned, we might note the following. In 1862, when unexpected numbers of Union troops died in battles in northern Virginia (near Washington), Abraham Lincoln and Secretary of War Edwin Stanton took steps to seize the estate of Robert E. Lee, overlooking the Potomac, in order to provide a burial ground for soldiers. On August 6, 1866, corpses of 2,111 unknown soldiers recovered from the battlefields at Bull Run and along the Rappahannock River were brought to Arlington and buried beneath a single monument in what would become Section 26 (fig. 3). These were the first combat Unknowns brought to the sprawling federal site soon to be known as Arlington National Cemetery.[26]

It is worth noting that the United States has nothing like Westminster Abbey in London. In 1889 the Reverend R. Heber Newton, an Epis-

*Figure 3.* Vignettes of Mount Vernon; the tomb of George Washington; graves of the 2,111 unknown soldiers—the first Americans buried at what became Arlington National Cemetery. Division of Prints and Photographs, Library of Congress.

copalian active in the Social Gospel movement, urged the creation of a national mausoleum in New York for illustrious Americans. The closest we came to that was a statuary hall of fame administered by New York University.

In 1945 the anthropologist and folklorist Zora Neale Hurston wrote to W. E. B. Du Bois, asking him, "Why do you not propose a cemetery for the illustrious Negro dead? Something like Pere Lachaise in Paris." She envisioned such figures as Nat Turner and Frederick Douglass and wanted it to be located in Florida because the vegetation there is green all year round. As she urged Du Bois and possibly others: "As far as possible, remove the bones of our dead celebrities to this spot. Let no Negro celebrities, no matter what financial condition they might be in at death, lie in inconspicuous forgetfulness. We must assume the responsibility of their graves being known and honored. You must see what a rallying spot that would be for all that we want to accomplish and do."[27]

Needless to say, neither Newton's nor Hurston's idea ever got off the ground (or, rather, into it). Yet the imperative of "repossessing our dead" lingers on in proactive and politicized ways in the United States. Witness the black MIA flags commonly seen flying right below Old Glory at many post offices and airports in the decades since the Vietnam War, and of course many bumper stickers on cars and trucks convey the same message. The desire to locate and repatriate the remains of military personnel still stirs strong emotions in many quarters.[28]

✠

The practice of exhumation and reinterment has had a long, complex, and intriguing history elsewhere in the world. Although a fear of disinterment was prevalent throughout the ancient Near East, in Egypt and especially in Palestine, reburials often became unavoidable. One authority on this subject has argued for an ongoing pattern of secondary burials even though these appear to have contradicted orthodox theology. Jews in antiquity collected remains of the dead and deposited them in individual receptacles. Ossuaries for bones were deemed all the more desirable because they could be used to transfer human remains readily, either to a family tomb or else to the Holy Land. It became incumbent upon Jews to bury their dead in Palestine, if at all possible.[29]

In ancient Greece, as we have noticed, there does seem to have been an overwhelming imperative to bring back the bones or remains of Homeric heroes who had perished far from their homelands or city-states, though the literary and archaeological evidence is not consistent on this point. With the American Civil War in mind for contrast, especially, it is worth remembering that at times the Greeks and the Trojans paused or interrupted battles in order to exchange dead and dying heroes and provide them with appropriate on-site interment.[30]

The culture of ancient Rome had very strong taboos against moving or dividing bodies—taboos that gradually receded, however, over a period of centuries. An official market in famous bones began in the year 787 CE. By the twelfth century, dividing and even distributing body parts for burial became a widespread Christian practice. Quite often, one person's remains might be buried in two different places in order to satisfy competition for pride of place, even though the major liturgical manuals denied the validity of doing so.[31] It is well known that the bodies of saints were divided up in order to maximize the distribution of relics. During the High Middle Ages, the stowing of redeemed relics in an altar meant that the saint was virtually present during celebration of the Mass. But as historian Caroline Bynum has remarked, "Enthusiasm for bodily partition affected not just the saints." By 1200, especially north of the Alps, the bodies of prominent ecclesiastics or nobles were often eviscerated, boned, or boiled after death, and the resulting parts were buried in several places, often near different saints. Gradually, as older graves were opened for practical purposes, such as making space for new arrivals, charnel houses became commonplace. Initially charnel houses were all about the relocation of skeletons; only subsequently did they become dumping sites for bodies during periods of plague and pandemics.[32]

As Johan Huizinga observed in a classic work on the later Middle Ages, the desirability of being buried in the soil of one's own country gave rise to practices that the Catholic Church interdicted as being contrary to canon law. In the twelfth and thirteenth centuries, when a prince or another person of high rank died in battle or on a crusade far from home, "the body was often cut up and boiled so as to extract the bones, which were sent home in a chest, whereas the rest was interred, not without ceremony, however, on the spot. Emperors, kings, and bishops have undergone this strange operation." Although Pope Boniface VIII forbade it, his successors sometimes gave dispensations. Numerous Englishmen who died in France during the Hundred Years' War were granted this "privilege" of being buried in more than one place. The Swiss historian Jacob Burckhardt observed that Pope Pius II decided to make Rome "the common refuge for all the remains of the saints which had been driven from their own churches." But he could not get all of them. The obsession with relics became especially strong during the sixteenth and seventeenth centuries, enhanced by the Council of Trent, which officially directed that the remains of saints be venerated.[33]

The body of Saint Geneviève (419/422–512), for example, was exhumed and enshrined on several occasions at various locations in Paris during the millennium following her death, mainly due to the number of sanctuaries and churches devoted to her memory as the city's patron saint, and to their occasional relocation. In 1793, however, revolutionary Jacobins removed her remains from the site of the newly secularized Panthèon and burned them.[34] It is not surprising that when the beloved St. Francis died in 1226, his followers buried him secretly in Assisi and very deep underground beneath a kind of premodern cement in order to prevent his exhumation and bodily desecration.

✠

The multiple reburials of René Descartes, the brilliant philosopher, mathematician, and natural scientist, are instructive and prescient for our purposes because they had so much to do with national pride, the sometimes lurid early modern obsession with sacred relics (*la précieuse relique*), hero worship, and pride of possession—securely controlling the remains of a genius and great man. Religion, or one might better say religious differences, also played a part. All of these considerations will be critically important to the interpretive spine of this book.

Descartes led a peripatetic life. A Frenchman who lived and did much of his most important writing in the Netherlands, he moved to Stockholm in middle age (1643), lured by the invitation and brilliance of young Queen Christina. Special patronage as a court intellectual at a time when such figures were valued had special appeal for a man grown weary of war-ravaged Europe south of the Baltic Sea, separating Scandinavia from so many sites of ceaseless conflict. It also put some distance between him and harsh critics of his empirical *Discourse on the Method*, which some construed as a scandalous challenge to orthodox Catholicism, even though that had not been his direct intent at all.[35]

When Descartes died in 1650, with his anger raging against a climate that had caused him to contract pneumonia, he was buried in the obscurity of a small, rustic cemetery outside Stockholm. Sixteen years later, when a new and ultra-nationalistic French ambassador arrived in Sweden, he found it deeply offensive that his famous Catholic countryman was buried in Protestant oblivion. So he negotiated the highly complex arrangements necessary to have Descartes translated to Paris for proper reburial. Once again, reputation and respect were prime motivations. When Descartes' remains were dug up in 1666, however, a few people with immediate personal access kept souvenirs. The ambassador himself modestly plucked the bones of one finger for himself, but a Swede actually took the philosopher's entire skull—somehow seemingly unnoticed at the time—and it remained in Sweden until 1821, when repatriation finally occurred because of serendipitous coincidences.[36]

A Cartesian cult had already surfaced in France by the 1660s, mainly among academics, so what remained of Descartes—a heap of bones confined to a copper box only thirty inches long—was reburied inside a venerable church right next to relics of Saint Geneviève. Although Louis XIV disapproved of Descartes' views, national pride prevailed. In 1792, however, amidst the chaos of the French Revolution, a dedicated soul named Alexandre Lenoir removed what he believed to be the philosopher's remains from the Church of Saint Geneviève for safekeeping, but made some small jewelry from a bone plate—actually considered a gesture of respect rather than a callous act.[37]

Late in 1793, with Robespierre's Terror running at full steam, the National Convention ordered that the great Descartes be honored by reburial in the deconsecrated Panthèon. Despite that order, however, the philosopher's bones remained safe and secret in a convent near the Seine. Subsequently, as the French polity calmed, Lenoir relocated Descartes to the garden of his *soi-disant* Museum of Monuments. In 1819, though, when it became clear that the Bourbon monarchy would continue, Descartes was relocated and reburied yet again, just a short distance along the Left Bank from the Church of Saint-Germain-des-Prés.[38]

All told, Descartes' body was buried once in Stockholm and reinterred at least three times in Paris, twice at venerated sites and once in a secular venue. Scholars have lost count because there was at least one reburial of the wrong bones. The detailed detective story of where and when, including false starts and misidentifications, has been told exceedingly well by Russell Shorto in his gripping narrative of great moments in the history of early modern science titled *Descartes' Bones*. The skull was bought at auction in 1819 by the owner of a Stockholm casino. In 1821 it was again sold at auction in Stockholm, but this time it was solemnly retrieved by a dedicated French biologist, Georges Cuvier, and deposited in the Museum of Natural History. The skull was actually misplaced in the horrendous Paris floods of 1911–12, yet somehow it miraculously reappeared in a pile of bones. It could be readily identified because in 1666 and subsequently various owners had inscribed their names on the skull and someone else had composed an entire poem in Latin on the top.[39] What could not be inscribed on that skull was "R.I.P.," because that would never be Descartes' destiny. To this day he rests in pieces rather than in peace. It is not even clear whether the remnants other than his skull are all actually his. But the saga of his migratory bones may very well be the most bizarre of all such tales.[40]

✝

During and after the French Revolution, funeral processions and a cult of heroes played a crucial role in shaping what became a new, secularized cult of tombs, cemeteries, and the dead in nineteenth-century France. The National Constituent Assembly established the desanctified Panthèon as a burial place for distinguished Frenchmen. One notable occasion involved the 1791 reburial of Voltaire's body with official honors in the Panthèon. (He had died in 1778, his views anathema to the church, so he was originally buried surreptitiously at a Cistercian monastery near Troyes.) But after the monarchy was restored in 1814, royalist fanatics stormed the Panthèon, opened the lead coffins, and disposed of Voltaire's remains in a pit of quicklime.[41]

Perhaps the single most famous reburial of all occurred in 1840, when Napoleon's remains were recovered from St. Helena and reinterred in the Dôme des Invalides in Paris—a momentous reversal in the politics of French memory. (We might recall two lines from Sophocles' *Oedipus Rex*: "The tyrant as a child of Pride / Who drinks from his great sickening cup.") His son, Napoleon II (1811–32), remembered as "L'Aiglon" (the Eagle), received the title King of Rome at birth but apparently died in Vienna of lead or arsenic poisoning at the hands of Prince von Metternich's governmental agents. In 1940 Adolf Hitler sought to win favor with the politically paralyzed French by having the remains of L'Aiglon sent to Paris for burial with his father at Les Invalides. He was subsequently moved to a separate crypt below Napoleon's. (His heart and intestines, however, remain in separate urns in Vienna.)[42]

Less well known than Napoleon's repatriation is the grim obsession of Jules Michelet, the prolific and popular nineteenth-century French historian. "I had," he explained, "a beautiful disease: I loved Death." His favorite walk in Paris was through Père Lachaise, the extraordinary cemetery for celebrities; and he enjoyed exhumations. He delighted in the ghastly story of Danton opening the grave of his wife in order to embrace her corpse. Danton recorded her disinterment in grisly detail. Necromancy at work again? We cannot be sure.[43]

During the 1790s the graves of two seventeenth-century English antimonarchical martyrs, John Hampden and Algernon Sydney (the former killed in battle against Charles I in 1643 and the latter beheaded by Charles II in 1683), were opened, the bodies examined and then reinterred. Emblematic of the rights of Englishmen, those two were much admired by Whig reformers. In 1828 Lord Nugent opened Hampden's tomb once again, studied the remains, cut off some locks of hair, and then described the incident for the *Gentleman's Magazine*. More than a century following the death in London of philosopher-theologian Emanuel Swedenborg in 1772, his remains were repatriated to Sweden. Only then was it discovered that a Swedish sea captain had removed Swedenborg's skull as a souvenir for his cranium museum. (Yes, the Descartes drama déjà vu.) The skull was eventually recovered and returned to the Royal Academy of Science in Stockholm. "It's a great relief to have it home," remarked a grateful academy official. "It's been a very macabre story."[44]

Such sagas may seem like mere curiosities, fabulations from *Ripley's Believe It or Not*. But the death and repatriation of Lajos (Louis) Kossuth, the Hungarian revolutionary, bear (and bare) a political punch portending the dramatic events that unfolded in Eastern Europe with the fall of Communism. After Kossuth's 1848 revolution against the Austro-Hungarian Empire failed, he fled into exile in Italy, eventually dying in Turin in 1894 at the age of ninety-two. When his body was brought back to Budapest for burial in early April of that year, half a million people attended the funeral, and Kossuth was lauded as the father of the nation. His funeral—held at the National Museum because Kossuth was Lutheran and the Catholic Church refused to display any symbols of grieving—launched a three-week period of mourning and became a pivotal moment in the construction of Hungarian national identity and historical consciousness. For his burial in Kerepesi Cemetery, clumps of soil were actually sent to Budapest from all the sites where the blood of patriots had been shed during the wars of independence in 1848. Kossuth would be revered as the soul and spirit of the nation, and when the anti-Soviet revolt occurred in 1956, Kossuth became the symbol of democratic socialism—his shield sewn on the flags of nationalists, foreshadowing what would follow in 1989.[45]

A parallel yet different portent took place in Paris and Poland during the 1880s. Adam Mickiewicz (1798–1855), the beloved romantic poet, became a freedom fighter in the unsuccessful uprising of 1848, when his native Poland was partitioned and dominated by neighboring Russia as well as the Habsburg Empire with its seat in Vienna. Much of his mature life was then spent in France, so when he died in Constantinople his remains were shipped to Paris for burial at the cemetery in Montmorency, where many other Polish émigrés had already been laid to rest. During the later 1860s, when changes occurred in the governance of the Austro-Hungarian Empire, Polish patriots began to consider—indeed, yearn for—the possibility of exhuming Mickiewicz and bringing his remains back to Krakow for an unprecedented reburial in the Wawel crypts beneath the cathedral there, the historic burial site of Polish kings, considered the "holiest shrine of the Polish nation."[46]

Sentiment for the translation of Mickiewicz's ashes built only slowly during the 1870s and early 80s, because Poles were themselves divided on the issue, at least initially. Liberal nationalists, intellectuals, and students supported the idea with enthusiasm and referred to the poet's remains as "relics" and the prospect of their return as "elevation" or "exaltation." Conservatives and Galician officials, however, were reluctant because of the permission required from Vienna (the emperor's opposition never actually became public), and the Polish Catholic Church was reluctant because of doubts about the integrity of the poet's faith. As momentum for repatriation increased during the mid-1880s, Galician officials at least wanted to control when and how the translation would take place. After all, the remains were most likely destined for a castle and cathedral belonging to the king of Galicia and grand duke of Krakow. The prospect for a nonobservant poet was unprecedented.[47]

In 1884 the cathedral chapter finally bowed to popular sentiment and offered its approval for use of the Wawel crypt, but then balked at making any further arrangements. After the emperor eventually relented, permission formally came from the Austrian minister of the interior, with the stipulation that the celebration "not take on the character of a political demonstration." It is crucial to keep in mind that unlike nearly all reburials in the United States, Kossuth's and this one involved delicate international negotiations, requiring Russian as well as Habsburg approval above all because Poland had been partitioned. Moreover, the Polish community of exiles in France had to consent to relinquish their control over Mickiewicz's remains.

Once their approval had been secured, he was exhumed on June 27, 1890, before a small group of family and dignitaries and placed in a new metal coffin. (The old one was promptly cut into small pieces—like holy relics—so that many people could have souvenirs.) The next morning, delegations of French, Poles, Hungarians, and Czechs along with members of the French press crowded into the cemetery to pay homage to the great poet.[48]

Significantly, the official French spokesman on that day turned out to be the noted historian Ernest Renan, formerly a professor at the prestigious Collège de France, where Mickiewicz had also lectured. Renan was less than acceptable to the conservative Polish Catholics, because he was regarded as an atheist. He is best remembered for his famous lecture at the Sorbonne in 1882, "What Is a Nation?" in which he declared that a nation is "a soul, a spiritual principle," and that its existence is a "daily plebiscite." Those were comforting sentiments to the partitioned and politically subordinated Poles. In his remarks on June 28, Renan explained that in moving Mickiewicz's remains to Krakow, Poles were voting for their nation. He elaborated: "To have shared glories in the past, a shared will in the present; to have performed great deeds together, to wish to perform still more—these are the essential conditions for the making of a people."[49]

The train bearing Mickiewicz in his new coffin passed through France and then Zurich, Switzerland, where it was met with fanfare, flowers, and speeches in six languages. When it reached Vienna, however, rallies at the train station were disallowed. Polish requests to speak and place wreaths were prohibited, and railroad officials transferred the coffin from the French train to an Austrian one without the poet's family even being present. But Krakow more than compensated with an extravagant reception, called by one scholar "the public event of the decade, if not the century." Poles arrived in record numbers to witness the procession and entombment in the largest manifestation of national unity since the January insurrection of 1863.[50]

On July 4, 1890, elaborate ceremonies began with the coffin being placed on an elevated catafalque in Wawel Cathedral, topped by a prominent cross and an image of the Mother of God, Queen of Poland. Poles had come from all over the country and showered the bier with flower petals as the procession, accompanied by Chopin's solemn *marche funèbre*, made its way to the cathedral. The event had immense populist appeal, with considerable involvement from Polish peasants manifest in the form of forty-four large wreaths sent from all across the land. The inscription on one of them read: "To Mickiewicz: from the Warsaw youth, born in bondage." The entire affair prompted an enormous burst of Polish nationalism.[51]

When the great poet William Butler Yeats died in the south of France early in 1939, the drama of his eventual return to Ireland measures up well in significance with Kossuth's narrative but even more with that of Mickiewicz, for religious reasons (or more precisely, doubts about the orthodoxy of both poets). One of Yeats's very last poems, published posthumously, made clear that he wished to be repatriated after death, and his wife and family wanted to honor his last request. But because he, too, was regarded by many as an atheist, even "satanic," and by some as "un-Irish," objections appeared in the Irish press and from the Catholic Church. Meanwhile, obituaries published in Britain claimed him as an "English poet," which enemies in Ireland used as a taunt. Plans for exhumation and interment in County Sligo actually went forward for many months, but the outbreak of World War II put all arrangements in abeyance for nearly a decade.[52]

Initially the delay occurred because Yeats and his wife had wanted his remains to lie in Roquebrune, France, for up to a year before being shipped back to Sligo; but the war and fierce objections from the Catholic Church in Ireland combined to complicate reburial amid secular as well as ecclesiastical red tape. There was also considerable confusion following the war at the cemetery in France: the curé there informed Yeats's widow that the temporary permit for burial had expired after five years and Yeats's remains had been removed to an ossuary. Some, especially French authorities, insisted that owing to wartime "disturbances" the body should remain at Roquebrune. Although it had indeed been exhumed without anyone informing the family, French officials eventually identified Yeats's remains and placed them in a new coffin with the original plate affixed. Rumors persisted for years that the wrong body had been shipped to Ireland, and legends endure of a mysterious reburial and even of an empty coffin.[53]

In any event, no one can doubt the powerful symbolism of Yeats's ceremonial return to Ireland in September 1948. The coffin was carefully removed from Roquebrune on September 6 and relocated with a military guard of honor to Nice, covered by the Irish national flag. At Villefranche it was placed on an Irish naval corvette for shipment to Galway, where it was met early in the morning by Yeats's widow and children. They were greeted at Sligo by yet another military guard of honor, though the family resisted the idea of a state funeral. A Church of Ireland service was conducted by the local rector despite doubts about Yeats's right to Christian burial. An enormous crowd assembled for the funeral, and the ceremony on September 17 proclaimed that Yeats's reputation "belonged neither to government nor family, but to the country whose consciousness he had done so much to shape," and which would declare itself a republic at the end of that same year.[54]

✝

As one anthropologist has written of ancestor-related rituals in Madagascar: "Ancestors are made from remembering them. Remembering creates a difference between the deadliness of corpses and the fruitfulness of ancestors. The ancestors respond by blessing their descendants with fertility and prosperity." A handy reminder of the constructedness of history! A visit to the Melanesia and Oceania galleries of any large art museum underlines the fact that ancestor worship plays a prominent role in the religious lives of many so-called primitive cultures. We see ancestor poles from the Asmat people of New Guinea and striking ancestor tablets from the Kerewa people of the Papuan Gulf. In Madagascar, when an ancestor becomes restless, he is removed from his tomb, dressed in silk, and paraded through the town; toasts are drunk to his health, and he is brought up to date on local gossip. Then the body is returned to its grave until it calls upon the living once again.[55]

In one form or another, the importance of acknowledging ancestors appears to be nearly universally felt. The notion of *repossessing* the dead for political purposes is also widespread but occurs under more particular circumstances, most often as a consequence of regime change. In the United States, however, for much of the nineteenth century ancestor worship was deemed inappropriate for a present-minded and future-oriented society. As Ralph Waldo Emerson declared in a widely heard lecture on the lyceum circuit, "The reverence for the deeds of our ancestors is a treacherous sentiment. Their merit was not to reverence the old, but to honor the present moment; and we falsely make them excuses of the very habit which they hated and defied."[56] Sentiments about ancestor veneration began to change more rapidly in Britain than in America, so that in 1878 Gilbert and Sullivan included some satirical dialogue and recitative in "The Pirates of Penzance" directed at social pretense in "acquiring other people's ancestors."

During the later nineteenth century, however, American sentiments about forebears began to shift rapidly, at least among the elite and upper middle classes, which created in the 1880s and 90s a series of hereditary and honorific patriotic societies like the Mayflower Descendants and Daughters of the American Revolution, followed swiftly by a burst of similar exclusive groups. Just after the turn of the century a rash of essays appeared in popular journals bearing such titles as "The Quest of Ancestors" (nonfiction) and "The Power of Ancestors" (fiction).[57] Nevertheless, Americans still did not regard statues as surrogate corpses, as many Europeans did, nor did they have a tradition of toppling or desecrating statues, despite the famous episode of pulling down the equestrian statue of George III in New York City in 1776. Unlike Europeans, Americans reluctantly relocate statues after they have become offensive for racial or political reasons.[58]

And yet the history of exhumation and reburial in the United States tells us much about the phasing and variability of ancestral idealization, about certain sites of collective memory and how Americans have felt about them. The phenomenon can even be related at times to revisionist historical writing, though not to the same degree that it has been in Europe, especially since 1989 in the countries once under Soviet control. Reburials have not been a major stimulus for the rewriting of history here in the United States. Yet in some instances dead bodies *have* served as the Protestant equivalent of Roman Catholic relics in medieval times, and quite often, as we shall see, dead bodies have indeed been deployed as potent American political symbols. Lincoln and Davis are among the most obvious examples. Statues and the bodies that lie near or beneath them (virtually more often than actually) do make the past more immediately present and vivid. And that is exactly what the makers of monuments and memorials had in mind.[59]

✝

Germane to our understanding of pan-Atlantic sentiments are the news items that Americans in times past could read in the press concerning the reburials for cultural or political reasons of notable Europeans who died in the "wrong place." The rise of intensely felt nationalism made it increasingly imperative for iconic figures to lie on native ground. In 1887, for example, the *New York Times* reported that the remains of composer Gioachino Rossini, who died in Paris in 1863, were disinterred at Père Lachaise Cemetery in the presence of dignitaries from the Italian embassy and musical admirers who included Jules Massenet, Leo Delibes, and Camille Saint-Saëns. Rossini's remains were taken to Florence, Italy, for reburial. By then, the notion of repatriation had begun to take hold in the United States as well. In 1852 the playwright and actor John Howard Payne, for example, died in Tunis, North Africa, where he had served as U.S. consul for a decade. In 1883 his body was exhumed and brought home to America for burial at the Oak Hill Cemetery in Washington, DC. How appropriate considering that he is best remembered for writing the enduring song "Home, Sweet Home" in 1822.[60]

Sergei Rachmaninoff, the great pianist and composer, fled Russia for the United States in 1918 because the Bolshevik Revolution disturbed the peace of mind he found essential for his work. When he died in 1943, burial took place at the Kensico Cemetery in the suitably named town of Valhalla, New York, where he was eventually joined by his wife and one of his daughters. By 1992, as the fiftieth anniversary of his death approached, speculation began to increase about the possibility of exhuming the trio for reburial in Novgorod, close to Oneg, the composer's birthplace. The inspiration for this move owed much to the removal of Bela Bartók, who also died in the United States during World War II and was first buried in 1945 at Ferncliff Cemetery in Hartsdale, a suburb of White Plains. In 1988 Bartók's two sons arranged for his remains to be reburied in Hungary, his native land—a politically motivated decision that actually pleased the Communist regime that had one year remaining before the velvet revolutions toppled governments throughout

Eastern Europe. As of this writing, however, Rachmaninoff remains in Valhalla, but for how much longer no one can be sure.[61]

In the wake of World War II, the American press provided numerous reminders that politically motivated reburials could bear immense symbolic significance. In 1949, for example, the body of Theodor Herzl, considered the founder of political Zionism during the 1890s, was exhumed from his burial place in Vienna (where he died in 1904) and flown to the new state of Israel for reinterment in Jerusalem. According to the media, this ceremony was perceived as the biggest event of its kind "since the burial near Nablus of the mummified remains of Joseph, which the Prophet Moses took along on the exodus of the Israelites from Egypt."[62]

Whereas the reburial of Herzl as a virtual founding father received unanimous acclaim, the 1964 reburial (on what became known as Mount Herzl) of Vladimir Jabotinsky would be quite controversial, because he had led what was called a Revisionist movement in Judaism. Upon his death in 1940 he was buried in the United States. Because Jabotinsky had been a particularly divisive figure, Prime Minister David Ben Gurion refused repeated requests from Menachim Begin that the Israeli government provide an official state funeral for his reburial, just as it had done for Herzl. Ben Gurion's successor relented, however, and Jabotinsky's remains received a full-dress state funeral in 1964, on the twenty-fourth anniversary of his death. That ceremony symbolized the normalization of relations between the Labor Party and political descendants of the conservative Revisionist movement, and marked the beginning of a process of political rehabilitation and legitimization for the latter.[63]

Somewhat less controversial, and a prime example of exhumation for purposes of national pride and regime building, was the state funeral orchestrated by the Begin-led government in May 1982 for remains reputedly belonging to the fighters and followers of Shimon Bar Koziba (popularly known as Bar Kochba), who led the second Jewish revolt against Rome in 132–35 CE. The remains had been discovered in 1960 by the noted archaeologist Yigal Yadin. The exhumation and ceremony twenty-two years later was understood as an attempt by Prime Minister Begin to establish political dominance for the Likud Party by means of ideological hegemony for what is called the New Zionism, closely identified with Begin and the period of his political leadership in Israel.[64]

✠

When we read about various funeral and burial practices in nineteenth-century Europe, especially the more macabre ones fetishized by people like Jules Michelet, we might wonder how Americans reacted when they had occasion to observe or learn about them. We don't have much information concerning firsthand American responses, but early in 1878 a group of upper-class women from Boston happened to be in Rome and found themselves spectators at a lurid display that became something of a tourist attraction. After King Victor Emmanuel II died in January, visitors could climb a long staircase to the grand salon of the palace, which was hung with crimson (not black) brocade. The sides of the room were lined with huge candles, and the king's body, "crowned and dressed in royal robes, was seated on the throne." The Boston ladies were utterly dumbfounded.[65]

Although nothing quite like that in U.S. history has come to my attention (so far), we do have from the mid- and later nineteenth century numerous accounts of men and women's attempts to visualize deceased family members, especially parents and children. The next best thing to ethereal or mystical contact was the presence of art intended to memorialize if not immortalize a loved one. But on occasion a family would reopen a recently buried coffin in order to gaze one last time at the visage of someone beloved, most often a child, but sometimes to attempt communication with or guidance from a parent. Ralph Waldo Emerson recorded the following in his journal on July 8, 1857: "This morning I had the remains of my mother and of my son Waldo removed [transferred] from the tomb of Mrs. Ripley to my lot in 'Sleepy Hollow' [cemetery in Concord]. The sun shone brightly on the coffins, of which Waldo's was well preserved—now fifteen years. I ventured to look into the coffin. I gave a few white-oak leaves to each coffin, after they were put into the new vault, and the vault was then covered with two slabs of granite."[66]

In 1704 in colonial Virginia, William Byrd II, who rapidly became a prominent planter, politician, and writer, lost his father. The father's will had expressed the clear hope that when his son returned from being educated in England, he would successfully follow his parent in running a major plantation on the James River. Byrd did so, "but his father's distant voice, urging him to improve and sending him specific tasks as agent of Virginia, was now silent." So Byrd made one final effort in the winter of 1709–10 to consult his father by exhuming the corpse for continuing counsel. The effort failed. The corpse remained obdurately silent, and consequently the heir was obliged to become totally self-reliant. He eventually surpassed his father as a planter, built one of the grandest homes in early America, became a notorious womanizer, and achieved immortality as a compulsive keeper of self-revealing secret diaries.[67]

An episode that took place in 1801 would have been much less likely to occur later in the century. Louisa Park of Salisbury, Massachusetts, wished to postpone the interment of her infant because her husband was away at sea and she wanted to wait for his return to make a final decision about how and where the little boy should be buried. Consequently she "borrowed" the vault of a wealthy friend for temporary interment. She recorded the following in her diary: "Captain Hoyt's politeness I shall never forget. . . . His consenting so readily to lay the corps [sic] in his tomb was a satisfaction to me. For some reason, to see him deposited there was not half so distressing to my feelings as it would have been to see him buried under the [ground]; and when his father returns he can see him, and remove him as he may think best."[68]

The nature and course of such shifts in sentiment and practice, as well as significant continuities, will become increasingly apparent in the chapters that follow.

— TWO —

# Heroes of the Revolution

## THE SITING AND RECITING OF PATRIOTISM

Land where my fathers died
Land of the pilgrims' pride . . .

✢ Samuel Francis Smith, "America" (1831)

$\mathcal{A}$lthough reburials of certain key figures from the age of the American Revolution tended to become politicized in several respects, these nineteenth-century episodes tell us more about patriotism than they do about nationalism or sectionalism, which will provide the focus of chapter 3. Distinguishing between patriotism and nationalism is difficult and subtle, but in the large literature devoted to those topics, a slender line sometimes suggests a valid and meaningful difference. The former, derived from the Latin *patria*, concerns love of country—its heritage, traditions, symbols, and institutions. The latter, nationalism, has more to do with what one wants a country to achieve in terms of policy initiatives and worldly standing in relation to others. Nationalism tends to be more chauvinistic and competitive. It has prompted aggressive action to acquire colonies and territory overseas, to be number one in an arms race, or to be the "top gun" in space.[1]

Patriotism takes pride in what has been—in past achievements that have shaped the present, legendary and mythic as well as historically recorded. Nationalism seeks validation in what should or might be— here and now, but also soon. Although nascent nationalism certainly helped to provide a potent impetus for the movement leading to American independence, its transformational manifestations would arise in the later nineteenth century in a different form, whereas patriotism achieved its full flowering earlier, well before the doctrine of Manifest Destiny set the United States on a course leading to the successful Spanish-American War of 1898–99 and its implications overseas.

Whereas patriotism is closely concerned with civic affiliation and cultural identity, nationalism has more to do with the State and its objectives in relation to other nation-states. Patriotism involves sentiments predicated upon a perceived past. Nationalism takes pride in ongoing achievements and future prospects. Patriotism fosters allegiance. Nationalism prompts competitiveness.[2]

This chapter will concentrate primarily on battle-tested heroes who died and received burial far from home, frequently giving rise to conflicts over just exactly *where* should most properly be considered "home." In some instances there could be no doubt where home was situated, yet disputes hinged upon the issue of which venue was more apropos: home or the site of a hero's greatest military triumph and contribution to American independence. At the close of this chapter we will also consider a few foreign-born figures, similar to Baron Von Steuben, who helped facilitate freedom in highly significant ways and died in the young United States—a circumstance that grateful Americans often felt needed to be rectified, though sometimes with disastrous results, as in the case of Tom Paine.

✠

We must begin with the sad, intensely politicized story of the "prison ship dead" and their unfortunate neglect. During the War for Independence, Americans taken prisoner by the British in the New York area, especially sailors, were detained under wretched conditions in prison ships anchored near Brooklyn. When they died of disease, malnutrition, and other causes—it is estimated as many as 11,500 in all—the corpses were placed in shallow graves on the shores of Wallabout Bay. Although their bones soon lay scattered and exposed, plans to honor the "prison ship martyrs" after the war elicited little interest. In 1807–8, however, a surge of attention occurred because of a potentially serious conflict with England, and thirty thousand spectators witnessed a solemn procession by barge and by wagon from Brooklyn to Manhattan and back, organized by the Tammany Society, which originated as a Jeffersonian Republican political club. Thirteen coffins filled with bones were ultimately taken to a Brooklyn burial vault, where prayerful eulogies by clerics accompanied the reinterment of "the relicks of our brethren."[3] Here we have just the first example among many that we will encounter of mourning rituals as political performance.

Hopes for the construction of a suitable monument rose and fell because Federalists condemned the attempt at memorialization as shameless posturing by the Tammany Society. From the Federalist perspective, what was going on amounted to partisan manipulation of the past, because passage of the Embargo Act in 1808 aroused sentiment that played to the anti-British feelings of Jeffersonian Republicans. Repeal of the Embargo Act one year later meant that this heated issue subsided and the prison ship victims would receive no monument. Those lost ghosts lapsed into total obscurity following the War of 1812 and peace with Great Britain. Nevertheless, the Tammany Society's cornerstone ceremony on April 13, 1808, followed by a special holiday declared on May 26, although less than a full-scale reinterment, included genuine funereal elements. There were floats, banners, and a considerable sequence of marchers. The Republican Greens performed the "Grand Wallabout Dead March," composed by Captain James Hewitt. As historian Robert Cray has observed, New Yorkers saw an "impressive display of sepulture immersed in pageantry."[4]

As Brooklyn grew rapidly during the nineteenth century and population spread quite close to the burial vaults, local residents typically blamed the inadequate entombments for what they considered impure air and gases believed to be capable of spreading disease. Anxiety concerning possible cholera outbreaks recurred periodically. Given the neglect of those bones in their poor housing, the aging Walt Whitman later lamented the situation, "mark'd by no special recognition," in his *Leaves of Grass*:

> Greater than memory of Achilles and Ulysses,
> More, more by far to thee than tomb of Alexander,
> Those cart loads of old charnel ashes, scales and splints of mouldy bones,
> Once living men—once resolute courage, aspiration, strength,
> The stepping-stones to thee to-day and here, America.[5]

So in 1873 the remains were removed to Fort Greene, and thirty-five years later in 1908 the Martyrs' Monument was dedicated, with President-elect Taft as the prime guest of honor. Federal, state, and municipal funds supplemented by private subscription made possible the construction of a 198-foot column above the new crypt where the peripatetic bones now reposed. Some twenty thousand spectators braved the elements to witness the dedication. But that was then. Within little more than a generation, the monument fell into neglect prior to World War II; by the end of the twentieth century it was "forlorn and forgotten."[6]

✛

One of the most representative episodes for our purposes involves the earliest martyr in the struggle for independence, Joseph Warren, president of the Massachusetts Bay Colony's Provincial Congress and Masonic Grand Master, shot in the head on June 17, 1775, at the Battle of Bunker Hill. According to legend, some British officers suggested decapitating him for being a despicable traitor to the Crown, but a more civilized fellow Mason intervened. So they buried Warren with several others in a shallow unmarked grave. On April 8, 1776, after the British had decamped from Boston, Warren's brothers and some friends exhumed his body, which was identified by Paul Revere, who had made two false teeth for Warren. After a public ceremony at King's Chapel, his remains were interred at the Granary Burying Ground. Almost half a century later, in 1825 a nephew undertook a quest to find the "lost" bones at the Old Granary. They were exhumed a second time and removed to a special crypt in the Warren family vault at St. Paul's Episcopal Church, where they lingered for thirty years until they were disinterred yet again for reburial in the new Forest Hills Cemetery at Roxbury, Warren's birthplace.[7]

The eulogy delivered by a minister at the first reburial in 1776 (and reprinted on the occasion of the third in 1856) is instructive for several reasons. Although it begins with the sentence "*Illustrious Relics!—What tidings from the grave? Why has thou left the peaceful mansions of the tomb, to visit again this troubled earth?*" it never mentions God, heaven, or anything remotely eschatological. Instead the emphasis, above all, is upon Warren's patriotism. "*Amor patriae* was the spring of his actions," the cleric intoned, and there are repeated references to "our patriot." The day before he died at Bunker Hill, Warren is said to have declared: "Dulce et decorum est pro patria mori" (It is sweet and becoming to die for one's country). A secondary motif in the eulogy concerns Warren's distinguished role as Grand Master of all Masons in Massachusetts (in 1794 a Masonic lodge in Charlestown erected a monument to his memory on the very spot where he fell in June 1775). The homily, given in Calvinist Boston, was totally secular.[8]

✠

Charles Thomson, a prominent Philadelphia patriot from 1765 onward and secretary of the Continental Congress throughout its existence from 1774 until 1789, was married in 1775 to Hannah Harrison, daughter of a wealthy Quaker landowner, Richard Harrison. Thomson requested that when he died he be buried with Hannah (who passed away in 1807) in the graveyard at Harriton, his father-in-law's estate, which was legally divided among Harrison's heirs, and where the Thomsons lived after 1781. Having been married in their forties, they had no children. Charles's wishes were honored in 1828. Eight years later, however, several prominent figures in Philadelphia, following the Mount Auburn model in Massachusetts, established Laurel Hill Cemetery on the banks of the Schuylkill River and expressed eagerness to acquire prestige (and new customers) by having historically important people reburied there.[9] One of the promoters called upon the owners of the Harriton estate, requesting permission to remove Thomson's remains from the family burial ground to the new cemetery. An elaborate cenotaph configured as a sixteen-foot obelisk in the shape of Cleopatra's Needle was prepared in advance to mark the site of Thomson's new, more publicly visible interment site.[10]

After various family members had considered the request, they decided that because Thomson had so explicitly asked to lie with his wife's ancestors, it would be inappropriate to agree to reinterment. Deborah Logan, a socially prominent near relative, raised particularly vocal opposition. There was, however, a nephew of Charles Thomson, unrelated to the Harrisons and apparently unfriendly to the new owners of Harriton. He had not been consulted, and he approved the removal on grounds that he had been his uncle's executor and nearest relative. Because taking Charles's body also meant removing Hannah's, and because the exhumers were not at all sure of the legality of their undertaking, it seems that the deed had to be done by stealth.[11]

On August 12, 1838, gravediggers assembled at a home in Bryn Mawr, about a quarter of a mile from Harriton in neighboring Merion Township. They expected to complete the task that night, but digging up the two (and possibly three) graves proved more difficult than expected. They were still finishing when dawn broke and were spotted by a farm laborer on his way to work. Hearing their voices and seeing their lanterns, he approached them, whereupon the diggers "were seized with a panic and hastily loaded the bodies in wagons which they had in readiness, and drove off rapidly, leaving the graves open, a high pile of earth, and other signs of their depredations. The facts were at once reported to the owners [of Harriton], but there seemed nothing to do but fill up the open graves and repair the damage done to the cemetery."

Because individual graves were not clearly marked in those days, especially at Harriton, and there had not been sufficient time for careful examination of the exhumed bodies, it is unclear whether the real Thomson remains were actually removed.[12] That will turn out to be an ongoing pattern in our narrative. "Did we get the right body?" became a great issue in the case of Daniel Boone's remains in 1845, as we shall see, and with many subsequent exhumations as well.[13]

As Mount Auburn enjoyed almost immediate popularity following its dedication in 1831, and because eminent figures who were logical prospects for burial there died conveniently in the early 1830s, the proprietary trustees felt less urgency about obtaining other men comparable to Thomson and General Hugh Mercer, also reburied in 1840 at Laurel Hill. Still, during the 1840s a number of eminent Bostonians, especially such prominent clergymen as the Reverend John Murray and Unitarian leader Joseph Buckminster, were exhumed from sites like the Old Granary and reinterred at Mount Auburn. Adding celebrities enhanced the sale of lots. Like attracts like, even the likely deceased.[14]

✠

Richard Montgomery was born in Dublin in 1738, served in the British army during the French and Indian War (most notably at the siege of Louisburg in 1758), and then returned home. In 1772, however, he sold his army commission and chose to relocate in New York, where he bought a sixty-seven-acre farm in King's Bridge, now part of the borough of the Bronx. Three years later he was elected to the New York Provincial Congress and married Janet Livingston, and in June 1775 he was commissioned a brigadier general in the Continental Army. He achieved swift promotion to major general on December 9 and along with Benedict Arnold led an American army into Canada, where he seized two British forts and the city of Montreal. On December 31, while attempting to capture the city of Quebec amidst a fierce snowstorm, Montgomery was killed. The British recognized his body and, quite unlike the episode involving Joseph Warren six months earlier, provided him with an honorable burial in Canada—an act that brings to

mind the military courtesies we recall from Homer's *Iliad*. Montgomery swiftly received romanticized recognition as another great martyr
to the American cause, and numerous towns and counties would be
named for him throughout the United States.

In 1794 Jedediah Morse wrote the first biography of Montgomery,
coupling him with the war's greatest hero, George Washington—a
pattern of pairing that would be repeated in histories and eulogies for
other leading generals, such as Nathanael Greene. When Washington
died in 1799, one widely published poem declared that *"Montgomery's
godlike form directs the way"* to heaven. Effusive praise for Montgomery, linked with Warren as the first great and lamentable losses,
appeared in every early history of the War for Independence. When
Anglo-American tensions began to intensify again in 1810, members of
Congress both for and against the prospect of war invoked Montgomery's memory in debating the issue. Once the war actually began in
1812, citations of his patriotism and bravery served quite effectively in
the enlistment of soldiers. As one recruiter in northern New York explained to his father, invading Canada might result in the loss of American lives, but it was better to "bleed on the tomb of Montgomery" than
submit to British intimidation.[15]

In 1814 the poet Alexander Coffin published a long ode titled *The
Death of Montgomery*, comparing him to such epic heroes as Hector and
Achilles. In the years following the war, veneration of Montgomery
increased even further, and his widow, Janet Livingston Montgomery,
who had never remarried, launched repeated efforts to have his body
returned. In 1816, at the age of seventy-four, she called upon her social
connections for support, and Sir John Sherbrooke, governor general
of Canada, consented to release the remains. In 1818 Janet used family
ties once again to prevail upon a former lieutenant governor and current assembly member to persuade New York to formally undertake
the necessary procedures. The legislature then passed a resolution authorizing the state to get final Canadian approval for exhumation, with
reburial to take place at St. Paul's Chapel in New York City.[16]

Governor DeWitt Clinton gave Janet's nephew the rank of honorary
colonel and sent him to Quebec to manage the project with assistance
from the man who had supervised the initial burial in January 1776.
Despite his eighty-nine years, he readily located the general's grave in

1818. Although the coffin had largely decayed, the skeleton was intact except for part of the lower jaw, which had been struck by grapeshot. As workers moved the remains, a musket ball fell from the skull. The coffin and skeleton were wrapped in a tarpaulin and placed in a heavy box for movement to New York. Following arrival at Whitehall south of Lake Champlain, cavalry units escorted the crate to Albany. Communities through which they passed held memorial services, with Revolutionary War veterans participating in the ceremonies. At Troy the remains were transferred to a large mahogany coffin bearing an engraved silver plate. On July 4 that coffin lay in state at the capitol building, guarded by an artillery company, and large numbers of citizens filed past to pay their respects to a fallen hero. On the morning of July 6 an even larger procession followed the coffin to the steamship *Richmond*, which carried it down the Hudson to Manhattan. Several aging men who had participated in the 1775 assault on Quebec marched in this ceremony. When the vessel passed Montgomery Place, the estate where Janet still lived, she felt overcome with emotion and fainted.[17]

Upon arrival in New York City the remains were taken to City Hall, and the funeral on July 8 was grander than anything that had preceded it there. "It began at dawn with cannon shots announcing a day of mourning." Businesses closed early, horse and wagon traffic was banned from the parade route, and flags flew at half-mast. In midmorning a huge procession made its way to St. Paul's. "The marchers walked in silence, accompanied by tolling church bells and booming salutes fired by the ships and forts in the harbor." Thousands of spectators lined the parade route or watched from windows overlooking it. This was the most elaborate and solemn ceremony since George Washington's death in 1799. Press coverage would be national because Montgomery's tragic loss had transcended the bounds of state and regional fame. As Andrew Jackson, himself a military hero of the War of 1812, would write: "The memory of the *patriotic* and gallant Montgomery is coeval with our liberty as a nation, and will exist in the heart of every *patriot* so long as our Republic exists."[18]

Phrases expressing gratitude and welcoming redemption from ingratitude appeared in many speeches and newspapers, but above all, the inspiration of patriotic pride was most frequently cited. As New York's adjutant general, Solomon Van Rensselaer, observed: "In rendering due honor to illustrious heroes and statesmen, we not only reward distinguished merit, but excite to new achievements of patriotism and glory." Seven years later Henry J. Finn produced a play, *Montgomery; or the Falls of the Montmorency*, in which the general makes only a brief appearance; but the use of his name in the title shows that it still held strong audience appeal.[19]

The Mexican War of 1847–48 intensified interest in the War for Independence and prompted an array of new publications. In George Lippard's highly popular *Washington and His Generals, or Legends of the Revolution* (1847), the author conveyed a widespread sentiment that Canadians might revolt against Britain and therefore should receive American aid: "Then perhaps some true American heart will wash out the blood of Montgomery from the rock of Quebec."[20]

Anthony Wayne, linked historically with Montgomery, was born in 1745 in Chester County, Pennsylvania. His vocation began as a surveyor and with work at his father's tannery. Like Montgomery, he became involved in late colonial politics as a patriot, serving as a member of the Pennsylvania legislature from 1774 until 1780. In 1775, however, he raised a militia and his regiment joined Montgomery's unsuccessful assault on Quebec. During the next eight years he commanded the Pennsylvania Line in a series of major battles at Brandywine, Paoli, and Germantown (near Philadelphia). He led the American attack at the battle of Monmouth, but the highlight of his military career came with his victory at Stony Point in 1779, a cliffside redoubt commanding the Hudson River—the triumph coming as a great boost to American morale at a time when there had been numerous losses.

Wayne then moved south, scored significant victories, and severed the British alliance with Native American tribes in Georgia. He successfully negotiated peace treaties with the Creek and Cherokee nations, for which the state of Georgia rewarded him with the gift of a large plantation. Following his final promotion to major general in 1783, he moved to Georgia in order to manage his plantation; but in 1793 President Washington recalled him from civilian life to head an expedition in the Northwest Indian War, where British support had made Indians living beyond the Appalachians a major problem for American settlers pushing west. In 1794 Wayne led a successful assault on the Indian Confederation at the Battle of Fallen Timbers, near Maumee, Ohio (just south of modern Toledo). Following that decisive victory ending the war, in August 1795 he negotiated the Treaty of Greenville, which ceded most of what is now Ohio to the United States.[21]

Fifteen months later Wayne died of complications from gout during a return trip to Pennsylvania from Detroit, and he was buried in a plain oak coffin in an isolated grave at the foot of the flagstaff next to the blockhouse at Fort Presque Isle (now Erie, Pennsylvania). In compliance with his request, similar to Von Steuben's, Wayne was clad in his best uniform—suitable attire for a man who had devoted most of his mature life to military affairs. Soon after the burial an austere stone monument was erected bearing the initials A. W., with a simple wooden railing surrounding the burial site.

Late in 1808, however, Thomas McKean addressed the Pennsylvania Assembly and lamented that his home state had largely ignored the graves and achievements of notable revolutionaries, especially Anthony Wayne.[22] That prompted Wayne's son and daughter to seek reinterment in the family's burial plot at St. David's Church in Radnor Township. When they sought advice from the venerable Dr. Benjamin Rush, he assured them that the remains had long since turned to dust; therefore the bones could easily be "taken up . . . put in a box in their natural order," and surrounded by wood shavings for safe and expeditious shipment home. "I rejoice," Rush added, "that public honor is at last to be done to one of the heroes of the American Revolution—I love his name—he was a sincere patriot, a brave soldier, and what is more, an honest man."

So Isaac Wayne went to Erie in August 1809, but feeling emotionally incapable of presiding over the exhumation himself, he commissioned a doctor who had also been a friend of General Wayne to do the work. When J. C. Wallace opened the grave, he found the body remarkably well preserved—contrary to Dr. Rush's assumption. Because it could not be transported in that condition (given that embalming was not possible), the doctor, with Isaac's approval, "dissected the body and boiled the parts in a large iron kettle to render the flesh from the bones. Thereupon the skeleton was cleaned, arranged in order in a new casket, and shipped home in that fashion." What remained in the kettle, along with the surgeon's knives used in the operation, was returned to the old coffin and placed in the original grave.[23]

At the end of a difficult 350-mile journey, Isaac Wayne's entourage was met by an honor guard of Pennsylvania militiamen drawn up to escort the boiled general to Waynesborough. The next day, accompanied by the same military guard, Wayne's new coffin was taken in "solemn processional" through roads lined with friends and relatives to St. David's Church in Radnor, where a minister delivered a suitably patriotic discourse. Subsequently the Society of the Cincinnati and three local militia companies erected a tall stone monument at the grave (fig. 4).[24] A handsome statue of Wayne now stands in the Valley Forge National Military Park, where the general endured the bitter winter of 1777–78. Fourteen counties in as many states are named in his honor, along with countless cities, including Fort Wayne, Indiana. According to legend, however, many bones were somehow lost during the arduous ride from Erie to Waynesborough. Every year on January 1, Wayne's ghost is said to wander the highway (now primarily Pennsylvania Road 322) searching for his missing bones.

✠

As the centennial of George Washington's birth approached in 1832, members of Congress began thinking of ways to memorialize him

*Figure 4.* Grave site of General Anthony Wayne, Radnor, Pennsylvania. From the *Freemason's Magazine*, September 1811. Courtesy of the American Antiquarian Society.

properly in the nation's capital. (The design of the Washington Monument on the Mall lay more than a decade in the future.) Serious proposals circulated to exhume the Father of His Country from his rustic tomb at Mount Vernon and rebury him in the crypt below the Rotunda of the U.S. Capitol. Washington's descendants, however, led by nephew Bushrod Washington, defeated that plan in court, arguing successfully that reburial would violate the president's wishes, stated explicitly in his will. At just that time, moreover, many assumed that the nation's capital might eventually be moved beyond the Appalachians and then to the Midwest as America's population spread westward. Would Washington have to be reburied in conjunction with each demographic shift? Consequently, what might have been the ultimate American reburial never took place.[25]

As late as 1889, the centennial year of Washington's first inauguration, a letter from Bushrod Washington to the governor of Virginia, written in 1816, suddenly surfaced. The Virginia legislature had passed a resolution requesting that Washington's remains be moved to Richmond, where a publicly funded monument would be built above the new tomb. Anticipating the 1832 controversy, Bushrod said that he was moved by the request and that if the decision were his alone, he would allow the transfer to occur. But citing the written terms of the will, he declared that it would be illegal to violate the late president's preference. It is unclear whether the avid congressmen had been aware of that exchange when they proposed reinterment in the nation's capital in 1831–32.[26]

✢

John Trumbull was born in Connecticut in 1756, the son of colonial governor Jonathan Trumbull. He served during the Revolutionary War as an aide to Washington, valued especially for his cartographic abilities. Resigning his commission with the rank of colonel, he spent 1778–79 painting and the following year went to London to study with the American expatriate Benjamin West. Trumbull was arrested there in reprisal for the execution of British spy John André in 1780 and spent seven months in prison. Following his release he continued his studies with West from 1782 until 1785. A year later, encouraged by Thomas

Jefferson, he began a series of historical canvases designed to illustrate major episodes in the American Revolution.

Noted for their liveliness and presumed authenticity in terms of detail, his early works included *The Battle of Bunker Hill* (1786), which he insisted he had witnessed from a distance (a dubious claim), and *The Death of General Montgomery in the Attack on Quebec* (1788), both located today in the Yale Art Gallery, the very first college art museum in the United States and one that Trumbull was instrumental in founding. Sensing what his mature mission and vocation would be, he spent the years from 1789 until 1794 traveling extensively around the United States making portrait studies of leading statesmen and collecting visual data for future paintings. He maintained a studio in New York City from 1815 until 1837; in 1817 he received the plum commission to paint four huge canvases for the rotunda of the U.S. Capitol. They were complete by 1824 and have been admired by many millions of visitors ever since. They include *The Declaration of Independence*, his most famous; *The Surrender of General Burgoyne at Saratoga*; *The Surrender of Lord Cornwallis at Yorktown*; and *The Resignation of General Washington at Annapolis*. From 1817 until 1836 he served as president of the American Academy of Fine Arts in New York. In 1831, despite being a Harvard graduate, he consigned his own collection of paintings to Yale (for an annuity of $1,000) and designed a gallery to house them. He lived in New Haven from 1837 to 1841 while working on his *Autobiography, Letters, and Reminiscences* (1841).

Soon after his pictures were installed at Yale, Trumbull declared to the noted scientist Benjamin Silliman, his devoted nephew-in-law, "It is my wish to be interred beneath this Gallery," adding that "these are my children—those whom they represent have all gone before me, let me be buried with my family. . . . Please, therefore, apply to your authorities of the College for leave to construct a tomb beneath this building—at my expense. I wish to have it large enough for two. I will remove the remains of my wife from New York and place them in it and when I die, I wish to be placed by her side. Let the tomb then be finally closed, not to be opened again until earth and sea shall give up their dead." The tomb was built accordingly, and Sarah Trumbull's remains were reburied at Yale in 1834.[27]

Nine years later the artist died in New York at the age of eighty-seven, and his body was transported by steamer to New Haven, where it was taken to Silliman's home and given a laudatory funeral. The artist was lowered into his allotted place well beneath his portrait of Washington, with portraits of Trumbull and his wife just below the general's. Under them were placed a trophy sword from the battle of Rhode Island and Trumbull's palette and brushes—art and war displayed in symmetry. Silliman soon added a black marble tablet with this inscription: "Colonel John Trumbull, Patriot and Artist, Friend and Aide of Washington." When Yale built a larger art museum in 1866, the college corporation voted to remove Trumbull's paintings to the new structure and that "the remains of Colonel Trumbull and his wife be also removed." Sixty-one years later Yale erected a third art museum, and the director found himself obliged once again to relocate both the pictures and the coffins. The "translation of the relics" was set to take place during the next spring recess in order to avoid any student demonstrations.[28]

At first it appeared to the assembled spectators, led by Trumbull and Silliman descendants, that the reburial would take place outside of and adjacent to the new museum. Then someone happened to suggest moving inside to a spot where the floor had been removed, revealing that a well-constructed brick crypt was prepared. Still resting outside, the coffin containing the thrice-buried Sarah was not in good condition, and when it was gently lifted, the bottom gave way. Her bones were moved to a new casket by waiting undertakers, who had been advised to prepare for any eventuality. The colonel's mahogany casket was well preserved, and "the two flag-draped coffins were carried across High Street, followed by a small procession, to the new impressive tomb in the still incomplete Gallery." A full account of what happened that day, along with the signatures of witnesses and extracts from Silliman's notes on the original burial eighty-five years earlier, were bricked up in the new and spacious vault.[29]

The press carried extensive reports in the following days, but within a decade distorted versions of what had happened in 1928 began to appear. In one wild account, Trumbull's own bones had tumbled out of a broken coffin, only to be swept back into the box by a crabby janitor using a broom and dustpan. In truth, however, on June 26, 1928, the 172nd anniversary of the "patriot-artist's" birth, a decorous memorial service was held directly above the new vault. President Angell presided over a distinguished gathering composed of Trumbull and Silliman descendants, friends, faculty, and students. The university chaplain reenacted the original service of 1843, and eloquent tributes were heard. Trumbull's request remained honored. He lies beneath his art, though not quite so close to it as he had envisioned.[30]

✣

The political and military career of Nathanael Greene paralleled those of Montgomery and Wayne. Born in 1742 in what is now Warwick, Rhode Island, he initially worked at his father's iron foundry and then in 1770 moved to Coventry, where he managed the family forge. He served in the Rhode Island General Assembly during 1770–72 and again in 1774–75. In May 1775 he helped raise a militia in his colony and was promptly named a brigadier general. Months later he achieved the same rank in the Continental Army and participated in the American siege of Boston. When the British evacuated that city in March 1776, he was placed in charge of Boston. In August he was promoted to major general and given command of the troops in New Jersey. Although he suffered defeats in Manhattan and at Fort Lee across the Hudson, he played a major role in the victory at Trenton late that year and subsequently at Brandywine and Germantown in 1777. Following the harsh winter at Valley Forge, Congress appointed Greene quartermaster general, and he established a system of supply depots for Washington's army.[31]

When Benedict Arnold's plan to surrender West Point to the British was discovered, Greene succeeded Arnold in charge of West Point and presided over the tribunal that condemned John André, the British spy, to die. After Horatio Gates was defeated in 1780 by the British at Camden, South Carolina, Washington gave Greene the command of Gates's army. After reorganizing the Southern Department, and following Daniel Morgan's victory at the Cowpens in January 1781, Greene nearly exhausted Cornwallis's forces by leading them on a hectic winter chase through harassment across North Carolina to Virginia.[32]

At the battle of Guilford Court House, Greene caused Cornwallis to suffer very heavy losses, and subsequently his troops completed the reconquest of the South. After the war the citizens of Georgia voted to give Greene, as they had to Anthony Wayne, a plantation there, and he spent the rest of his life moving back and forth between Georgia and Rhode Island trying to restore his finances. Greene died near Savannah in June 1786 and was buried there in what became known as the "old cemetery" and later the "Colonial cemetery," first established in 1758 as the burying ground for Christ's Church (Anglican).[33]

At the close of the nineteenth century, a time of increasing veneration of ancestors, especially heroes of the Revolution, sentiment grew quite strong in Rhode Island to have Greene exhumed and to repatriate his remains for reburial in his native state. Colonel Asa Bird Gardiner, president of the Rhode Island Society of the Cincinnati, led a delegation to Savannah not only to negotiate for Greene's return but to search for his burial place, by then totally obscure. As Savannah grew, burials had ceased in the "old cemetery," and it fell into disuse and sad neglect, the graves heavily overgrown. Boys had entered and desecrated some of the tombs, and when Sherman's army camped in Savannah during the close of the Civil War, soldiers had emptied out some of the major family vaults in order to use them for shelter. Further desecration resulted from their disregard for the final resting places of Southern families.[34]

Colonel Gardiner's committee came to Savannah in March 1901. It needed to secure permission from the vestry of Christ's Church and the mayor of the city to open and intensively examine a line of four major vaults known to contain the remains of distinguished persons buried during the later eighteenth century. Because there was no visible exterior marker for Greene's likely grave, intuition and careful study were employed to eliminate three of the four. Along with local cemetery staff, Gardiner's committee worked through massive brickwork at the Graham family site to get below an upper level of coffins to several that had fallen apart. Good fortune favored them. Amidst gravel and rubble they found part of a coffin-plate on which the numbers "1786" appeared. Very close by they found not one but two sets of bones intermixed, the skeletal remains of a grown man and those of someone either an adolescent or a teenager. The Rhode Islanders knew that Nathanael's son, George Washington Greene, had drowned in the Savannah River at the age of eighteen in 1793. Clearly, he had been buried in this vault close by his father. Mingled with the bones of the adult the searchers found three metal buttons from a military uniform, and on the bony hands, heavy French silk gloves had survived intact. Experts recalled that when Lafayette revisited the newly independent United States in 1824–25, he invariably presented French silk gloves to the generals he had known and worked with during the war. Perhaps he had done so a generation earlier for Greene and others. The committee felt confident that it had found the remains of Nathanael Greene and his son. The bones were separated and placed in two zinc-lined boxes.[35]

Those boxes of relics (with new coffin-plates suitably inscribed) were then placed in a vault of the Southern Bank of the State of Georgia, subject to the joint order of Colonel Gardiner and Alfred Dearing Harden, representing the Society of the Cincinnati, awaiting a decision about what to do next. Greene's widow had remarried a few years after his death and moved to a plantation on one of the Sea Islands. By 1901 there were numerous direct descendants scattered all over the United States, but mainly in Georgia and Rhode Island. When officials and family in the latter requested the remains for reinterment in Greene's home state, all the living descendants were consulted. An overwhelming majority preferred that his bones be buried in Savannah, close to their original location. Interestingly, the three exceptions expressed a preference for the battlefield of Guilford Court House in North Carolina, the site of Greene's most brilliant tactical decisions.[36]

Representatives from all the patriotic organizations in Savannah formed an ad hoc group simply called the Association of Patriotic Societies. They chose Johnson Square, where the cornerstone for a monument to Greene had been placed in 1825. The association exercised full control over the ceremonial reinterment on November 14, 1902, and decided to place the remains of father and son beneath flagstones on the south side of the monument.[37] The expense for that event would be borne by voluntary subscriptions from the citizens of Savannah, with no funds requested from either the state or the municipality. The mayor issued a proclamation requesting all merchants to close their places of business on November 14 between 2:00 and 6:00 p.m. "in order to give their employees an opportunity to be present and participate in the ceremonies incident to the occasion, and all persons having flags are requested to display the same at half-mast between the hours of three and six." Great numbers of people did, in fact, turn out to march in the procession and line the streets as spectators. The crowd was swelled by local and visiting members of the recently formed DAR.[38]

Greene's new casket, made of Georgia curly pine, was placed upon a caisson by a detail from the Chatham Artillery and accompanied by troops to the "old cemetery" (fig. 5).A bronze tablet was placed upon the original Graham family vault, declaring, "Here rested for 114 years the remains of MAJ.-GEN. NATHANAEL GREENE." Following the procession to Johnson Square, a prayer, and the playing of a dirge, the new permanent tablet to be placed upon a memorial shaft of granite was presented on behalf of Greene's descendants to the municipality. Walter G. Charlton, president of the Georgia Society Sons of Revolution, declaimed: "To-day come again the people of Savannah, and with them the distinguished sons and beautiful daughters of other parts, that, with *pride and reverence*, new honors may be paid to the memory of Nathanael Greene. We who will look upon the procession solemn, yet, triumphant . . . need no incentive to keep in our hearts and memories the services of this great soldier, whose strong arm and stout heart bore the burden of Georgia's fate in one of the darkest hours of her existence."[39]

*Figure 5.* Caisson bearing the remains of General Nathanael Greene, rolling to his reburial in Johnson Square, Savannah, Georgia, November 14, 1902. From *Remains of Major-General Nathanael Greene* (Providence: Committee of the Rhode Island General Assembly, 1903).

*Figure 6.* Monument to General Nathanael Greene, Johnson Square, Savannah, Georgia. Photograph courtesy of Mike Dover.

After the two coffins had been situated in their new crypt, the governor of Rhode Island stepped forward while the tribute from his state was placed upon the monument: "a large wreath of bronze galex, crossed with cycus palms, tied with rich purple ribbon on which were embossed in gold" the state arms of Rhode Island (fig. 6). The wreath stood on a tripod at the base of the shaft. Greene's great-great-grandson unveiled the memorial tablet, which declared General Greene second only to George Washington in greatness. After the playing of "America," the principal oration was given by the man who had initiated the search and exhumation, Asa Bird Gardiner, president of the Rhode Island Society of the Cincinnati.[40]

The Association of Patriotic Societies had been determined "to make the occasion a patriotic one, and to avoid giving it, as far as it was possible to do so, a funereal aspect." They succeeded admirably. Patriotism had been paraded with military exercises at two separate sites in Savannah, and solemnity had been achieved without grimness or maudlin words. On July 4, 1902, Colonel Gardiner had given a satisfying report of the exhumation and reburial plans to the Society of the Cincinnati in

Newport. Both sides seemed satisfied—and it is no accident that all of this occurred at a time when there was great emphasis upon sectional reconciliation and strengthening the Union.[41]

Although Daniel Morgan's origins were more humble, his military career would be closely linked with Greene's. Born in 1735 in Lebanon Township, New Jersey, Morgan was also the son of a forge worker, but he quarreled with his father and left home at age sixteen. After working at odd jobs in Pennsylvania, he moved down through the Shenandoah Valley and settled near Charles Town in what would become West Virginia a century later. Morgan, seemingly inexhaustible, worked mainly as a teamster; but when the Continental Army called for the formation of ten rifle companies, Virginia's House of Burgesses asked Morgan to organize one. He quickly recruited ninety-six men and marched to support the siege of Boston in 1775. Because of their effectiveness, his group came to be known as Morgan's Sharpshooters.

Late in 1775 Benedict Arnold chose Morgan to lead his own company and two others on the ill-fated expedition to Quebec in which Richard Montgomery lost his life. Morgan was captured by the British and remained a captive until early in 1777, when he received his freedom in an exchange of prisoners. Promoted to the rank of colonel, he played an important role in the defeat of General Burgoyne at Saratoga. Because he mistrusted the Continental Congress and did not curry favor with anyone, he was repeatedly passed over for promotion until late in 1780, when he became a brigadier general under Nathanael Greene, who instructed him to harass Cornwallis's army in the south.

Cornwallis chose to send Banastre Tarleton's British Legion to track Morgan down. He did so successfully, but Morgan devised a brilliant plan to maximize the effectiveness of his outnumbered men as guerrilla fighters and excellent shots with muskets and rifles. He chose to make his stand at a place known as the Cowpens, South Carolina, on January 17, 1781. Knowing that his foe tended to be precipitous, Morgan lured Tarleton into making a premature charge against a carefully arranged triple defense of riflemen, cavalry, and infantry. The outcome was an immense victory. Of Tarleton's 1,076 men, 110 died and 830 were captured. Although Tarleton himself escaped, Morgan's forces gained control of all his equipment.[42]

Following the war, Morgan returned to Charles Town, invested in land, and eventually acquired 250,000 acres. He joined the Presbyterian Church in 1782 and built a new house in Winchester, Virginia, which he named Saratoga. In 1790 Congress awarded him a gold medal to commemorate his great victory at the Cowpens. Four years later he returned to service by leading militia units to suppress the Whiskey Rebellion in Massachusetts. Elected to Congress in 1797–99 as a Federalist, he died in Winchester at his daughter's home in 1802 and was buried in the local Presbyterian graveyard. In 1881, the centennial anniversary of that astonishing triumph at the Cowpens, a statue of Morgan was erected with congressional funds in the central town square of Spartanburg, South Carolina. The square and the statue remain in place to this day.

At Morgan's funeral he was eulogized as the others had been, with resounding sentiments that Winchester would always remember its "Beloved Patriot and Hero." As early as 1843, however, a patriotic weekly titled *Brother Jonathan* ran this item: "In the graveyard at Winchester, Virginia, says a Southern paper, the traveler will find a grave overgrown with grass, without a stone or an inscription to preserve the ashes of its inhabitant from insult. Within the grave reposes the remains of the brave General Morgan, whose name ranks in the annals of the Revolution second only to that of Washington."[43]

One year later, however, as part of the "rural cemetery" movement begun at Mount Auburn in 1831, the new Mount Hebron Cemetery was dedicated in Winchester. On that occasion in June 1844, the principal speaker promised that "the tomb of Morgan shall be here. . . . Near, too, will be the graves of Soldiers and Patriarchs who fought and struggled in the early conflicts of our country. So that the youthful volunteer will have no need to make a pilgrimage to the plains of Marathon or the pass of Thermopylae, to inhale *patriotic* fervor."[44] Morgan's renown would be restored and respected once again, and the new cemetery would have a celebrity, just as Laurel Hill in Philadelphia had achieved two with the 1838–40 reburials of Charles Thomson and Hugh Mercer.

The full text of this highly representative eulogy illustrates two other points of importance. First, William L. Clark's totally secular address also called attention to the paramount significance and distinguishing feature of the new phenomenon of the public cemetery, because it portended the democratization of interment. "No man of proper feelings can be insensible to the final disposition of that tabernacle in which he hath abided during his earthly pilgrimage," he declared. "But to receive proper interment ourselves, we must extend it to others."[45]

The second point emerges from an introductory address given on the same occasion by Reverend A. H. Boyd, which is totally different in its tone and texture, indicative of the distinction mentioned in chapter 1. The body, Boyd explained, "is destined to rise from the tomb, and to be reunited to the deathless soul, to enhance either its happiness or misery. And thus it shall be, my hearers, with all the bodies that shall be placed within this enclosure. In their appointed time, they shall leave this hallowed spot . . . where they may have been reposing for centuries in undisturbed silence, and shall enter another abode, which their Creator has prepared for them."[46] The two sets of remarks on this occasion, Boyd's being much briefer, marked a careful separation between the secular and spiritual spheres. At most reinterments, however, only the first was heard.

Unfortunately, Morgan would not lie undisturbed forever. During the Civil War his remains were removed because of the fear that Yankee soldiers in that hotly contested valley might carry them away—assuming that they could find them! In 1868 he was reinterred in Mount Hebron Cemetery, and the six Virginians responsible each took away a handle from the original coffin as a personal memento—a latter-day reminder of what had once been done with the body parts of disassembled saints. Morgan's gravestone had become chipped, however, the words weathered and difficult to read. As the cemetery expanded, the older portion where Morgan's casket was located came to be neglected, and once again grasses grew up around the marker. In 1900 the firemen of Winchester initiated a movement to memorialize Morgan properly, but nothing came of it.[47]

In July 1951 Winchester received a rude awakening. Having learned of Morgan's lapsed renown and the neglect of his grave, the DAR chapter in Spartanburg enlisted support from local civic groups to launch a campaign to have Morgan disinterred and reburied in or near Spartanburg, where they believed he would be accorded greater respect. But when a delegation of determined gravediggers from South Carolina, armed with picks and shovels, arrived at Mount Hebron, an alert caretaker called the Winchester and county police. Very quickly a crowd of

*Figure 7*. Monument to General Daniel Morgan, Mount Hebron Cemetery, Winchester, Virginia. Photograph courtesy of Steven Dunn.

"patriots" gathered at the cemetery, hotly determined to retain their nearly forgotten hero's relics. Outnumbered, the South Carolinians retreated and headed for home. *Life* magazine recounted the episode in a lively article titled "Who Gets the General's Body?"[48]

Morgan's memory would ultimately be vindicated in 1953, when the Winchester-Frederick County Historical Society proceeded to erect an impressive granite monument bearing the general's likeness over the grave (fig. 7). Children descended from members of Morgan's first rifle company saluted the monument, and the congressman representing the district unveiled it. Thus, having been exhumed during the deadliest of all American wars, the remains of "the Old Wagoner," as Morgan was once known, were belatedly rescued by his adopted community rather than being removed to the site of his greatest triumph and ultimate source of fame.[49]

✠

The battle for Button Gwinnett's bones also took place at midcentury, but in this instance the conflict involved two competing communities in Georgia: Savannah, once again, and Augusta as a determined rival—the latter much less gracious than Rhode Island had been about its native son Nathanael Greene. The conflict began to heat up in 1957, but the phase of greatest intensity occurred between 1960 and 1964. Like Daniel Morgan, Gwinnett had been born in 1735 but in Gloucestershire, England. His odd first name came from his godmother, Barbara Button, his mother's cousin. Because of family need and a feisty disposition he would not repay a loan, decided to cross the Atlantic, and settled in Savannah in the mid-1760s. Gwinnett purchased a sea island south of Savannah and became a planter and a lumberman. After taking an interest in politics, he became a member of Georgia's colonial assembly and decided to support the Patriot side when push came to shove with Britain. As an ardent Whig, in 1776 he was sent to Philadelphia as a delegate to the Continental Congress, where he strongly supported the Declaration of Independence and signed it. Once back in Savannah, he became speaker of the new state assembly.[50]

Gwinnett also had military aspirations, but in the spring of 1777 his fiery temper led him to challenge a suspected traitor to a duel. They met in a meadow on Sea Island Road near Savannah and faced off with pistols at a distance of only four paces. Each man was shot only in the leg, as honor required, but Gwinnett's wound in the left thigh became gangrenous, and he died just three days later at the age of forty-two. Because of his early death, his signature is the scarcest among all signers of the Declaration. There is no known portrait of him that can be certified, though spurious ones have surfaced. For many decades, amateur historians played detective in trying to locate his unknown burial place, but without success. In 1957, however, a retired school principal from Savannah, Arthur J. Funk, who had been intrigued by Gwinnett ever since 1913, began the process of serious sleuthing.[51]

At the Chatham County courthouse in Savannah, Funk found the original accounting by the executor of Gwinnett's will. A bill indicated payment for erecting some sort of monument to the deceased, and the only plausible site turned out to be the same neglected "old cemetery" of Christ's Church where Greene had been buried. Exploring the renamed Colonial Cemetery, Funk found a brown stub of stone situated seven paces from the grave of Georgia's first governor. After receiving park department permission, Funk very carefully removed soil from beneath the stub and made out a few letters on the face, including a *G*, a *T*, and a *7*, which certainly suggested the likelihood of Gwinnett's grave. An archaeologist from New York who happened to be in Savannah at the time urged Funk to dig further and open the casket to see whether the leg was broken at the knee. Funk decided to seek help from the Georgia Historical Commission, which sent its own archaeologist to excavate the site and examine the remains.[52]

They found the skeleton of a man about five feet six inches tall whose left femur exhibited a section of damaged bone in the area immediately above the knee. Although Funk felt jubilant, a Savannah physician who was also an expert on Indian remains argued that the evidence was inadequate. He may very well have been piqued that after so many years of fruitless searching by others, Funk had found his man so easily. With Funk's consent, the damaged femur was sent to the Smithsonian Institution in Washington; specialists sent back a skeptical report, speculating that it was actually a female skeleton. Funk and his supporters responded angrily, calling attention to the gravestone evidence that had been ignored and a plait of hair on the skull that seemed to belong to a male. When Funk showed the bones to a ballistics expert in Georgia, the latter declared that the wound had clearly been inflicted prior to burial and most likely by a "circular device" such as a pistol ball.[53]

By then much of Savannah was intrigued and intensely divided, so Funk appealed to the mayor for an impartial investigation. The mayor turned the matter over to the Savannah-Chatham County Historic Site and Monument Commission, an agency of state government chartered by the Georgia legislature in 1949. In September 1959 the commission issued a thirty-four-page report and added some information of its own. Essentially, it supported Funk's view that the grave as well as the skeleton was indeed Gwinnett's. Funk stored all of the exhumed remains in the guest room of his home and awaited the next phase of the controversy: the claims of rival Augusta to Gwinnett's bones, on the grounds that it already had the bodies of Georgia's other two signers of the Declaration of Independence entombed beneath a granite obelisk, erected in 1848, known as the Signers' Monument. Shouldn't all three rest in peace together?[54]

In April 1960, Mayor Millard Beckum of Augusta began his campaign to have Button's bones removed there. Augusta's case hinged heavily upon the authenticity of a portrait believed (by some) to be the only known likeness of Gwinnett, signed by the painter Jeremiah Theus. It had been purchased by Atlanta's Fulton Federal Savings and Loan Association from a New York gallery for five thousand dollars and then acquired by Augusta as a kind of surrogate for Gwinnett's actual remains. After citizens of Savannah made a compelling case that for various reasons the portrait could not be genuine, the city appropriated funds for the erection of a proper Gwinnett monument, thereby dashing Augusta's hopes for relocating the bones (fig. 8). The people there took their loss gracefully under the circumstances, because reburial of Gwinnett locally would have required digging up the wife of one of the other two signers, and everyone seemed to agree that that was no way to treat a very old lady.[55]

*Figure 8.* Monument to Button Gwinnett, Savannah, Georgia. Photograph courtesy of Kurt Lau.

In October 1964 a crowd gathered in the Colonial Cemetery to witness Gwinnett's reinterment, quite satisfied that they possessed the correct set of bones and had commemorated him in a dignified manner. Present for this patriotic occasion were representatives of the Georgia chapters of the Sons of Revolution, the DAR, the Society of Colonial Wars, and the Colonial Dames of America—each member waving an American flag. There were many chuckles when a leading collector of rare American manuscripts from Joliet, Illinois, declared: "We no longer need to ask, 'Button, Button, who has the Button?' Button has been found." Arthur Funk then proudly unveiled an appropriate bronze tablet; taps was sounded, and a detail of ROTC cadets fired three volleys into the air.[56]

✢

We turn next to episodes concerning four individuals, each European born, who figured dramatically in the history of Revolutionary America—all of them involving issues and controversy over exhumation and reburial, and most culminating in confusion or fiasco, but in two cases sad neglect followed by fortuitous redemption: one might even say a satisfactory second ending.

Complex and historically convoluted is the story of George Augustus, Lord Viscount Howe, a principal leader of the British attack early in July 1758 on the French fortification at Ticonderoga, located just south of Lake Champlain. He turned out to be the most prominent martyr fighting on behalf of the colonies in the French and Indian War, so the location of his burial prompted considerable research and controversy, especially between 1889 and 1911. In October 1889 some laborers digging a sewer in the town of Ticonderoga found a tombstone that appeared from cryptic lettering to be a battle-site memorial to Howe, along with a skull and some disintegrated bones. The discovery caused a local sensation, and the laborers had to prevent people from ripping away pieces of the coffin (such as it was) in order to carry off relics.[57]

This discovery sparked a battle among local historians and archaeologists that would eventually be clarified, though not definitively, with a lengthy publication in 1911. Howe was serving under General Abercromby on July 6, 1758, when the decision was made to launch a frontal assault on the French lines defending their fort. Howe was shot through the chest and died at the scene of battle. His partially embalmed body was carried south of Lake George to Fort William Henry on a "rude bier," where preservation of the body was completed prior to its being sent by wagon to Fort Edward. After that it went by bateau to Albany and from there, presumably, to be shipped down the Hudson River and then to England for final burial. That much is known largely from the papers of Major Philip Schuyler, who was in charge of moving the corpse, and from oral history within the Ingalsbe family. The ancestor of one member is known to have accompanied Schuyler with Howe's body to Albany.[58]

When the corpse reached Albany, however, its condition was so poor that General Stanwix felt obliged to have it buried there in St. Peter's Church. What is known as its "church book" survived several major fires and contains entries regarding use of the church pall (or coffin drapery). Those who believe that Howe was buried elsewhere contest the validity of that evidence. But accounts of Howe's death and burial appeared swiftly in New York and Boston newspapers. (Albany still lacked its own paper in 1758.) When the old church was taken down in 1802, there are eyewitness accounts of Howe's remains being placed in a special coffin with a rich silk damask cerement, seen and handled by the historian Elkanah Watson and his assistant, formerly a British officer residing in Greenbush, New York, who knew the exact location of the grave. Howe was then reburied beneath the second St. Peter's Church along with twenty-four other bodies that had been interred at the original structure.[59]

When the second church was in turn demolished in 1859, Lord Howe's coffin was disinterred once again, distinguishable by a black silk ribbon referred to in Watson's account, and reburied under the vestibule of the third church. That is where matters stood when the accidental discovery in Ticonderoga of an apparent headstone and some bones occurred in 1889. Subsequent expert investigation determined that the memorial headstone had no characteristics of such stones from the mid-eighteenth century and that the remains bore no indications of a person of high rank and social status. Moreover, these remains had been found in a venue to which the British had absolutely no access at the time of the battle and defeat.[60]

Adding to all this uncertainty concerning Howe's whereabouts, some people have cause to assume that he must be buried in Westminster Abbey. How could that be? Only with the arrival of a fresh and stronger British force under Lord Jeffrey Amherst in 1759 would the British and their colonial allies begin to repulse the French occupation of northern New York and turn the tide. Meanwhile, the General Court of Massachusetts had appropriated 250 pounds for a monument to be erected in Howe's honor at Westminster; this compounded the confusion, leading many to believe that the military hero surely must be buried there rather than remaining in Albany, despite two recorded exhumations and three burials.

✠

An English officer who conspired *against* the Patriot cause two decades later did come to rest at Westminster Abbey, but that didn't come about easily. When Major John André was captured by American irregulars in 1780 while disguised in civilian clothes, papers concealed in his boot revealed that he was negotiating with Benedict Arnold for the betrayal of West Point to the British. George Washington ordered that André be hanged as a spy rather than shot as an officer and a gentleman— an injustice bitterly resented by the British, and by quite a few Patriot women who admired young André for his bravery and good looks. They pleaded for his life in vain, nor were they able to upgrade him from the status of a common criminal in his execution.[61]

In August 1821 James Buchanan, the British consul in New York, risked life and limb by visiting Tarrytown, where André had been buried. He managed to disinter the corpse and examine it before a large gathering of townspeople. When they learned that Buchanan intended to return in order to retrieve the body for reburial in England, they objected vehemently: any honor bestowed on the spy would constitute a stain on the reputation of General Washington for having ordered him to be hanged and stripped of his officer's uniform prior to burial. Eventually, Buchanan did manage to take the remains to New York City and then to London, where a monument had already been erected to André's memory at Westminster Abbey. In 1833 Buchanan even published an account of the intensely politicized episode.[62]

What makes this saga especially noteworthy is that Hezekiah Niles, editor of *Niles Weekly Register*, promptly and correctly assumed that Buchanan's efforts had been inspired, or at least prompted, by the return of the remains of General Richard Montgomery from Canada and his reburial in New York in 1818, as well as William Cobbett's removal of Thomas Paine's bones in 1819. Buchanan reported that he had been "hourly annoyed by contrasts drawn from the conduct of the state of New York as to the remains of General Montgomery—while those of the British soldier, who was sacrificed in the service of his country, in the flower of his youth, (*by a doom, which, in the judgment of many, might have been commuted*), were abandoned and neglected." Exhuming Major André became a political quid pro quo.[63]

What transpired with the remains of Thomas Paine, the English émigré corset maker, the author of *Common Sense* in 1776, and one of the most influential (but also controversial) tract writers of all time, may well be the reductio ad absurdum among all these strange stories. Near the end of his life, Paine expressed the fear that his bones might eventually be dug up for malevolent reasons. When he died on June 8, 1809, in New York City, impoverished and by then rather obscure if not forgotten by the public, his corpse was arrayed in a shirt, a muslin gown tied at the neck and wrists with black ribbon, and stockings. A cap was placed beneath his head as a pillow because he never slept in a nightcap. He reposed in a mahogany coffin with his name and age engraved on a silver plate carefully attached and was buried in New Rochelle. His request for interment in a Quaker burying ground had been denied because he wrote the deistic *Age of Reason* (1794–96), so he was laid to rest in a corner section of his own farm. Because his friends surrounded the grave with a wall twelve feet square and planted four special trees, the site could be readily located. Ten years later William Cobbett, once Paine's bitter foe and an avidly pro-British journalist who wrote tracts under the pseudonym Peter Porcupine, went to New Rochelle, managed to dig up Paine's bones, and carried them off to England (fig. 9).[64]

After Cobbett died bankrupt in 1835, all of his property had to be submitted for public auction in order to satisfy his creditors. When the auctioneer refused to include Paine's bones in the proceedings, Cobbett's eldest son and executor petitioned the lord chancellor for relief, but the request was denied. What happened after that is anyone's guess. The son reputedly sold the bones to a neighboring Hampshire day laborer, but they more likely fell into the receivership of farmer George West along

*Figure 9.* "A Radical Reformer." Cartoon of William Cobbett carrying a sack of bones of Tom Paine from New Rochelle, New York, to England (1819). From Craig Nelson, *Thomas Paine* (New York: Viking, 1996).

with the remainder of Cobbett's unsold estate when the son himself was imprisoned for debt. Either the laborer or the farmer then sold Paine's remains to a London furniture salesman and onetime Cobbett secretary, who in turn seems to have sold at least part of the skeleton to an orthodox Anglican priest who insisted in 1854 that he owned the skull and the right hand but refused to let anyone see them. When a Paine disciple and researcher pursued this lead, he was told that the bones had been lost—which is the most familiar version of how the saga ended—but in fact those bones had apparently been taken by the priest's son to be examined by the Royal College of Surgeons, where an anatomist insisted that the putative skull was too small to have been a man's head.[65]

Meanwhile, the American press caught wind of what had happened following the failed auction and in 1837 expressed increasing outrage at the disgraceful treatment of a determined Revolutionary figure who had done so much to activate public sentiment in favor of independence early in 1776. The Philadelphia *Public Ledger* declared, "One of the grossest acts of indecency of which we ever heard, was the exhumation and transportation to England, of the remains of Paine. Nor can we regard with greater disgust, the still greater indecency of keeping them without internment [sic]." The *Ledger* demanded burial in either England or the United States "out of common Christian decency" and proclaimed the whole affair "disgraceful to both countries."[66]

Stories soon began to emerge that buttons had been carved from Paine's bones, and a rumor circulated for a while that his rib cage had surfaced in France, where Republicans felt indebted to his memory because of his antimonarchical tract *The Rights of Man* (1791–92). According to one other story, recorded in Cobbett's archives, some of Paine's hair and his blackened brain, taken from Cobbett's home in 1833, were later passed along to several other families and were eventually sold to Moncure D. Conway, Paine's American biographer (the biography was published in 1892), who gave them to a physician, who interred them in 1905 beneath an obelisk belonging to the Paine National Historical Association in New Rochelle. The dispersion and loss of Paine's remains is, indeed, one of the most bizarre and perplexing stories in the entire history of politically motivated exhumation.[67]

Adding more than a bit to the mystery, in July 1976 a seven-foot obelisk inscribed "in memory" of Thomas Paine was unearthed by a backhoe at Tivoli, New York, a town north of New Rochelle on the Hudson. It lay several feet beneath the roots of a hemlock tree and was uncovered only because a man had been asked to dig a ditch for a new septic field next to the home of a highway equipment operator. What has always been assumed to be Paine's true tombstone is much smaller and resides at the Thomas Paine Cottage and Museum in New Rochelle. Heightening the mystery, when the "new" obelisk was found, its top was broken and it also contained the name of John G. Lasher, a man descended from Palatine Germans who had first settled in the Tivoli area around 1710, and who died in 1877 at the age of eighty. Someone must have decided to "recycle" this imposing marker that had blank space to spare, just as Paine's remains got recycled in a different sense owing to their ongoing and seemingly perpetual mobility.[68]

It feels apt as well as ironic that while Paine was still very much alive and writing his impassioned installments of *The American Crisis* (December 1776–November 1778), he touched upon the topic of death and appropriate burials in a republican polity. In the fourth installment he addressed himself directly to General Sir William Howe, commander of British forces in North America: "The usual honours of the dead, to be sure, are not sufficiently sublime to escort a character like you to the republic of dust and ashes; for however men may differ in their ideas of grandeur or government here, the grave is nevertheless a perfect republic. Death is not the monarch of the dead, but of the dying. The moment he obtains a conquest he loses a subject, and, like the foolish King you serve, will, in the end, war himself out of all dominion."[69]

Paine had begun his life in that "foolish" monarchy and ended it in a republic, however imperfect. Yet in most surviving accounts his bones would haplessly disappear in the monarchy he had despised.[70]

✠

A sad story with an upbeat outcome will close this chapter devoted to the posthumous fate of famous figures from the Revolutionary era. Pierre L'Enfant, an artist, architect, and civil engineer, came to America in 1776 in order to serve in the Continental Army under George Washington's command. His cartographic skills made him invaluable, and he endeared himself to Washington. When New York City was selected in 1789 to serve as the new nation's temporary capital, Washington felt that L'Enfant was best qualified to redesign Federal Hall in lower Manhattan as a suitable site for the inaugural government. Because he accomplished that challenge quite successfully, Washington then invited L'Enfant to draw up a plan for the newly designated capital city on the Potomac, after Congress reached the compromise decision to have it located and built there between 1790 and 1800.[71]

The headstrong L'Enfant achieved a brilliant and enduring design in 1791–92 but was dismissed less than one year later by Secretary of State Thomas Jefferson because of disputes over the optimal schedule for publishing an engraved plan, which affected the value of house lots in the village and privately owned plots of land that would become the District of Columbia. In the years that followed, L'Enfant imprudently rejected the commission offered by Congress in payment for his services and demanded far more. Later, when he became willing to settle for a modest fee, an irritated Congress refused to pay him at all. He became the victim of his own arrogance, and the remainder of his life, like Paine's, devolved into a bitter struggle against poverty and obscurity.[72]

Benjamin Henry Latrobe, the gifted architect appointed by Jefferson to serve as the first surveyor of public buildings and to oversee "public construction" in the new capital, blamed L'Enfant for every setback and delay that occurred during the 1790s. He called his rival "this singular man, of whom it is not known whether he was ever educated to the profession, and who indubitably has neither good taste nor the slightest practical knowledge." Rather than returning to France, L'Enfant remained and continued to petition Congress for payment while living on sufferance at the estates of others. In 1824, when his final petition was nearing failure and he was forced to leave yet another temporary residence, a letter of salvation reached the old man from a nephew of Thomas Digges, inviting him to take up residence at Green Hill, a medium-sized plantation located along the "Eastern Branch" of the Potomac (the Anacostia River), just outside the Federal district that L'Enfant had so elegantly designed.[73]

The planner ended his days there as a "kind of eccentric elderly relative," spending much of his time tending flowers, studying the sky, intending to go into the city to pursue his claims but somehow never doing so. He died at Green Hill on June 15, 1825, just shy of his seventy-first birthday, and was buried at the base of a newly planted cedar sapling near the graves of servants and slaves to the Digges family. There was no public funeral, and only one obituary (little more than four hundred words) in the *National Intelligencer*, which lamented the absence of adequate materials for a biographical sketch. It acknowledged his plan for the capital but added that "he thought himself ill remunerated for this service, and, because full justice was not, as he thought, measured to him, he refused to receive what was tendered, and lived a life of sequestration from society, and austere privation, which attracted respect, whilst it excited compassion."[74]

Out of sight and very much out of mind for most of the nineteenth century, L'Enfant slowly began to regain public attention after 1881, when an anonymous article about him appeared in the *New-York Tribune*. Meanwhile, a retired Washington banker who now owned Green Hill decided to organize the architect's remaining effects, especially letters and documents of various sorts. In 1887 the Library of Congress published a facsimile edition of L'Enfant's plan for the District, and two years later Washington's newly organized Columbia Historical Society devoted its second volume of records to the origins of the city, including transcriptions of a selection of L'Enfant's memorials to Congress. By 1901–2 President Theodore Roosevelt had become quite friendly with Jules Jusserand, the French ambassador, who had strong interests in history and literature; they often played tennis together.[75]

Among Jusserand's goals while he enjoyed easy access to Roosevelt was calling greater attention to the role of French heroes during the Revolutionary era, ranging from Lafayette to L'Enfant. The crusade would prove effective: in May 1908 Congress allocated one thousand dollars "to remove and render accessible to the public the grave of Major Pierre Charles L'Enfant." Going even further, and quickly, in December of that year the secretary of war approved a prime grave site in Arlington National Cemetery. The process of giving L'Enfant his due, at least in terms of glory, was now under way. On April 22, 1909, the remains were exhumed—after a prudent pause until lightning and thunder abated. According to the *Washington Post*, witnesses found that a sadly decomposed coffin with "a layer of discolored mold three inches in thickness, two pieces of bone, and a tooth were all that remained of the great engineer."[76]

Those few surviving pieces were placed in a metal casket wrapped in an American flag and conveyed to Mount Olivet Cemetery along the Bladensburg Road, the route by which L'Enfant would have approached the village of Georgetown in March 1791 for a planning session with George Washington and others. On April 28, 1909, the casket arrived in Washington, escorted by an Army Corps of Engineers honor guard. It was brought into the Capitol rotunda and placed upon the very same catafalque that had supported the coffin of Abraham Lincoln (fig. 10). L'Enfant lay in state there, the very first foreign-born person and only the seventh individual to be given such a high honor. President William Howard Taft and his wife arrived at 10:30, surrounded by members of the Society of the Cincinnati and other dignitaries. Ambassador Jusserand praised his countryman for demonstrated skill and devotion. "For Major L'Enfant," he proclaimed, "the planning of the city of Washington was a work of love. . . . The streets were unexampled anywhere; gardens, parks, fountains, statues to famous men—all were devised in view of a great and powerful nation, the nation of today."[77]

Around noon, eight army engineers carried the casket out to the east front of the Capitol and placed it on an artillery caisson pulled by six bay mares. Cavalry from Fort Meyer across the Potomac led a cortège of five hundred persons and the Corps of Engineers band. The procession followed Pennsylvania Avenue to M Street in order to cross the Key Bridge in Georgetown, because the Memorial Bridge would not

*Figure 10.* Pierre L'Enfant's body lying in state in the Rotunda of the United States Capitol, April 28, 1909. Courtesy of the Washingtoniana Division, DC Public Library.

*Figure 11.* The dedication of Pierre L'Enfant's tomb and memorial at Arlington National Cemetery, April 29, 1909. Division of Prints and Photographs, Library of Congress.

be completed until 1929. Flags flew at half-mast along the way while children and teachers, given a holiday, lined the route to see the horse-drawn cart and its "solemn cargo." The new grave that awaited it had been situated on the highest promontory in Arlington Cemetery, beneath a huge oak standing less than twenty yards from the front steps of Arlington House, Robert E. Lee's former mansion. The view of the federal city from that spot is marvelous. In 1824 Lafayette had called it the greatest vista in the world (fig. 11).[78]

The grave into which the casket was lowered still lacked a permanent memorial cover; this had been authorized by Congress in 1908 but was still awaiting completion in Tennessee. Two years later it was ready, and in May 1911 several hundred distinguished visitors returned to gather on the porch of the Lee Mansion to witness L'Enfant's "second day of belated apotheosis." President Taft observed in his tribute, "There are not many who have to wait one hundred years to receive the reward to which they are entitled until the world shall make the progress which enables it to pay the just reward." Taft candidly alluded to L'Enfant's "highly artistic temperament" along with "the defects which not infrequently accompany that temperament."[79] The president made no bones about the handful of bones that had just been eulogized by the rector of St. Patrick's Church, where L'Enfant had once been a communicant.

The very large limestone cover for the grave had been carefully carved with an elaborate text, and at the top it displayed a part of the designer's own plan for the city that lay below, across the river. It is an exceedingly handsome tribute to this prickly genius who loved his adopted country despite rebuffs from his first patron, George Washington, rebukes from Secretary Jefferson, and repeated rejections by Congress. All of that now lay largely forgotten in the past, just as L'Enfant himself had been for almost a century.

✠

I find it remarkable that so many graves of Revolutionary heroes turned out to be sadly neglected yet were ultimately contested and then properly restored. Patriotic pride usually became the key determinant when people finally decided to do the right thing, including British patriots in the cases involving Major André and Thomas Paine. Although the Paine saga was sui generis as theater of the absurd, in general we can say that conflicts became intensified when partisans had divergent perceptions of what patriotic duty required.

The problematic search for reliably authentic first burial sites is another common denominator (see the Warren, Thomson, and Gwinnett scenarios), as is the competitive role of site-specific prestige in many instances. Finally, very substantial crowds turned out for many of the reburial events, most notably for the Wallabout martyrs, and for Montgomery, Greene, and even Button Gwinnett. These were highly public reburials, civic events that sparked sincere participation—perhaps more consistently so than many others that we will examine.

During the century between the partisan Republican notice taken of the prison ship victims (1808) and L'Enfant's federal restoration to a place of honor (1909), some of the reburials that took place owed their stimulus to sectional pride, though by the time of L'Enfant's memorialization, national reconciliation and a resurgent nationalism would prompt several of the most remarkable and notable of all American reinterments.

— THREE —

# Honor, Dishonor, and Issues of Reputation

## FROM SECTIONALISM TO NATIONALISM

"And this too shall pass away." How much it expresses! How chastening in the hour of pride! How consoling in the depths of affliction.

✚ Abraham Lincoln, address to Wisconsin State Agricultural Society, Milwaukee, September 30, 1859

*A*lthough issues of historical reputation and problems of group pride remained highly important with mid- and later nineteenth-century figures, narratives of neglected or forgotten burial sites became less common and less prominent, except of course for the many thousands of Yanks and Rebs who had the misfortune to die in the wrong region during the Civil War. Because the latter topic has been discussed recently and well by others, it will be dealt with mainly in passing here.[1] Pride of place and the growing significance of sectionalism and regionalism during much of the nineteenth century dominate the episodes that follow because survivors could not let the Civil War lapse from memory despite increasing calls toward the close of the century for sectional reconciliation. Reinterments often occurred because political and military leaders who died received burial far from home or else, once again, too far from the special site deemed most pertinent to their historical significance.

By the end of the nineteenth century and turn to the twentieth, however, sectionalism began giving way to nationalism as the main motive for several of the most notable exhumations and reburials in American history. Indeed, it is apropos to reference Theodore Roosevelt's New Nationalism here, because he will be a principal player and outspoken figure participating directly in our final two episodes.

Following the tragic conflict that took place from 1861 until 1865, it came to be accepted, at least among Northerners, that the federal government should bear responsibility for permanently honoring American military heroes. Hence the creation of Arlington National Cemetery, though not without considerable controversy and resentment from Southerners. But the kind of national pride that led to the reburial of adopted Virginian John Paul Jones in 1906 involved a whole different order of magnitude and symbolic meaning.

The achievement of belated recognition for sectional as well as national heroes provides us with a picture patterned with illumination as well as shadowy areas. The primary cause of such variations involves not only competing venues but also issues of overdue honor (or compensation for dishonor) among a galaxy of presidents and generals, admirals and justices. Gender also became an important factor, most notably in the South, where women aggressively insisted upon taking responsibility for ensuring proper burials in communities that had lost loved ones—loved ones who then became communities of the dead looked after by an array of proactive ladies' associations.

Resting in peace did not seem possible unless a personage reposed in just the right place. So the shared motif or common theme for American heroes, as the nation shifted back from sectionalism to nationalism, would be pride of place as compensation for death in the wrong locale. To some survivors the key issue remained, quite simply, "they shall not have died in vain." The Lost Cause lingered, to be sure, for more than a generation. But for others, mainly as the century reached its close, bestowing honor upon the deceased also meant achieving symbolic laurels for the United States as a whole. For persons imbued with that ideal, the motivation was not a lost cause so much as a *new* cause—the new nationalism that gave the twentieth century its jump-start.[2]

✠

James Monroe, a Virginian who became fifth president of the United States, married a New Yorker who predeceased him. Bereft and in ill-health by 1830, he decided to live with his daughter and moved to Manhattan, where he died on July 4, 1831, the same sacred day so rich in symbolism that had witnessed the demise of Adams and Jefferson in 1826. Officials in New York City asked Monroe's family for permission "to bury him, with appropriate honors, at the public cost." The funeral, held on July 7, became an elaborate affair. An honor guard escorted the body from the Gouverneur family residence of his children to a draped platform where the president of Columbia College delivered a moving eulogy. Following funeral services at St. Paul's, the procession moved up Broadway toward the Marble Cemetery at Second Street. Church bells tolled, guns sounded, and mourners in the cortège included members of the Society of the Cincinnati, national and local officials, foreign ministers and consuls. Although representatives from Virginia did not attend, a special church service was conducted in Richmond by the Episcopal bishop there.[3]

A quarter-century later, Virginians experienced a surge of new pride in their Revolutionary-era statesmen. But the initial idea to honor Monroe on the one-hundredth anniversary of his birth came from a transplanted Virginian living in New York who proposed that a monument be erected there to Monroe. While a Manhattan Council member agreed to seek municipal funding for it, Governor Henry A. Wise of Virginia was asked whether his state also had plans to honor the late president. Virginians apparently had not even considered the matter, but they mobilized swiftly. The General Assembly promptly passed a resolution appropriating two thousand dollars "for the removal of the remains of James Monroe . . . to the cemetery at the city of Richmond . . . for interment, provided that upon enquiry [the governor] may deem it proper, and such removal may meet with the approbation of the family." New York officials accepted the request graciously, and it pleased Monroe's children and grandchildren, who asked only for simplicity and privacy—neither of which would ultimately be provided.[4]

The Common Council of New York appointed a committee of arrangements that agreed the ceremonies should straddle July 4, which fell on a Sunday in 1858. They chose to exhume and ship Monroe's remains on July 3 for burial in Richmond on July 5; twenty-five hundred dollars was appropriated for the disinterment ceremonies, which included an offer by the Artillery Corps of Washington Grays to march in the funeral procession along with the New York Light Guard—a clear indication that sectional unity would be an ancillary goal (fig. 12). Once New York made it clear that pride of place would prompt the rituals there to be elaborate, Virginia clearly felt that it must follow suit, so the Monroe family had no choice but to allow public participation. When New York's socially elite Seventh Regiment announced that it would accompany the body to Richmond and stop in several cities on the way back, including Washington, where it would be reviewed by President Buchanan, the intensified current of regional tensions began to be felt. As one New York paper remarked of the regiment's journey to Richmond: "This handsome offer cannot but give the Southerners a higher opinion than they are accustomed to expect of the liberality and fraternal feeling of the people of the North. We trust in the future they will be disposed to accord to Northern chivalry a place in their vocabulary of compliment."[5]

*Figure 12.* Exhuming President James Monroe in New York, July 3, 1858. Wood engraving from *Harper's Weekly*, July 17, 1858. Division of Prints and Photographs, Library of Congress.

In Richmond, meanwhile, Governor Wise negotiated with Hollywood Cemetery, then still situated in a rustic area, to purchase not one but *three* prime lots on a hill in an ideal space reserved for very special dignitaries. The governor had an ambitious vision and scheme: to exhume what remained of Thomas Jefferson at Monticello and James Madison at Montpelier and rebury both founders along with Monroe as a kind of Old Dominion triumvirate. Descendants did not share this vision and declined, of course, just as George Washington's family had thirty-six years earlier.

On July 2 a delegation from Virginia joined with New York Virginians as well as Monroe's relatives and their guests for the opening of his tomb. The lead coffin was removed from its original casing and placed in a new, silver-handled mahogany casket. After the nameplate was transferred to the new container, it was surrounded by thirteen stars symbolic of the original states. The coffin, draped with a black pall, was then carried to a waiting hearse and taken to the Church of the Annunciation on West Fourteenth Street. At three in the afternoon, about ten thousand people who had gathered were admitted to view the coffin. A few hours later the coffin was replaced in a glass-covered hearse and became the focal point for an elaborate procession to City Hall, where it remained overnight with the Eighth New York Regiment as an honor guard.[6]

At eleven the next morning the mayor committed Monroe's remains to the Seventh New York Regiment, resplendent in dress uniform, along with the Virginia committee designated to accompany the body "home," even though home would not be his beloved Loudoun County. At Pier 13 the steamer *Jamestown*, newly painted and draped in mourning, awaited its 1:00 p.m. departure. Standing on the quarterdeck, Congressman John Cochrane delivered a farewell address on behalf of New York, to which the son of Virginia's governor responded with an apparent defense of his state's apparent delinquency in properly honoring Monroe: "James Monroe's head was bowed down to the grave, partly by a series of personal animosities and political acerbities, which chased him even to the tomb. Was it not, then, appropriate, exceedingly proper, that every memory of dissent, every voice of dissonance, and every discordant tone, should be allowed to die away, and be obliterated from the minds of men, before Virginia proceeded, in the fullness of time, to pay the merited honor to the remains of her illustrious dead?"[7] The firing of minute-guns from government forts continued until the *Jamestown* finally left the dock at 3:00 p.m.

The ship reached Norfolk late on Sunday afternoon, greeted by militia companies and large crowds. Following speeches, punch, and mint juleps, it proceeded up the James River to Richmond, where it was eagerly met on the morning of July 5. Flags hung at half-mast on buildings in town and ships in the harbor. Artillery salutes were fired from Capitol Square, and dockside ceremonies took place as the New York delegation was greeted by a host of Virginians. After an elaborate procession out to Hollywood Cemetery, Governor Wise delivered a eulogy that traced and celebrated Monroe's fifty-five-year career of distinguished public service. Welcoming the New Yorkers who had traveled that distance for the funeral of a hero they had gracefully surrendered, Wise once again alluded to the sectional differences so evident by 1858: "Who knows this day, this hour, here around this grave, that

New York is of the North and that Virginia is of the South? . . . They are one even as all the now proud and prominent thirty-two [states] are one" (fig. 13).[8]

Following the burial with prayers and powerful salvos, the Virginia militia accompanied the New York Regiment and many others to the huge Gallego flour mill, the only site in Richmond large enough to seat a vast throng for a celebratory banquet. A series of toasts saluted Independence Day first, then George Washington, then Monroe, and the fourth, given by a Richmond lawyer, mentioned Monroe's marriage to a New Yorker and finished with a tribute that captured the subtext of the entire event: "New York and Virginia, United in glory, united by interest and united by marriage, nothing but fanaticism can separate them."[9] As conflicting political positions soon gathered momentum, foretelling a brewing storm, that was not a sound prediction.

What remained to be done? The selection of a suitable monument. Governor Wise chose an elaborate gothic revival design by an Alsatian living in Richmond, a cast-iron structure that critics called the "bird

*Figure 13.* The ceremony at the grave of President James Monroe, Hollywood Cemetery, Richmond, Virginia, July 5, 1858. Wood engraving from *Harper's Weekly*, July 17, 1858. Division of Prints and Photographs, Library of Congress.

*Figure 14.* The tomb of President James Monroe, Hollywood Cemetery, Richmond, Virginia (1859; photo from 1908). Division of Prints and Photographs, Library of Congress.

cage," inspired by the delicate iron grills found around many statues located in or adjacent to European cathedrals (fig. 14). The twelve-foot-tall structure was placed above the new tomb late in 1859, almost the eve of the imminent and bitter Civil War that made such a mockery of all those vocal expressions of sectional harmony and cooperation.[10]

✠

On December 2, 1859, soon after his unsuccessful antislavery raid on Harper's Ferry, John Brown was executed by hanging in Charlestown, Virginia (soon to be West Virginia)—as ordered by the very same Governor Wise. The gallows had been set up in an open field outside of town. The doomed man rode there on a wagon, seated on his own coffin, accompanied by an armed escort. At the site, fifteen hundred cavalry and militia along with hundreds of spectators gathered to watch the grimly satisfying event. Observers on this occasion included one

John Wilkes Booth, standing in the ranks of the First Virginia Regiment and viewing the radical abolitionist with scorn: men like Brown were "the *only* traitors in the land." When authorities in charge removed Brown from the scaffold, they placed his body in a black walnut coffin, and most Southerners felt that justice had been done.[11]

One recalls a venerable, anonymous quotation that William Shakespeare incorporated into *Othello* as Iago's song: "It's pride that puts this country down; / Man, take thine old cloak about thee" (2.3.93).

While Southern sympathizers rejoiced, in the North many abolitionists bitterly lamented the death. At the widely publicized time of his execution, officials in Albany, New York, fired a one-hundred gun salute to honor Brown's martyrdom, and church bells tolled from New England to Kansas. In Lawrence, Kansas, antislavery settlers adopted eleven resolutions, three of which praised Brown's intentions at Harper's Ferry and asserted that "he had given his life for the liberty of man." At just the same time, Henry David Thoreau offered an address in Concord honoring the "crucified hero." Soon after, William Dean Howells, Edmund Clarence Stedman, Herman Melville, and Walt Whitman all wrote poems intended to immortalize Brown.[12]

When the train bearing Brown's body reached New York, a friend of the family decided that the martyr should not be buried in a *Southern* coffin and transferred the body to one made locally: a significantly symbolic "translation" even though not an ordinary exhumation. As the train headed to and through the Adirondacks, bells tolled with pride in every town and people gathered to observe the procession. When it reached Elizabethtown, New York, near North Elba, an honor guard stood watch until dawn, and then the coffin was placed in the main room of the Browns' farmhouse at North Elba so that neighbors could view their friend and hero for the last time. On December 8, 1859, final services were conducted at the home, and Wendell Phillips, an ardent abolitionist, gave the eulogy for that "marvellous old man" who "has loosened the roots of the slave system; it only breathes—it does not live—hereafter" (fig. 15).[13]

Historian Gary Laderman has observed that the meanings ascribed to John Brown's body "were related to the political strife, cultural dissension, and emotional turmoil erupting over the future of slavery in the years before the war—his corpse became a virtual arena where

*Figure 15.* John Brown's grave at North Elba, New York (c. 1897). Photograph by Seneca Ray Stoddard. Division of Prints and Photographs, Library of Congress.

larger social conflicts were represented for all sides in the debate."[14] In that sense and for those reasons, the politicization of his execution, funeral route home, and ultimate burial—in this instance there was no reburial, only the ideologically driven coffin change—foreshadowed the ideological politicization of reburials that took place in Europe following the fall of Communism in 1989.

✝

The grim narrative of Abraham Lincoln's assassination on Good Friday and subsequent death just before Easter Sunday, 1865, has been extensively related and analyzed.[15] Equally familiar is the mournful train trip home to Springfield, Illinois, with numerous stops in cities from Washington to New York and then west to Chicago so that a host of cities and citizens could express their grief. (The Lincolns' late son Willie, who had died at the age of eleven, was disinterred from Georgetown's Oak Hill Cemetery and sent along to be buried with his father.) The sixteenth president would be commemorated in death far more than he was ever celebrated in life. Less familiar to us today are the recorded sightings of country folk digging symbolic graves and burying the president "virtually" all along the funereal route.[16] Then there would be fierce conflicts over just where he should be buried and memorialized: in Chicago or at Springfield, as Mary Todd Lincoln defiantly demanded, and then in the heart of Springfield, as many residents preferred, or in the new Oak Ridge Cemetery situated on the outskirts, as Mary also insisted (figs. 16–17)?

Ultimately his remains would be moved numerous times, several of them for unexpected and bizarre reasons. The Lincoln Memorial Association swiftly emerged in Springfield to raise money for a suitably honorific tomb in Oak Ridge, with a hall inside the capacious structure that could serve as a museum and a caretaker to maintain decorum at the site and answer the questions of visitors, who eventually arrived in vast numbers. By the 1920s, so many people were making pilgrimages to visit the tomb that Chicago journalist Lloyd Lewis declared that more "pilgrims" came to pay their respects at this burial site than at any other in the world. More people may have visited Mount Vernon, but they did so primarily to see Washington's home, not his grave.[17]

On the night of November 7, 1876, a gang of four thugs working for a ring of big-time counterfeiters attempted to break into Lincoln's

*Figure 16.* Abraham Lincoln's magnificent hearse on the street at his funeral in Springfield, Illinois (May 4, 1865). The hearse was borrowed from the livery stable of a Mr. Arnot of St. Louis. Photograph by Samuel Montague Fassett. Division of Prints and Photographs, Library of Congress.

*Figure 17.* Abraham Lincoln's burial service at Oak Ridge Cemetery, May 4, 1865, Springfield, Illinois. Wood engraving after a sketch by W. Waud. *Harper's Weekly*, May 27, 1865. Division of Prints and Photographs, Library of Congress.

crypt to steal the body for a ransom of $200,000 in order to get the most skillful counterfeiter of them all out of jail. They intended to cart the remains all the way to the Indiana dunes and bury them there until the ransom was paid. Little did they know that one of their number, Lewis Swegles, was also an informer. The notified authorities waited in the ominously dark tomb until the grave robbers arrived, but then they bungled the capture: a police gun went off accidentally and gave the would-be robbers an opportunity to escape. They were soon apprehended in Chicago, however, through careful police work and imprudent behavior by the thieves—they had foolishly gathered at their favorite saloon.[18]

But what followed made the situation even stranger. The devoted caretaker, John Carroll Power, and a covert group of self-appointed guardians from Springfield became so nervous about the possibility of another attempt at theft that they removed Lincoln's coffin from its sarcophagus and reburied it, unmarked, at ground level where no one could conceivably find it. People living in Springfield could not keep a secret, however, and rumors circulated for years that the sarcophagus

*Figure 18.* The Lincoln tomb and monument as it appeared in 1883, when the president's body lay concealed in a shallow grave in the basement. Courtesy of the Abraham Lincoln Presidential Library and Museum, Springfield, Illinois.

on the main level was actually empty (fig. 18). So on April 14, 1887, the twenty-second anniversary of Lincoln's death, members of the Lincoln Monument Association opened the lead-sealed coffin to make sure the body was still inside (it was) and then rendered a proper reburial in its original sarcophagus.[19]

In order to minimize body snatching by medical students and doctors making anatomical studies, Illinois had passed a statute in 1845 making it a crime to disinter a body or remove a grave. The penalty was one year in prison. In 1879 the legislature augmented that law and changed the penalty to ten years for disturbing a grave or exhuming a body.[20]

Meanwhile, Robert Todd Lincoln, the president's only surviving son, escaped from his boredom as ambassador to England by taking on the presidency of George Pullman's Palace Car Company in Chicago. The despotic Pullman knew that he was hated by many people, and he feared that his remains might be dug up someday by those who had despised him in life, so he left explicit instructions to be buried in a steel-caged coffin beneath tons of cement. Robert Lincoln decided that that might be just the right solution for his father's apparently vulnerable remains. His advocacy led to the Springfield monument's redesign, and Lincoln, encased in lead and a cage of steel, found permanent repose beneath tons of Portland cement (fig. 19).[21]

That reburial took place on September 26, 1901, but the saga doesn't end there. In 1930 it became apparent that the Lincolns' tomb needed significant repairs. As one writer has explained, "This time the coffins stayed put; but before the contractors went to work, everything else fragile or valuable was cleared out of the tomb." During the process the

*Figure 19.* The removal of Abraham Lincoln from his temporary tomb, April 30, 1901. A crowd gathered around the crate containing Lincoln's coffin. Division of Prints and Photographs, Library of Congress.

sarcophagus that had once held Lincoln's coffin was not locked away in a storage shed but left exposed out of doors. Alas, vandals once again entered the Oak Ridge Cemetery after dark, smashed the sarcophagus to bits, and carried off pieces, presumably as souvenirs. At least the Lincolns remained deeply secure.[22]

✠

Jefferson Davis served in the Black Hawk War (1832) but resigned his U.S. Army commission in 1835 to marry a daughter of General Zachary Taylor and became a planter in the Mississippi Delta. After leading the Mississippi Rifles in the Mexican War and participating in the Battle of Buena Vista, he entered the U.S. Senate and became chairman of the Committee on Military Affairs. In 1853 President Pierce made him secretary of war; but in 1857 he returned to the Senate, and eventually he became a reluctant secessionist. Soon after Mississippi left the Union, he accepted a major-generalship to prepare his state for defense, and in February 1861 he was unanimously chosen president of the Confederacy. Initially he tried to settle sectional differences peacefully around a conference table, but when Lincoln sent armed ships with reinforcements to Fort Sumter in Charleston harbor in April 1861, Davis tried unsuccessfully to enlist the support of Britain and France on behalf of his section's cause.

When the war ended in 1865, Davis and his cabinet fled southward from Richmond. He was captured by Federal forces in Georgia, imprisoned at Fort Monroe (named for the recently reburied fifth president) from 1865 until 1867, and indicted for treason but never actually brought to trial. His health shattered, he went to Canada and then Britain but was eventually allowed to return to the United States, where he settled on the Gulf Coast and completed his *Rise and Fall of the Confederate States* (1881).[23]

When Davis died late in 1889 after a lingering illness, people came to New Orleans from all over the South to pay their respects and participate in last rites for their historic leader. He was accompanied by the governors of nine states to what turned out to be a temporary tomb in Metairie Cemetery, as noted in this book's introduction. During the winter months of 1890, Southern legislatures all held solemn memorial sessions. More than three years following his death, in response to a request from citizens of Richmond, capital of the Confederacy, Davis's body was exhumed and taken to Hollywood Cemetery for burial on Memorial Day. Large crowds heard fond eulogies from men who had known him well, and in 1907 a statue honoring Davis (clothed as a cavalry commander) was erected at the west end of Monument Avenue, a kind of pendant to the great equestrian statue of Robert E. Lee already located at the east end.[24]

Albert Sidney Johnston, born in Kentucky, lived most of his life in Texas as a planter and soldier. Like Davis, he served under Zachary Taylor in the Mexican War. Although posted in California when the Civil War began, he swiftly returned eastward, and in May 1861 his friend Davis appointed him a general and commander of the Western Department. After several unsuccessful battles, he mounted a massive surprise attack on Ulysses S. Grant's forces at Shiloh in southwestern Tennessee and rallied his troops courageously, riding up and down the lines in a manner that made him legendary—especially after he was killed (most likely by friendly fire) on April 6, 1862. Davis considered him the finest Confederate general prior to the emergence of Robert E. Lee two months following the struggle at Shiloh. Johnston turned out to be the highest-ranking officer on either side killed during the Civil War.[25]

Following his death, Johnston's staff requested permission from General P. G. T. Beauregard to carry his body from the little church at Shiloh to New Orleans for burial. When Beauregard consented, a doctor injected whiskey into Johnston's blood vessels in order to preserve the body during the long journey south by wagon. A somber cavalcade accompanied the hearse to Corinth, Mississippi, where the remains were properly prepared for burial. At New Orleans the coffin was met by the mayor and the commander of Confederate troops defending the city. The body lay in state at City Hall for two days, after which Johnston's staff served as pallbearers and buried him in the St. Louis Cemetery.[26]

For nearly five years, Johnston's body remained there even though it was well known that he preferred burial in Texas. He had remarked to his brother-in-law, "When I die I want a handful of Texas earth on my breast." In the autumn of 1866, having secured the approval of Johnston's family, a joint resolution of the Texas legislature determined to bring Johnston to Austin for reinterment and appointed a committee of distinguished Texans to be the escorts for the body. On January 23, 1867, a religious service was held beside the tomb in New Orleans amidst a crowd of mourners and admirers. The pallbearers accompanying the body were all former Confederate generals.[27]

These were the early years of Reconstruction, however, and federal officials feared a demonstration of Confederate sympathy; consequently they had prohibited the funeral procession planned by Johnston's former comrades. This, however, served only to arouse Southern outrage. So thousands of people filed past the coffin once again as it lay on the wharf at Galveston, and the same response occurred when the body passed through Houston. When it reached Austin on February 1, Governor James W. Throckmorton welcomed it with an oration. While it lay in state at the capitol, vast numbers filed past the bier and covered the coffin with laurel and flowers. The next afternoon Johnston was laid to rest in a place of honor in the Texas State Cemetery. He had assisted in the founding of Austin, had lived there when it was the frontier capital of the independent Republic of Texas, and still later had liked living there with his family. In 1839 he had written to a friend: "Austin is in the . . . most beautiful & lovely country that the 'blazing eye' of the sun looks upon in his journey from the east to the west." Johnston had come home. In 1907 Elisabet Ney designed a graceful gothic monument, smaller but strikingly similar to James Monroe's "gilded cage," to be erected at his grave site.[28]

✠

The burials, reburials, and woefully neglected improper burials of the 620,000 combatants who died fighting in the Civil War constitute a very large and complex story that has been the subject of no fewer than five quite admirable recent books.[29] As early as 1862 Congress enacted legislation authorizing the president to purchase land "to be used as a national cemetery for the soldiers who shall die in the service of the country." That led to the requisition of Lee's Mansion and the eventual creation of Arlington National Cemetery. The following year General Lorenzo Thomas ordered the creation of a local cemetery for Federal troops who died in the prolonged battle of Chattanooga, and yet another for those killed at Stone's River, marking a transition from burial for convenient reasons of proximity to battle, and health considerations, to burial for purposes of commemoration as well.[30]

The narrative of Civil War reburials is also complex because the movement of bodies followed varied patterns in different phases as well as diverse locations, and persisted for more than a full generation following 1865. The Northern states whose men had fought at Gettysburg, for example, took the initiative in establishing the famous cemetery there; but the federal government assumed responsibility for its maintenance and gradually became the custodian of seventy-four national military cemeteries that served as the final resting places for well over 300,000 Union war dead (and eventually thousands of veterans of subsequent wars as well; fig. 20). Others who died in battle, usually coming from more affluent families that could pay searchers to locate bodies and bring them home, were taken back to their communities. Of the 5,100 Union soldiers killed or mortally wounded at Gettysburg, some 1,500 would be interred or reinterred in their hometown cemetery or family graveyard.[31]

*Figure 20.* Collecting the remains of Union soldiers for reinterment in national cemeteries. Wood engraving after Alexander Gardner, *Harper's Weekly*, November 24, 1866. Division of Prints and Photographs, Library of Congress.

The class and socioeconomic status of bereaved families made a considerable difference in the arrangements that might be worked out to respect the deceased and final wishes of their families. Late in 1864 General Larkin Dickason received seventy dollars and a request that a Union soldier who died in an Alexandria hospital be sent to his home: "Will you be kind enough to see that the body is properly exhumed and forwarded to my address. . . . The sum enclosed has been raised here by [the soldier's] friends out of respect for him and his relatives who are poor."[32]

In contrast, Stillman King Wightman of New York, who had connections with some important officials, resolved to find, collect, and ship home the remains of his son, who had died at Fort Fisher in North Carolina. After receiving a special pass from his old friend Secretary of the Navy Gideon Welles, Wightman made the long and difficult journey to the mouth of the Cape Fear River in North Carolina, found the marked grave of his son, Edward, and consulted with a surgeon, who explained that a lead coffin would be needed and might take months to procure. When Wightman refused to leave without the body, the surgeon conceded that it could be transported "in tolerable safety" if he used a regular coffin but filled all of the empty spaces with salt and rosin. Wightman attended to the exhumation and had the body wrapped in tent-cloth with pitch applied on the outside and then placed in a coffin that in turn was nailed shut inside a larger box. The body was then shipped to New York City at considerable expense and interred in the family burying ground next to the young soldier's sister.[33]

When the Gettysburg cemetery was created, it was assumed that only Union dead would repose there. A Gettysburg resident, F. W. Biesecker, won the contract to bury fallen soldiers at the rate of $1.59 per corpse; it stipulated that when ordered, "he shall open up graves and trenches for personal inspection of the remains, for the purpose of ascertaining whether they are bodies of Union soldiers, and close them over again when ordered to do so." Most of the soldiers who eventually received burial in the seventy-four national cemeteries had initially been placed in temporary graves, exhumed, and then reburied. Between 1865 and 1870 intensive efforts were made to reinter all Union dead in the newly created national cemeteries, which meant a great deal of checking based upon jackets (Federal blue), shoes (which differed by section), and even underwear (the quality of cotton varied North and South).[34]

Race mattered greatly, of course, though the practices varied inconsistently. For the most part, however, colored troops were buried with Union whites in national cemeteries, though often in separate sections. When Robert Gould Shaw, commander of the Negro Fifty-fourth Massachusetts Volunteers, was buried with his men in a mass grave at Fort Wagner, South Carolina, where they fell, many who knew of this were appalled, but the antislavery Shaw family in Boston totally approved and insisted that such an arrangement was exactly what he would have wanted. Shaw and his men were later exhumed and presumably buried as "unknowns" at Beaufort National Cemetery in South Carolina. Needless to say, integrated burial grounds were not acceptable in the South.[35]

What happened there, and to Southerners who died in the North, provoked the greatest amount of controversy, bitterness, and vexed reburials (fig. 21). At Antietam, for example, where the bloodiest single day of fighting occurred, a separate section was set aside for Confederates killed in Maryland (unlike the initial policy at Gettysburg). Rumors persisted in the North, however, that Southerners not only separated their own dead from Union losses but also severely abused

*Figure 21.* Graves of Confederate soldiers with board markers in Oakwood Cemetery, Richmond, Virginia, 1865. Division of Prints and Photographs, Library of Congress.

the bodies of fallen Federal troops. One Northern minister angrily insisted, "Not satisfied with the victory won, to add ignominy to defeat, the rebels buried our men with their faces downward, and took their bones for drumsticks and finger-rings, and their skulls for goblets and punchbowls."[36]

But bitterness over issues of reburial and memorialization lingered far longer in the South. In 1895, for example, Chicago's Ex-Confederate Association obtained permission from the secretary of war to erect a memorial within the soldiers' section of that city's Oak Woods Cemetery. During the war there had been a military prison in Chicago where at least forty-five hundred Confederates died from an outbreak of smallpox. After the war these Southerners were exhumed and reburied at Oak Woods, but largely in unmarked graves. The Ex-Confederate Association spent nearly twenty-five thousand dollars for a monument and appropriate dedication ceremonies. The monument displayed a soldier above a shaft of Georgia granite, rising from a broad plinth.[37]

From the close of the war onward, Southerners remained exceedingly vexed by what they considered the spiteful disrespect and indifference to Southerners who died in the North, especially in Pennsylvania and New York. (Southerners, of course, were deemed no more respectful of Yankees who died in the South.) Gettysburg became the greatest locus of anger, and provisional arrangements were made in 1869 for Confederates who had been buried in shallow mass graves there to be exhumed for reburial at Hollywood Cemetery. In 1872 the first group of 708 Confederate bodies reached Richmond. Five more shipments occurred during the next fourteen months, and eventually there would be 2,935 identified men and yet another 3,000 unknown dead.[38]

What remained the most distinctive feature of respect for deceased soldiers in the South was the very active role played by ladies' memorial associations, which insisted upon controlling everything to do with reburials and cemetery maintenance. The Hollywood Memorial Association in Richmond was one of the most active, of course, and largely managed the Gettysburg reinterment project. Long before the United Daughters of the Confederacy became politically active near the close of the century, these community-based associations of women operated independently, though they interacted for mutual support. They eventually relocated and reinterred the remains of 72,250 Confederates killed in the war, and they erected markers wherever possible, especially if the deceased could be identified.[39]

In 1900 and 1901 the United Daughters of the Confederacy, an organization then only six years old, bitterly contested the creation of a separate Confederate section at Arlington National Cemetery. Fearing that veterans belonging to the Grand Army of the Republic might still desecrate Confederate graves, they pleaded for the return of all Southern bones to their respective home states. For the most part they lost that struggle, mainly because programmatic sectional reconciliation was well under way by the start of the twentieth century.[40] In 1909 the widow of General George E. Pickett became the first woman and the second Confederate to deliver the annual Memorial Day address at Boston's Tremont Temple. In 1914 a Confederate memorial, built by the UDC, was erected at Arlington with Northern support and dedicated in a ceremony respectfully attended by federal authorities drawn from both camps, blue and gray.[41]

Variations on this theme and related ones persisted throughout the twentieth century and into the twenty-first. During the Civil War centennial, for example, the president of a historical society in Kansas City, Missouri, sent a proposal to President Lyndon B. Johnson aimed at marking Memorial Day in 1965 as the culmination of centennial observances. He felt that symbolic action was needed to minimize differences that still persisted between North and South. So he suggested the following: "Obtain permission from the families of the last survivor of the Union and Confederate Armies respectively, to have their bodies removed from their present resting places and placed side by side in a tomb to be erected in Arlington National Cemetery on the slope between the Lee Home and President Kennedy's tomb. . . . Not only would it be a reminder of, and a memorial to, the everlasting unity of the North and the South, but it would be a further tribute to the memory of our late President."[42] When the proposal was referred to Professor Bell Wiley at Emory University, a Civil War scholar and consultant to the commission, he responded with disdain: "I don't react positively to the idea of disinterring the remains of the last survivors and removing them to Arlington. Surely some more meaningful and appropriate ceremony can be arranged, and one that would not necessitate the transfer of bones and the erection of an expensive tomb." The proposal swiftly sank from view.[43]

In 1980 a more radical but also pragmatic proposal was implemented because the only national cemetery in West Virginia had been full for twenty years and veterans of World War II and Korea became concerned about whether they would be able to receive honored burial in a military cemetery. Many hundreds of Civil War soldiers, mostly unknown, were exhumed from the small national cemetery in Grafton, West Virginia, and all of their remains were reburied in one mass grave with a large and solemn memorial monument. The Veterans Administration speculated that if this project turned out to be successful, it might be expanded to include some 150,000 unknown Civil War soldiers across the United States. That does not seem to have happened, even though the concept did not cause a massive outcry.[44]

As recently as 2008, however, a thrust in the opposite direction—to *prevent* reburial—occurred. During the Civil War escaped slaves fled their plantations to join the Union Army and fight for freedom. More than three hundred who died during and after the war were buried in Talbird Cemetery on Hilton Head Island in South Carolina. By the twenty-first century the small plot of land where they lay had been overshadowed by multimillion-dollar condos and a private marina, signs of the transformation of a once predominantly black town into a cluster of gated communities for the very wealthy.

Yet for Howard Wright, the great-great-grandson of a former slave who fought in the war, Talbird was important to his family's heritage and, as he insisted, "an integral part of American history that should not be forgotten." Consequently he launched a campaign to get the Department of Veterans Affairs to provide proper headstones for the more than three thousand blacks in South Carolina who served in what was called the U.S. Colored Troops. Early in 2008 he received more than three hundred markers from the department, including one for his great-great grandfather, Caesar Kirk-Jones, who died in 1903 at the age of seventy-four.[45]

✝

More than any other writer from the Civil War era, Walt Whitman (who served as a hospital nurse for three years) is best remembered for his ruminations on what might help to redeem or countermand the catastrophe of mass death and the psychological consequences of terrible, lingering losses. Regarding the former, Whitman and others noted the positive effects of a "heroic-eminent death." With Abraham Lincoln very much in mind, he viewed a unifying and tragic loss, such as the president's, as "the cement of a death identified thoroughly with that people, at its head, and for its sake." Each ordinary soldier's death would also qualify as "heroic-eminent" if citizens could identify it with a just cause in defense of a people and on their behalf. Yet "strange, (is it not?)," he concluded, "that battles, martyrs, agonies, blood, even assassination, should so condense—perhaps only really, lastingly condense— a Nationality."[46]

When Ulysses S. Grant died of throat cancer in July 1885, his death qualified as "heroic-eminent" on several grounds. His reputation as the general who did the most to secure Union victory had grown steadily and eclipsed the corruption scandals and lapses of his presidency. His death also seemed heroic because he had bravely completed his memoirs while suffering from a most painful terminal illness. Because the memoirs became a best-seller, he achieved financial security for his family. In 1885 no one doubted that the burial place for such an American hero would have to be special and quite grand, but there would be rancorous disputes over the appropriate design for such a tomb, the campaign to raise a massive sum exceeding a million dollars, and above all, *location*. The Grant Monument Committee formed within a week of his death, mainly consisting of wealthy and prominent New Yorkers who seemed to assume that New York City must be the inevitable choice.[47]

In 1885 the body was placed in a temporary tomb in Manhattan, but as of early 1890, a suitable design had not yet been selected. Moreover, where to put him permanently remained equally vexing. He had died a resident of New York, but he had not lived there at all until returning from his much-touted tour around the world in 1879. In July 1885, not long before his death, Grant handed his son a slip of paper listing three possibilities: Illinois, his home state where he received his first general's commission; West Point—problematic because his wife could not be buried with him there; and New York, because, in Grant's words, "her people befriended me." Meanwhile, a U.S. senator from Kansas, a Civil War veteran himself, introduced a bill proposing the removal of Grant's remains to Washington for burial at Arlington National Cemetery. That suggestion met with strong approval on the grounds that many more people would visit the grave at the national cemetery with greatest prestige.[48]

During the course of 1890 the bill for reburial in Arlington was defeated, however, after intense bickering and high-pressure tactics exercised by a powerful coalition of New Yorkers. The latter, having raised the most money, felt determined to have their way, dodged the democratic logic of having an open design competition, and invited five prominent architects to submit plans. From that group it selected John H. Duncan, the designer of Brooklyn's Soldiers' and Sailors' Memorial Arch. Duncan's accepted plan took as its model the Roman mausoleum of Hadrian, a square Doric temple surmounted by a great granite dome. Five years earlier several journalists had suggested that a design from the middle period of Rome's imperial grandeur—a phase that fascinated Americans at the time—would be suitable, and now they saw their wish fulfilled.[49]

One more major decision remained: where in New York City should the memorial be placed? The committee took Grant's sons to three possible sites: on Central Park's Mall, on Watch Hill near Eighth Avenue and 110th Street, and in the new Riverside Park overlooking the Hudson. The Grant family chose the third, and when the tomb was dedicated in 1897, the crowds that gathered to mourn and celebrate General Grant would rank among the largest New York had ever seen. As historian Neil Harris has noted, Grant's Tomb "would become an important part of the city's public landscape, an anchor for great ceremonies." On April 27, 1897, nearly twelve years after his death, the Monument Association turned the tomb over to New York City (fig. 22). With sixty thousand marching troops, a parade of ships sailing up the Hudson River, choral societies, and bands, President McKinley and many other high-profile dignitaries reburied Grant. As one retired general wrote, "Since the transfer of Napoleon's remains from St. Helena to France, and their interment in the Hôtel des Invalides," no function had equaled "in solemnity and importance" the dedication of Grant's Tomb.[50] The sense of justice being done, along with commemorative euphoria, did much to overcome the disappointment felt by those who would have preferred Galena, Illinois, or Washington, or a structure that smacked less

*Figure 22.* Grant's Tomb, New York City (1901). Division of Prints and Photographs, Library of Congress.

of imperialism. The full realization of American empire lay two years in the future following the outcome of the Spanish-American War.

✢

Because of Southern disinterest in memorializing the victor of Appomattox, Grant's final entombment basically remained a sectional celebration, even though American nationalism had already begun a powerful and soon to be widespread revival. In President William McKinley's 1901 inaugural address he declared, "We are reunited. Sectionalism has disappeared." Although that insistence was not exactly true, it represented what a great many Americans wanted to believe at the dawn of the twentieth century.

In terms of reburials, three quite different episodes during the first decade of the new century epitomized the resurgence of interest in figures who had made special contributions. Each episode is indicative of diverse sentiments and motives, yet they reflect the rediscovery of pride in cultural institutions that served the nation ( James Smithson), constitutional law (James Wilson), and above all, American maritime strength (John Paul Jones). Senator Charles Sumner of Massachusetts may have been just a generation premature when he pronounced the following in an 1867 address in New York City: "There is the national flag. He must be cold, indeed, who can look upon its folds rippling in the breeze without *pride of country*."[51]

Smithson, an illegitimate son of the widow of James Macie, was a direct descendant of King Henry VII, founder of the Tudor line in England. Educated at Oxford as an experimental chemist but barred from noble recognition at home because of his illegitimate birth, he spent most of his adult life in France and Italy. When Smithson died in Genoa in 1829, his will specified that his inherited fortune be left in trust to his bankers, with the income paid to his nephew. If the nephew died without heirs, the entire estate would go to the "United States of America, to found at Washington, under the name to [sic] the Smithsonian Institution, an establishment for the increase & diffusion of knowledge among men." The nephew built a handsome monument over Smithson's grave, but when he died childless in 1835, Smithson's bequest came to the United States in the form of a thousand gold sovereigns filling each of 105 bags, a fortune worth $508,418.46—a very considerable sum at the time.[52]

Early in the twentieth century the French consul at Genoa informed American officials of unsettling news. The city was building a huge jetty to protect its economically essential harbor, and stone for it was being quarried from the hill where the cemetery stood. Quite soon, the ground beneath Smithson's remains would disappear, and all of the bodies would be removed to unknown locations. When the Smithsonian regents learned of this, they responded with only mild interest—except for Gilbert Grosvenor, a son-in-law of Alexander Graham Bell and an energetic editor of what would shortly become the *National Geographic*. Grosvenor carried the case for reburying Smithson in the United States to the public by way of a carefully reasoned but impassioned letter to the New York *Herald*. The institution's regents then took the idea seriously and appointed Bell a committee of one to arrange for Smithson's bones to be brought to Washington "quietly" and "privately."[53]

Bell defied those low-key instructions and took the case to President

*Figure 23*. American Consul William Bishop holding the skull of James Smithson at the British Cemetery in Genoa (1904). Division of Prints and Photographs, Library of Congress.

Theodore Roosevelt, later noting in a letter, "I am proud of him [TR], for I am sure that the people of the United States recognize that it was the proper thing to do to accord a *national* reception, to the remains of the founder of the Smithsonian Institution." Bell and his wife arrived in Genoa late in December 1903, worked with the American consul there to cut through a tangled bureaucracy, and had Smithson's grave opened just as blasting and digging was beginning to erode the cemetery's hillside. After the last slab of stone covering the grave vault was removed, Smithson's skull stared up at the small group that had gathered to observe the proceedings (fig. 23). The coffin had crumbled to a reddish dust, but the bones remained dry and remarkably well preserved. They were carefully placed in a metal casket and stowed in a chapel for several days. The container was then wrapped in an American flag, nailed up in a heavy wooden box, and loaded aboard a German steamship bound for the United States. When it arrived off Sandy Hook, New Jersey, the USS *Dolphin* fired salutes and winched the casket aboard for the trip to Washington.[54]

On the morning of January 25, 1904, the Navy Department provided "as large a force of Marines as may be available" to escort the Marine Band as Smithson's casket, draped with American and British flags, was lifted from the *Dolphin*'s deck and carried slowly to the gate of the Navy Yard, where a troop of the Fifteenth Cavalry waited to escort carriages down Pennsylvania Avenue in a procession swelled with Smithsonian regents, the British ambassador, and a representative of President Roosevelt. Because Congress had not yet approved a final resting place for the remains, the casket was covered with a large American flag in a quiet upstairs room at the reddish sandstone Castle on the Mall. Soon after, the regents were authorized to place the casket in a handsome tomb situated at the main entryway to the Castle, surrounded by much of the original monument from Smithson's grave in Genoa (fig. 24).

*Figure 24.* James Smithson's crypt at the Castle of the Smithsonian Institution, Washington, DC. Courtesy of the Smithsonian Institution.

The regents, Congress, and the president had done their duty to what was rapidly becoming the nation's premier institution devoted to scientific research and museums of several kinds.[55]

+

Less than two years later a very different story of exhumation and reinterment took place, one that helped restore the sullied reputation of an American nationalist who had been present to sign both the Declaration of Independence and the U.S. Constitution. James Wilson of Pennsylvania, associate justice of the first Supreme Court, died disgraced in 1798, fleeing from his creditors and on the verge of impeachment. Yet his significant role in drafting the Constitution had been second only to that of James Madison; a lawyer who attracted many clients, he was also regarded as a distinguished teacher of the law. The passion that proved to be his undoing was the accumulation of "private landed property," an ambition widely shared by prominent men of his generation — though few handled their financial affairs as badly as Wilson did. His downfall resulted from greed and imprudent investments in schemes to develop his land.[56]

In 1793, by then a widower in his early fifties, Wilson had married a nineteen-year-old woman. Three years later the general financial panic of 1796 caused his personal fortunes to collapse. When his work on the judicial circuit finished in 1797, Wilson and his young wife fled to Bethlehem, Pennsylvania, in order to escape angry creditors in Philadelphia. He promptly moved out of the state to New Jersey but was imprisoned briefly there because of the applications of a relentless creditor. Early in 1798 Wilson fled to Edenton, North Carolina, and sought refuge with his Supreme Court colleague Justice James Iredell, but he was still pursued by men to whom he owed substantial sums. His wife soon joined him, but malarial fever and high anxiety caused his death on August 21, 1798 — a demise that saved him from certain removal from the Supreme Court by impeachment and conviction. Wilson was virtually destitute by then.[57]

Only a handful of mourners accompanied Wilson to his grave in the small rural cemetery close to Edenton, and Iredell, who returned home from Philadelphia (still the nation's capital in 1798) on the very day of Wilson's death, promptly informed the secretary of state of the vacancy on the Court and urged prompt appointment of a successor because so many cases were then pending. Newspapers made little mention of Wilson's death, and his colleagues on the bench did not even see fit to offer a eulogy. They seemed to be relieved that political embarrassment had been avoided. So Wilson remained largely forgotten—out of sight, out of mind, and disgraced—until late in the nineteenth century, when restoring his reputation was taken up as a cause by S. Weir Mitchell, a Philadelphia physician widely consulted for his rest-cure remedies for female neurasthenia but equally famous for his immensely popular historical novels about the Revolutionary era.[58]

Early in 1904 Mitchell approached the dean of the University of Pennsylvania Law School, urging him to mobilize his colleagues and Philadelphia lawyers more generally on behalf of a plan to bring Wilson's remains home for reburial in a "very great state affair" involving little public expense. The dean referred the matter to the chancellor of the Law Association, who lacked enthusiasm for the project because as a Democrat he feared the prospect of an elaborate state ceremony in which the Republican Theodore Roosevelt might participate or even preside. Given Wilson's best-known opinion for the Court, *Chisholm v. Georgia* (1793), which Congress soon reversed with passage of the Eleventh Amendment protecting state sovereignty, he might be viewed as an apostle of the New Nationalism and an advocate of implied powers granted to the federal government under the Constitution.[59]

Weir Mitchell then acquired an energetic ally, however, in Burton Alva Konkle, an independent writer who decided to "give my life . . . to put Pennsylvania into national history as she ought to be." Disregarding the weak response to Mitchell's appeals, Konkle organized a James Wilson Memorial Committee, served as its secretary, and persuaded many prominent people to serve, including the chancellor of the Law Association. Konkle also recruited an equally energetic young member of the Philadelphia bar, Lucien H. Alexander, to act as his assistant. Alexander planned an entire agenda for the Wilson memorial proceedings: bringing Wilson's remains to Philadelphia on a warship provided by the secretary of the navy; carrying Wilson's coffin to Independence Hall, where it would lie in state; a solemn cortège of dignitaries who would accompany the remains to Christ Church; and the delivery of an address by a member of the Supreme Court, preferably the chief justice himself.[60]

Early in 1906 Alexander went to Hot Springs, Virginia, where Andrew Carnegie was vacationing, to appeal for his endorsement of the plan along with that of the St. Andrew's Society. Carnegie had come from the very same shire of Fife in Scotland that had been Wilson's birthplace. In June, Konkle and Alexander went to see Roosevelt in order to brief him on their plans and request that he attend the commemoration in Philadelphia. They also conferred with Chief Justice Fuller and the U.S. attorney general to secure their participation, and the secretary of the navy to gain his approbation. Only a short time before, in 1905, Roosevelt had played a prominent role in bringing the bones of John Paul Jones back to the United States from France, so 1906 marked a kind of apogee for such nationalistic reburials.[61]

When Roosevelt came to Harrisburg in October to dedicate the new state capitol building, he incorporated sentiments that had been handed to him by Konkle and Alexander: "I cannot do better than to base my theory of governmental action upon the words and deeds of one of Pennsylvania's greatest sons, Justice James Wilson." According to Roosevelt, Wilson had foreseen the need for a strong national government that had "full and complete power to work on behalf of the people."[62]

Early on November 18 the USS *Dubuque* steamed from Philadelphia to Norfolk with a Pennsylvania delegation on board, including Konkle, Alexander, a representative of the governor, and a special casket donated by the St. Andrew's Society. The delegation, swiftly expanded with other dignitaries, proceeded to Edenton with an honor guard from the Society of the Cincinnati and the Sons of the Revolution. North Carolina's lieutenant governor gave permission to exhume Wilson from his unmarked grave, a cordial luncheon took place at a nearby mansion, and the *Dubuque* steamed home with a grand salute from all the vessels in Norfolk's harbor, whose flags flew respectfully at half-mast. When the ship reached Philadelphia, the reception turned out to be even grander. A convoy of small craft moved out to meet the *Dubuque*, guns boomed in Wilson's honor, foreign vessels lowered their flags, and bells in the city began to toll.[63]

Sailors from the *Dubuque* carried the casket in a solemn procession to Independence Hall, where it was placed on a catafalque in the very room where Wilson and his fellow delegates had once gathered to discuss the Declaration and debate the Constitution. Previously this immense honor had only been bestowed upon the remains of John Quincy Adams, Henry Clay, and Abraham Lincoln. After citizens filed past for several hours, Wilson's coffin was escorted to a memorial service by three justices of the Supreme Court, led by the chief justice and Oliver Wendell Homes Jr. Christ Church was filled beyond capacity, and the justices sat in the pew that had belonged to George Washington during his two administrations. Speakers included Governor Samuel W. Pennypacker, Samuel Dickson as spokesman for the lawyers of Pennsylvania, the dean of the law faculty at Penn, where Wilson once taught, S.Weir Mitchell representing the realm of humane letters, Andrew Carnegie speaking for Scottish Americans, and Alton B. Parker, Roosevelt's Democratic opponent in 1904 and president of the American Bar Association, who tactfully praised Wilson's role in what had become "the greatest court in history."[64]

The U.S. attorney general, representing Roosevelt on this occasion, showed somewhat less finesse when he confessed, "It is one of the mysteries of history, which I have not been able to solve, why [Wilson's] fame has not kept pace with his service." The attorney general of Pennsylvania compensated with lavish praise for *Chisholm v. Georgia* as a masterpiece that "must be regarded as the climax of Federalism," even though it barely marked the beginning. A brief service followed in the venerable Christ Church graveyard at Fifth and Arch streets, the final resting place of such luminaries as Benjamin Franklin and Benjamin Rush. Wilson's remains were then lowered into the ground next to those of his first wife. By then Konkle and Alexander had become bitter enemies over who deserved the lion's share of credit for this triumphant outcome. Their mutual recriminations were noticed by the press, which ran such headlines as "Row Spoils Holy Rite."[65]

David W. Maxey, a Philadelphia attorney and historian by avocation who has pieced this story together, suggests in his conclusion that the entire episode "corresponds in strikingly similar ways, to the translation of the relics of saints in late antiquity and the medieval period. The modern mind may resist this comparison, but the continuities are there, including the discovery of the saint and the verification of sainthood, the ceremonies associated with the translation, the speeches given, the erection of a monument, and what an acute observer of this phenomenon has dubbed the 'impresarios' of the cult of saints."[66] Wilson's greed, financial collapse, and flight from his creditors were apparently forgiven if not fully forgotten. His reputation cleverly manipulated and miraculously restored, then raised from the dead like Lazarus, he rejoined the founding fathers as an American immortal.

There is an intriguing irony that must be added as a postscript to this strange story. In 1790 James Wilson delivered an important series, Lectures on Law, at the College of Philadelphia. Almost at the outset he declared that his new nation urgently needed a pantheon in Philadelphia so that her "patriots and her heroes" would be duly honored and remembered. Although no such hall of fame had been planned, he could envision it so clearly.

> The glorious dome already rises. Its architecture is of the neatest and chastest order: its dimensions are spacious: its proportions are elegant and correct. In its front a number of niches are formed. In some of them statues are placed. On the left of the portal, are the names and figures of Warren, Montgomery, Mercer [each one a patriot eventually exhumed and reinterred, as we have seen]. On the right hand, are the names and figures of Calvert [religious liberty], Penn, Franklin. In the middle is a niche of larger size, and decorated with peculiar ornaments. On the left side of it, are sculptured the trophies of war, on the right, the more precious emblems of peace. Above it, is represented the rising glory of the United States. It is without a statue and without a name. Beneath it, in letters very legible, are these words—"FOR THE MOST WORTHY." By the enraptured voice of grateful America—with the consenting plaudits of an admiring world, the designation is unanimously made. Late—very late—may the niche be filled.[67]

President George Washington sat in front when that lecture was delivered. He understood full well for whom the niche was envisioned. Perhaps James Wilson also imagined that one day, somewhere in his adopted city, there might also be a niche for himself.

✶

The story of John Paul Jones's exhumation in 1904 and trans-Atlantic reburial two years later is perhaps the most elaborate and grandly nationalistic in the entire American sequence of such episodes. Born in Scotland in 1747, Jones initially served on English ships engaged in the

slave trade and then rose to command a merchant ship in the Carib-
bean. In 1773, however, he emigrated to Virginia, was commissioned by
the Continental Congress two years later, and commanding the *Providence* he captured sixteen enemy ships. By 1777 he was carrying out crucial raids on British commercial shipping. In 1779, having remodeled
an older French vessel that he renamed the *Bonhomme Richard*, Jones
captured the *Serapis*, a more powerful British warship than his own, off
the east coast of England and became the greatest American naval hero
of the war.

Historically considered the first commodore (ultimately called vice-
admiral) of the new American navy, he gave valiant and brilliant service during the War for Independence, often made possible by financing
from King Louis XVI. In 1783 he went to Paris to arrange for settlement
of prize monies for ships he had captured in European waters, but the
complex legal procedures dragged on for several years. In 1787 Congress
awarded him a gold medal. One year later he accepted a commission as
rear admiral in the navy of Queen Catherine the Great of Russia, seeing
action against the Turks; but when Jones's relationship with Catherine
soured, he returned to Paris in 1790 and died there in 1792, amidst the
political chaos that followed the first phase of the French Revolution.

According to some enthusiastic and intensely patriotic early
twentieth-century accounts, both France and the United States claimed
Jones as a national hero; French admirers are said to have proposed
reburial in the Panthèon. In 1805 Napoleon lamented Jones's death,
and a century afterward comparisons would be made between Jones's
reinterment in the United States and the return of Napoleon's ashes
from St. Helena to Paris in 1840. That brings to mind two sentences
penned generations later by Charles de Gaulle: "Every man of action
has a strong dose of egotism, pride, hardness, and cunning. But all those
things will be forgiven him, indeed, they will be regarded as high qualities, if he can make of them the means to achieve great ends."[68]

The American minister to France in 1792, Gouverneur Morris, explaining rather lamely that it would be imprudent to spend the limited
resources of the United States and Jones's heirs on a grand funeral, said,
"I desired that he might be buried in a private and economical manner,"
which meant in the very modest Protestant cemetery in Paris. Even
that involved considerable bureaucratic hassling in a Roman Catho-

lic country, however, though a commissary for Louis XVI paid the 462 francs for public interment as fitting tribute to a man who felt grateful to the king and had earned royal respect by humiliating the archrival British navy. Jones's burial actually marked a new era of religious toleration within the highly unstable republican regime that was emerging in 1792, the very year Louis XVI was imprisoned. Despite objections that Jones was a Calvinist, he became the first Protestant to receive any sort of public interment in France.[69]

The ceremony turned out to be considerably more impressive than one might have expected under the circumstances—despite the fact that Morris felt his many social obligations (inconsequential, as it turned out) prevented him from attending. At eight o'clock in the evening on July 20, three primary groups appeared. First, a deputation from the French National Assembly was accompanied by a detachment of grenadiers, a bishop, and a vicar. A second group came from the consistory of Protestants in Paris, including a pastor chosen to make an address. And third, there were a number of friends and associates who had hovered over Jones during his final illness.[70]

With the passage of time, unfortunately, the small cemetery became densely crowded. Deceased persons were buried very close together, sometimes even two or three deep. Within a century the graveyard underwent so many changes and suffered from such neglect that it became nearly impossible to recognize who was buried where, and inaccurate reports eventually circulated that Jones may well have been relocated in either of two other graveyards, including Père Lachaise, famous for its flock of celebrities. In 1899 an American journalist, Julius Chambers, publicized the desirability of locating Jones's remains and taking them home. That led to a resolution's being introduced in Congress supporting such a plan, yet it died in committee. Undaunted, Chambers hired an agent at his own expense to seek out the exact location of the grave.[71]

During his term as ambassador to France, General Horace Porter followed Chambers's lead and made it his mission to locate Jones and take him back to the United States for proper burial. As he wrote when he launched the search, "Here was presented the spectacle of a hero whose fame once covered two continents, and whose name is still an inspiration to a world-famed navy, lying for more than a century in a forgotten grave, like an obscure outcast, relegated to oblivion in a squalid corner of a distant foreign city, buried in ground once consecrated, but since desecrated." The efforts that Porter went to in order to find Jones's remains in the abandoned and overbuilt St. Louis Cemetery were genuinely heroic, exceeding virtually any comparable quest on every measure: funds expended, supervision of the work, verification of the bones, arranging for the autopsy, "repackaging" Jones, and organizing an elaborate parade.[72]

Relying upon careful historical research and advance work done by Chambers's agent, associates recruited by Porter identified the correct cemetery. They knew from a letter written in 1792 that Jones had been buried in a "leaden coffin." Looking in what seemed to be the logical spot, they dug deep and found five leaden coffins, three of which bore the nameplates of other men. A fourth contained the skeleton of a person too tall to have been Jones, but the fifth held the remains of a man just the right size with a cap on which there appeared to be the initials *J* and *P*, the latter with an open loop when it was inverted. Anthropologists and pathologists then discovered kidney lesions, "which presented the appearance, very clearly, of chronic interstitial nephritis," the condition responsible for Jones's final illness and death. Twelve individuals, American and French, witnessed the site, the examination, and the identification (also relying upon samples of hair; fig. 25). They unanimously concurred that these were surely the remains of John Paul Jones.[73]

When news reached Washington in 1905, the government dispatched four war vessels, led by the USS *Brooklyn*, which remained in perfect column formation for the entire trans-Atlantic cruise and landed at Cherbourg in time for an elaborate French welcome and Fourth of July celebration. Two days later, the anniversary of Jones's birth, his remains were accompanied through Paris by five hundred American sailors and marines, a formal transfer of the body from French to American custody took place, and the decision was made to strike a note of victory rather than sounding a funereal tone. In remarks delivered as part of the service held at the American Church on July 6, special emissary Francis Loomis gave a speech celebrating Jones's achievements but acknowledging that "America unfortunately exemplified the adage that Republics are ungrateful, for in the stress and struggle of building a new country, she forgot for a time her departed hero."[74]

*Figure 25.* The place where the body of John Paul Jones was found in 1904. General Horace Porter seated at the left. A workman holds the point of his pick over the spot where he struck the lead coffin. From *John Paul Jones: Commemoration at Annapolis, April 24, 1906*, comp. Charles W. Stewart (Washington, DC: Government Printing Office, 1907).

That lament would echo Alexis de Tocqueville in his two-volume *Democracy in America* (1835–40), where several times he called attention to the memory lapses of a present-minded and future-oriented society. But at the farewell dinner arranged in Paris for General Porter, Colonel Henry Watterson proclaimed that Porter had "rescued John Paul Jones from fiction and restored him to history. He [Porter] ends his career in Paris by the rescue from a forgotten sepulcher of an immortal sea fighter."[75]

At five o'clock on July 6 a grand procession formed and proceeded along the Avenue de l'Alma to the Champs Elysées. The cortège bearing the coffin on a caisson included two regiments of French infantry with their orchestral bands, one regiment of cuirassiers, two batteries of artillery, two companies of American marines, and six companies of "blue jackets" from the four American warships. Enthusiastic and reverent spectators lined the route, which culminated at the Esplanade des Invalides, where the coffin was placed on a bier in a specially con-

*Figure 26.* The ceremonies in honor of John Paul Jones at the Naval Academy, July 24, 1905. From *John Paul Jones' Last Cruise and Final Resting Place. The United States Naval Academy* (Washington, DC: George E. Howard, 1906).

structed pavilion, under the flags of both countries and a profusion of flowers. Ambassadors and dignitaries from many nations surrounded the catafalque and listened respectfully to national anthems and a reading of the resolution by which Congress ordered a medal to be struck and presented to Jones in 1787, along with a letter written to the unfortunate Louis XVI informing him of that fact.[76]

A funeral train then carried the coffin and well-wishers from both countries to Cherbourg, where a French admiral gave a flowery address on July 8. The remains were then transferred to the *Brooklyn*, which steamed westward and was met by a naval escort of honor as it approached Hampton Roads, Virginia, at the mouth of the Chesapeake, where it docked on July 22. Two days later the coffin arrived at the Naval Academy in Annapolis, where it was placed in a temporary vault to the accompaniment of Chopin's funeral march (fig. 26). The final, triumphant commemorative ceremonies took place on April 24, 1906—the exact anniversary of Jones's glorious capture of the *Drake* off Carrickfergus in 1778—in the new Memorial Chapel whose cornerstone had been placed by Admiral Dewey, revered hero of the Spanish-American

War, on June 3, 1904, more than a year before the completed exhumation in Paris.[77]

The two-year time-lag between preparation of the new chapel and the final entombment was not at all unusual for Anglo-American state funerals, which required meticulous preparation of an elaborate burial site deemed to have sufficient national significance. I have already noted that to have been the case with Grant's Tomb during the 1890s. Also, a delay often occurred when mourners waited for a special anniversary occasion that seemed symbolically suitable or propitious. Well after the 1861 death of Queen Victoria's husband, Prince Albert, his coffin was brought from the royal vault beneath St. George's Chapel at Windsor and placed in a temporary sarcophagus in December 1862. It remained there until placed in an extraordinary gothic tomb in 1868.[78]

The planning and preparation for the final entombment of Jones could not have been more elaborate. The event coincided with the annual meeting of the Daughters of the American Revolution in Washington. On April 21 a French squadron of three armored cruisers arrived at Annapolis. Two days later the ranking officers of that squadron were welcomed at a White House reception, followed by two other receptions at the Navy Department and the War Department. In the evening many guests joined the French officers for dinner at the White House, followed by yet another reception. On April 24, the commemorative day, the presidential party and others were welcomed at a luncheon given by the superintendent of the Naval Academy. The next day, hardly an anticlimax, the secretary of the navy hosted a luncheon for the French officers, and that evening a gala dinner and reception took place at the French embassy. On April 26, French Ambassador Jules Jusserand (Roosevelt's favorite tennis partner) and Rear Admiral Paul Campion attended the laying of a cornerstone at Annapolis to honor French sailors and soldiers who had died in the American Revolution. The next day the French squadron departed from Annapolis toward home.[79]

The most important day during that weeklong celebration of Jones and the two nations was April 24, when President Roosevelt spoke for thirty minutes at Annapolis followed by Ambassador Jusserand, the indefatigable General Horace Porter, and Governor Edwin Warfield of Maryland, then a closing prayer by the chief naval chaplain. Roosevelt would use the occasion of James Wilson's reburial in Philadelphia to praise the expansion of national power, and he voiced similar senti-ments at the permanent entombment of Jones. The primary focus of this recent winner of the Nobel Peace Prize for his mediation in the Russo-Japanese War was military preparedness.

> We can afford as a people to differ on the ordinary party questions; but if we are both farsighted and patriotic we can not afford to differ on the all-important question of keeping the national defenses as they should be kept; of not alone keeping up, but of going on with building up of the United States navy, and of keeping our small army at least at its present size and making it the most efficient for its size that there is on the globe. Remember, you here who are listening to me, that to applaud patriotic sentiments and to turn out to do honor to the dead heroes who by land or by sea won honor for our flag is only worth while if we are prepared to show that our energies do not exhaust themselves in words.[80]

Within the imposing new chapel, the walls of the crypt surround-ing Jones's sarcophagus displayed, in recessed cases, memorabilia from his extraordinary career: his gold sword presented by Louis XVI, his service sword, his captain's commission of October 10, 1776, signed by John Hancock, and the two steel dies for his gold medal authorized by Congress in 1787 (fig. 27). Close by stands one of the original plaster busts of Jones executed during his life by Jean Antoine Houdon in Paris. In addition to this handsome and moving memorial, in 1912 a bronze statue of Jones was unveiled near the Tidal Basin in West Potomac Park. The commission for that work went to the American sculptor Charles Henry Niehaus, and the model for its handsome head would be the fine bust by Houdon.[81] Following more than a century of distance and ne-glect, John Paul Jones had been doubly immortalized in the nation's pantheon of larger-than-life heroes.

✠

Needless to say, nineteenth-century Americans were quite often in-clined to be more than sentimental about death, despite its prevalence, especially among the young. Some have even referred to a nineteenth-century American "cult of death" that is readily seen in domestic ico-nography, especially "mourning pictures," and the writings of such major figures as Bryant, Poe, and Whitman on Lincoln, Emily Dickin-

*Figure 27.* The sarcophagus and memorial to John Paul Jones in the chapel of the U.S. Naval Academy. Courtesy of the U.S. Naval Academy.

son, and others.[82] The artist William Sidney Mount (1807–68) received numerous commissions to paint the visages of recently deceased people, particularly women and children. One written request, for example, asked him to work from a "daguerreotype likeness, as I have one or two of my child that I lost about two months since [the child, not the likeness]. She was ten years old and the likenesses are very strong ones. I shall remove her from the vaulted grave in which she now rests to a family vault that we shall build as soon as the spring opens and will be ready about the first of May and then she can be seen if it will assist any in the painting of it as her coffin is so fixed that she can be looked at without exposing her to the air." Mount disliked these assignments but accepted this one and numerous others because they paid so well.[83]

Sentiments and episodes of that nature seem to have been common-place during the mid-nineteenth century.[84] By the close of the nine-teenth and start of the twentieth, however, as the vogue for spiritualism and necromancy waned, the impulse to immortalize by visual means gradually became less romantically ghoulish and gave way to memorial portraits as we now know them and the celebration of notable individuals in the interest of glorifying the nation and its institutions. Lurid voyeurism could take still other forms, though. The commercialization (even commodification) of dead celebrities and the idiosyncratic demands of survivors, most often family members, prompted still more instances of exhumation—the stimuli sometimes being just as much social or economic as political, and deeply personal as well.

— FOUR —

*Problematic*
*Graves, Tourism,*
*and the Wishes*
*of Survivors*

We cannot know how much we learn
From those who never will return,
Until a flash of unforeseen
Remembrance falls on what has been.

✠ Edward Arlington Robinson, *Flammonde*

$\mathcal{B}$eyond the orbits of American statesmen and warriors, founders and fallen heroes, there are significant exhumation episodes involving an array of legendary figures, especially in literature and the arts—distinctive individuals like Edgar Allan Poe and Mark Rothko. What many of them shared in common beyond exhumation and reburial, or the restoration of a neglected gravesite, is that civic and personal survivors (most notably mothers and spouses) felt that the deceased had either not been interred properly or else, most important, not in the most appropriate location. Survivors (or members of the next generation) frequently insisted—sometimes despite evidence to the contrary—that the deceased had really wanted to be buried in a spot other than the one initially chosen, often for reasons of convenience at the time. Arguments over where the most appropriate site might be frequently persisted for decades, and in certain cases even longer.

With some significant exceptions, graves of the persons discussed here were not disinterred because a change had occurred in their reputations as historically significant individuals: few went from being utterly forgotten to being dramatically rediscovered. On the other hand, opening or moving graves, or else erecting new and more imposing monuments, did tend to enhance reputations and revitalize interest in the individuals' careers and contributions to American life and culture. In a few instances, most notably that of Daniel Boone, whose reburial would be among the most bitterly contested of all, interstate rivalry and pride figured prominently but also profits to be made from commercial tourism. Curiosity seekers, disciples, and pilgrims have played prominent parts in prompting reinterment. And they have often thrived in its aftermath. The outlaw Jesse James, the architect Frank Lloyd Wright, and the scout, explorer, and colonizer Boone provide prime examples, along with many others.

Boone was born in 1734 near Reading, Pennsylvania. As a young man he migrated south through the Appalachians to the frontier portion of North Carolina; in 1775 he led a group of settlers westward into what later became Kentucky and erected a fort at Boonesborough. As that region was still a very remote county of Virginia, Boone was elected to the Virginia state legislature in 1780 and became a sheriff and surveyor who speculated in land and often received payment for his services in land. Because he repeatedly failed to file and secure fair title to his real estate—Boone was as lackadaisical about matters of business as he was brilliant as a guide, woodsman, and, when necessary, Indian fighter— he lost control of all his holdings in Kentucky (by then a state) and moved to Missouri, where he lived on land given to him by Congress for his valiant services in defending against the British and their Indian allies during the War for Independence.[1]

When Boone died near St. Charles, Missouri, in 1820, he was buried near his beloved wife Rebecca in her Bryan family graveyard on Tuque Creek, a typical frontier burying ground at that time: "a small, unkempt, and unfrequented space into which the deceased members of the Boone settlement were crowded." Most of the graves, including Boone's, were initially unmarked—a predictable source of trouble and contestation.[2] Because Boonesborough had been the site of a wildly dramatic battle during the war, a commemorative celebration took place there in 1840. After the governor of Kentucky gave a rousing oration about Boone and his heroic legacy, some prominent Kentuckians proposed erecting a statue dedicated to Boone and the early settlers there. Meanwhile, St. Louis newspapers mentioned the possibility of placing a monument at the site of Boone's grave in what became Charette, Missouri, where the overgrown Bryan family farm was situated.[3]

In 1845, however, before the slow-moving Missourians had taken any action, Kentucky's legislature passed a resolution authorizing the reinterment of Boone's remains near the state capitol in Frankfort. The scheme actually originated with the proprietors of a new capital cemetery company, an entrepreneurial group improving a site perched high on a hill overlooking the city. While seeking the assistance of various prominent state figures, the proprietors appealed to Nathan Boone for permission to relocate his father's remains. Although Daniel Boone had left very clear instructions concerning his burial, which did *not* include Kentucky because he had refused to set foot in the state since 1799,[4] the state treasurer wrote to Nathan "that his remains were deposited in a remote village in Missouri. This should not be." A former governor declared that "Kentucky (and none other) is the place to contain the remains," adding that he felt certain that if Boone and his immediate relatives could speak "from the other world . . . they would prefer being buried in Kentucky to any part of the globe."[5]

In Missouri officials promptly appropriated five hundred dollars to erect a monument over Boone's grave and dispatched their own appeals to Boone's son to leave Daniel's body alone. At that point Boone's many grandchildren, his nephews, and others descended from his large family began to take sides, because some had remained in Kentucky while the larger group lived in Missouri. Harvey Griswold also became a crucial figure in the conflict, because he had purchased the Bryan farm on Tuque Creek. Griswold declared that he was "opposed to a removal of said remains from the place selected by the said Boone in his lifetime, and to any act which may deprive Missouri of the credit of doing appropriate honours." Nevertheless, a prominent Kentuckian, Senator John J. Crittenden, later the author of the 1861 Crittenden Resolves that sought to avert the Civil War, claimed in response that William Boone had produced "satisfactory evidence that the immediate relations to Col. Boone had been consulted and had given their written consent."[6]

The aggressively determined Kentucky organizers hired three local African Americans in Missouri to excavate the Boone family graves for them. At that point a series of bizarre developments began to unfold. Some years after Boone died, family members had placed markers where they *believed* the scout and his wife had been interred. More than thirty witnesses now gathered around those stones and watched the diggers turn up pieces of bone, shroud, and decayed coffins. Many of the bones disintegrated, but what could be salvaged was placed in pine boxes, while locals picked up and walked off with teeth and bits of bone scattered around the excavated site and kept them as relics. No one even bothered to backfill the graves, and such markers as there were fell over and cracked. A St. Louis paper then reported that assembled members of the Boone family had declared that the bones "were freely given up" with the expectation that Kentuckians would "faithfully carry out their object of doing suitable honors to the remains of their illustrious ancestor."[7]

Meanwhile, as historian John Mack Faragher has recounted, the Frankfort cemetery proprietors planned an elaborate reburial ceremony "under as imposing auspices as the occasion should demand."

On the evening prior to the celebratory day, prominent Kentuckians came to the capital to observe the transfer of the collected remains into appropriately new coffins. A youngster who had been present recalled much later that Boone's presumptive skull "was handled by the persons present and its peculiarities commented upon." As we have seen with Descartes, Swedenborg, and others, the skulls of famous men seem to exude a certain fascination—even prior to the Victorian generation's obsession with craniology.[8]

On Saturday, September 13, 1845, several thousand people gathered in the streets of Frankfort to watch marching bands, state officials, military companies, and fraternal organizations parading from the capitol building across the river and up the hill to the cemetery, preceded by four white horses drawing the hearse that bore the Boone coffins. At the grave site overlooking the Kentucky River valley, the authoritative Crittenden, so crucial to this disinterment of the great guide from Missouri, delivered an elaborate tribute to Daniel Boone.

Within a month, the Frankfort cemetery group announced the first public sale of lots and enjoyed quite a brisk business. The enterprising proprietors, however, failed to erect the pledged monument. A few years later when a group of proud Kentuckians tried to raise a private fund to underwrite such a monument, they met with indifference. Only in 1860, when the state legislature put up two thousand dollars for the purpose, did a monument to Boone finally materialize (fig. 28).[9] While the monument was being prepared, some workers uncovered the graves and opened the coffins, and an observer lamented that they shoveled up remains "as carelessly as if they had belonged to any ordinary mortal." One person, eager for a souvenir himself, fled with a fragment of what he believed to be one of Boone's vertebrae in his pocket.

During the half-century that followed, tourists chipped away at the monument until it was nearly ruined. In 1910, under pressure from the Rebecca Bryan Boone Chapter of the DAR, the Kentucky legislature appropriated funds to restore the monument, and cemetery officials surrounded it with a substantial fence to protect it from what Faragher has labeled "Boone's adoring public."[10]

Meanwhile, bitterness had been brewing in Missouri. According to the St. Louis *Globe Democrat* in 1888, Boone's original grave had been "desecrated to gratify a spasm of Kentucky pride." Soon, some Boone

*Figure 28.* Daniel Boone's grave and monument, first erected in 1860, Frankfort Cemetery, Frankfort, Kentucky. Following restoration in 1910, cemetery officials surrounded the monument with a substantial fence to protect it from souvenir hunters. Courtesy of the Kentucky Historical Society, Frankfort.

descendants began spreading rumors that the Kentuckians had actually failed to retrieve Boone. They insisted that when Boone was buried in 1820 another coffin already occupied the spot next to Rebecca's, so Daniel's coffin was placed at her feet. At the disinterment, therefore, angry descendants from Missouri had allowed the Kentuckians to uncover the wrong grave. According to this version, the family "considered it a smart deception and justifiable." Other members of Boone's extended family, however, dismissed this face-saving account. In October 1915, at the dedication ceremony for a DAR monument to Boone at the Tuque Creek graveyard before an assembled crowd of two thousand, a Boone descendant publicly repudiated the revisionist tale.[11]

Historians have observed that according to contemporary comments, the immediate family's consent was "freely given" and that despite disintegration, the coffins lying side by side in 1845 seem to have been identical. Yet one Missouri-based Bryan bitterly resented the imputation that family members might have been privy to a shameful deception, though the highly ambiguous assertion that he made seems more an act of faith than empirically grounded: "For shame!" he cried. "There was not a single body buried here that was not [connected to] some one living near to whom the memory was dear." So doubts lingered in Missouri, and they have endured. On several occasions Missouri officials have requested the return of Rebecca Boone's supposed remains from Kentucky so that she could be reinterred in her rightful place next to her husband, who they claim never left. In 1987 officials in Warren County, where the Bryan graveyard is located, asked the governor of Missouri to issue a proclamation declaring that Daniel Boone's bones had not departed from the state. He declined to do so.[12]

More than just pride of place was at stake in all this. Tourist dollars also mattered. To complicate matters and keep the controversy alive, in 1983 Kentucky's forensic anthropologist carefully examined the plaster cast of Boone's skull that had been made at the time of his death and announced that not only could it not have been Boone's but more likely "this really could be the skull of a Negro." He acknowledged that it was not a very good cast, but that did not prevent wire services from picking up the story and having it reprinted in newspapers all across the country. The record keeper at the cemetery in Frankfort insisted that "his remains are here"; but who knows?[13] No one does for certain, even if no devious trick was played on the Kentuckians in 1845, because both Boones were buried in a small and crowded space without reliable markers. Daniel Boone's mythic stature may be larger than life, but the tangible reality that remains is much less.

✠

Born in 1809 and orphaned at the age of three, as an adult Edgar Allan Poe led a peripatetic life as a writer of poetry and detective and horror stories, and as the literary editor for various journals. He called himself a "magazinist" and clearly had a precocious and wide-ranging intellect. In 1829 he moved to Baltimore, which became his home despite significant stints of work in New York and Philadelphia. In 1835 he married a cousin, Virginia Clemm, who was not quite fourteen at the time, and some later believed that her premature death upset his emotional balance. Accounts of his alcoholism and possible use of opium seem to have been exaggerated, though both may have contributed to his own early death in 1849.[14]

Although Poe's life story is starkly different from Boone's, some striking similarities are relevant because they call attention to certain patterns in nineteenth-century American culture, irrespective of differences between urban and frontier conditions. I have in mind, for example, the practice of unmarked graves for so many, though by no means all, and the persistence of poorly tended graves, even for individuals who had achieved a degree of fame or notoriety. The initial failure to erect monuments for such figures also recurs, as does the ongoing difficulty in raising public funds for memorials even when attention is called to this lamentable lapse. The desire to move the remains of people to a more prominent place of honor commonly arose within one generation after death; and because various permissions to move coffins or bodies are usually required, it was often difficult to achieve a consensus about *whether* to reinter, and if so where. Finally, and once again predictably, many more people are likely to be present for a ceremonial reburial than for the first funeral.

In 1844 Edgar Allan Poe published one of his less familiar stories in a little-known Philadelphia periodical called *Broadway Journal*. Titled "The Premature Burial," it begins with this sentence: "There are certain themes of which the interest is all-absorbing, but which are too entirely horrible for the purposes of legitimate fiction." It recounts a variety of episodes that had been reported in the press worldwide, sounding like bizarre items from *Ripley's Believe It or Not*, about people who were inadvertently buried alive and then tried to battle their way out of their grave, most often without success but in some cases causing a coffin to topple off its temporary supports. The sixth and seventh paragraphs in this piece concern the wife of a widely respected citizen, "a lawyer of eminence and a member of Congress."

> The lady was deposited in her family vault, which, for three subsequent years, was undisturbed. At the expiration of this term it was opened for the reception of a sarcophagus;—but, alas! How fearful a shock awaited the husband, who, personally, threw open the door. As its portals swung outwardly back, some white-appareled object fell rattling within his arms. It was the skeleton of his wife in her yet unmouldered shroud.

A careful investigation rendered it evident that she had revived within two days after her entombment—that her struggles within the coffin had caused it to fall from a ledge, or shelf, to the floor, where it was so broken as to permit her escape.[15]

The nature and preoccupations of this journalistic-seeming story, rather than its particular and horrific mix of narratives (some American and others European), provide an eerie but figurative anticipation of what happened some years after Poe himself died in Baltimore on October 7, 1849. He was buried the very next day in an unmarked grave at the Poe family plot behind the Westminster Presbyterian Church in Baltimore. The Reverend W. T. D. Clemm, a relative of Poe's wife and her mother, read the burial service, and George W. Spence officiated as sexton. Only eight or nine people attended the brief rites.

In 1873 Paul Hamilton Hayne, a southern poet of some renown, visited Poe's grave and felt so distressed by its unkempt condition that he wrote an article for newspaper publication in which he urged people to clear the grave of weeds and erect an appropriate monument. Hayne's article was widely reprinted and helped to revive lagging efforts to raise money for a suitable memorial. His hortatory essay was duly noticed not only throughout the United States but also in Europe, where Poe had achieved an admiring readership. A Baltimore teacher of elocution in the public schools led the two-year crusade for funds, using newspaper publicity along with Poe-related entertainments given by her students; but only when a Philadelphia philanthropist provided the final $650 was it possible to commission a suitable marker.[16]

The result was a large monument initially located in the back of the churchyard. The marker even bore a medallion with a portrait of Poe, based upon an image of him in the possession of a family member. The total cost of the monument and medallion exceeded $1,500. But in order to provide an adequate foundation for such a large monument, it became necessary to exhume Poe's remains and place them in the grave of his mother-in-law, Mrs. Clemm, who died in 1871 and had adored "Eddie." Late in October 1875 a reporter for the Baltimore *American* described the exhumation.

The laborers employed to perform the task, upon digging to a depth of about five feet, discovered the coffin in a good state of preservation, after having lain in its place nearly 26 years. The lid was removed, and the remains curiously examined by the few present. There before their gaze, was extended the skeleton, almost in perfect condition, and lying with the long bony hands reposing one upon the other, as they had been arranged in death. The skull bore marks of greater decay, the teeth from the upper jaw having become dislodged, but those in the lower were all in place, and some little hair was still clinging near the forehead. Beyond what has been described nothing was to be seen. The coffin was inclosed in another, and reinterred.[17]

Spence, the sexton who had officiated in 1849 supervised the exhumation as well. Three years later he told a visitor to the grave that when it was first opened in 1875 he lifted the head of Poe's skeleton and "his brain rattled around inside just like a lump of mud, sir." Meanwhile, the monument committee deferred to what it believed to be popular sentiment and agreed to relocate the burial site from the rear of the churchyard to the front, which meant a far more prominent spot at the corner of Fayette and Greene streets (note the honorific names of two Revolutionary War heroes). Descendants of the original owners of two large lots gave their permission, so Poe was exhumed once again and moved, along with Mrs. Clemm (fig. 29).[18]

Although the reinterment and transfer of the monument were achieved on November 6, 1875, the unveiling and formal dedication occurred eleven days later (fig. 30). In order to accommodate the large crowd and special guests, the dedication actually took place at the Western Female High School, where members of the Baltimore Philharmonic Society played and sang. The president of Baltimore City College made the principal address, and Sara Sigourney Rice, who had launched and led the fund-raising campaign, read aloud from laudatory letters written by such American and English literati as Henry Wadsworth Longfellow, Oliver Wendell Holmes, William Cullen Bryant, Algernon Swinburne, and Alfred Lord Tennyson.

The memorialists then moved to the actual grave site, where a carefully draped cloth was removed from the monument, revealing wreaths of ivy, lilies, and evergreens. A floral tribute in the shape of a raven, made from black immortelles, was placed upon the tomb by the acting company of Ford's Grand Opera House in Baltimore, as a way of honoring Poe's biological mother, who had been an actress in the Holliday

*Figure 29.* The grave of Edgar Allan Poe, Westminster Burial Ground, Baltimore, Maryland. Photograph courtesy of R. Owens, Westminster Preservation Trust, Inc.

Street Theatre. After the ceremonies ended, Walt Whitman approached the monument and, as a mark of respect for Poe, asked for and received a leaf of laurel and a half-opened bud. As one writer remarked, "The atmosphere of the occasion was rather that of a grand triumphal pageant than of a funeral service, [and] strictly religious exercises were conspicuous by their absence."[19]

In 1883 William F. Gill of Boston and New York, one of Poe's earliest biographers, visited the cemetery in Fordham, New York, where Virginia Clemm Poe had been buried in 1847, and he arrived just in the nick of time. Part of the cemetery was being razed, and, according to his report decades later in the Boston *Herald*, Gill encountered a sexton with Virginia's bones on a shovel, about to be thrown away because he knew of no one who wished to claim them. With the sexton's cooperation, Gill placed the bones in a small box, took them to his home in New York, corresponded with Poe family members in Baltimore, and eventually took the container there to be placed in a bronze casket and laid on Poe's left side. On January 19, 1885, the seventy-sixth anniversary of

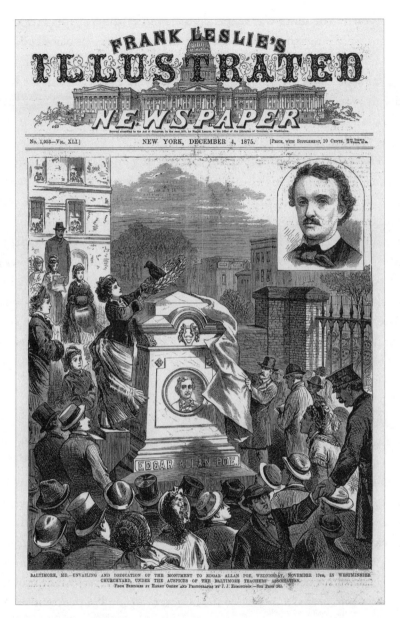

FRANK LESLIE'S ILLUSTRATED NEWSPAPER

No. 1,053—Vol. XLI]     NEW YORK, DECEMBER 4, 1875.     [Price, with Supplement, 10 Cents.

BALTIMORE, MD.—UNVAILING AND DEDICATION OF THE MONUMENT TO EDGAR ALLAN POE, WEDNESDAY, NOVEMBER 17TH, IN WESTMINSTER CHURCHYARD, UNDER THE AUSPICES OF THE BALTIMORE TEACHERS' ASSOCIATION.—FROM SKETCHES BY HARRY OGDEN AND PHOTOGRAPHS BY J. J. EDMONDSON.—SEE PAGE 221.

*Figure 30.* The unveiling of the Edgar Allan Poe Monument, November 15, 1875. Woodcut engraving from *Frank Leslie's Illustrated Newspaper*, December 4, 1875. The woman leaning against the monument, and placing a wreath with a raven on top, is Sara Sigourney Rice. In 1875 the monument stood on a grassy plot. The gate and a brick walkway were added in 1910. Image courtesy of Jess Savoye and the Edgar Allan Poe Society of Baltimore.

Poe's birth, the tomb was reopened once more, and Virginia Poe's remains were interred. It is unclear whether her casket was placed *next* to
her husband's or, perhaps more likely, on top of his and her mother's.
(That would not have been quite so quirky as it may sound. He had
deeply loved them both.) The sexton who had officiated at the very first
burial in 1849 and at the exhumation in 1875 was present yet again at the
rites that reunited the trio in 1885.[20]

There is an intriguing epilogue. Starting in 1949, a mysterious
stranger began placing the same birthday gift on Poe's grave every
year: a half-full bottle of cognac and three red roses—the absence of a
fourth rose signifying less than a full bottle of whiskey? According to
the tour director for the Westminster Preservation Trust, an organization with oversight of the graveyard where Poe is buried, "It's a very
personal tribute and we have never made any attempt to discover his
identity." Every Halloween the Westminster Hall and Burying Ground
Association provides a Poe impersonator who reads a work by the celebrated godfather of ghost stories.[21] Clearly, symbolic and sentimental tourism has become an increasingly significant part of the reburial
phenomenon.

✝

If the adventures of Boone's and Poe's remains seem somewhat bizarre,
an episode in 1889 provides a rather different example of attempts at
bodily identification at a time when putting up memorial markers to
historical personages was very much in vogue. During the summer of
that year, *Mayflower* descendants in Massachusetts intended to dedicate
a major monument to Miles (aka Myles) Standish, the Pilgrims' military adviser and defender immortalized by Longfellow in his romanticized narrative poem *The Courtship of Miles Standish* (1858). The monument was expected to be one of the largest of its kind in the country. As
with many figures who died in the distant and storied past, the location
where Standish had actually been laid to rest in 1656 remained utterly
obscure several centuries later.

But in 1889 it came to light that a man who had died eighteen years
earlier at the age of ninety-five had given testimony that Standish lay
buried in a South Duxbury cemetery. How did he know? When he was a
lad in Revolutionary times, his father had pointed out Standish's grave

to him. Consequently, during the third week in April (when the Boston Marathon is now run to commemorate Paul Revere's heroic ride in 1775), the grave (*some* grave, at least) was dug up so that authorities could try to ascertain whether the skeleton found there might possibly be that of Miles Standish. Professor Albert Bushnell Hart of Harvard, an esteemed authority on early American history and especially New England's, joined various pathologists in this fruitless undertaking. The outcome was inconclusive, of course, but it received attention in the press because interest in Standish and the Pilgrim "fathers" was so intense at the time.[22]

Yet another episode from that period involves less romanticism and consequently may seem less intriguing, perhaps, than the never-ending Boone and Poe sagas. It is far more representative, however, because Americans were often exhumed either because an influential survivor preferred them to be permanently in a place most prominently associated with them historically or else because a such a person decided that they should be reunited in death with the spouse deemed to be the most appropriate—the "right" one or the "original" one.

Robert Dale Owen was born in Scotland in 1801, the son of a highly successful, wealthy, and reform-minded manufacturer. The family came to the United States in 1825, when the father, Robert Owen, bought and briefly took control of a thriving utopian community that had been created at New Harmony, Indiana, by German Rappites in 1805. The idealistic senior Owen was too busy with other concerns, political and entrepreneurial, to administer his colony effectively, despite help from a son strongly committed to his socialist views. After this second and less well managed phase of the utopian community failed, young Owen went back to Europe briefly, then moved to New York and wrote the first book published in the United States advocating birth control (by means of coitus interruptus), titled *Moral Physiology, or A Brief and Plain Treatise on the Population Question* (1830). Owen returned to Indiana in 1833 and served two terms in the State House of Representatives. In between he was elected to two terms in the U.S. Congress (1843–47) and drafted the bill providing for creation of the Smithsonian Institution.[23]

In 1853 President Franklin Pierce appointed Owen U.S. minister at Naples. After that he remained active in public life in various ways, mainly through his deep commitment to abolitionism and emancipation. In 1865 he submitted a radical early draft of the Fourteenth Amendment that, with modifications by others, became the basis for the final version. As a strong believer in spiritualism (despite being hoaxed at least once), he wrote two widely read works on the subject: *Footfalls on the Boundary of Another World* (1859) and *The Debatable Land between This World and the Next* (1872). After his wife died, his efforts to communicate with her failed, so very late in life he remarried.[24]

When Owen passed away in 1877 at his summer home on Lake George in the Adirondacks, he was buried in the quiet Caldwell community cemetery across the lake. Simple private services were conducted by the same Presbyterian minister who had performed the wedding ceremony a year before, "mute testimony that a once outstanding infidel had learned to live in peace with orthodoxy." On his gravestone, however, the titles of his two spiritualist works were carved. Owen remained in that serene lakeside spot for sixty years, until his aged daughter decided to disinter and move him back to New Harmony in 1937, on the banks of the Wabash, next to his first wife and deceased children.[25] Survivors have a way of prevailing in the long run.

✛

The death and ultimate resting place of the brilliant inventor John Ericsson warrants inclusion here because, in key respects, it harks back to the John Paul Jones saga, though in reverse—a trans-Atlantic passage from west to east. It sheds interesting light on ceremonial uses of the U.S. Navy in peacetime, when warships are readily available for ceremonial purposes.

Born in 1803, Ericsson was a Swedish mechanical engineer best known for devising the caloric (or hot air) engine during the later 1820s; his invention eventually made him a very wealthy man. He moved to New York in 1839 and between 1840 and 1842 oversaw the development of a new frigate class for the U.S. Navy. In 1843 the USS *Princeton* won a speed competition against the paddle steamer, regarded until then as the fastest ship afloat. In 1862 Ericsson designed the USS *Monitor* for the Union side, responding to Confederate development of the *Merrimack* and resulting in a memorable confrontation between the first two ironclad warships. The American Academy of Arts and Sciences promptly awarded Ericsson the Rumford Prize, a very considerable and well-deserved honor.

When Ericsson died of Bright's disease in New York City in March 1889, ripe with years and honors, some said that "he had so separated himself from his fellows, and so far outlived the era of his best known works, that few realized the historical significance of his death until they read the record of his achievements in the biographical notices filling the papers." On the day of his funeral, however, thirty-two pall-bearers, personal friends and representatives of various societies, especially Swedish American, gathered at his house and proceeded with little ceremony to Trinity Church on lower Broadway, where the burial service was read and the choir sang the familiar hymn "Lead, Kindly Light." His body was then carried to the Marble Cemetery, where James Monroe had been initially buried back in 1831. The procession was a simple one, and nothing in the nature of a civic funeral occurred. The coffin was placed in a receiving vault to await a decision about Ericsson's final resting place. A funeral hymn was sung by a Swedish glee club, and the Odd Fellows of Ericsson's lodge, the Amaranthus, performed their basic, rather secular rites.[26]

Various suggestions emerged for his final interment, including a proposition to place his remains in the Livingston Vault of Trinity churchyard right next to those of Robert Fulton, the "other" inventor of a steamboat. In May the New York state legislature passed an act authorizing the city to spend ten thousand dollars to erect a monument to Ericsson in one of the public parks. Congress passed two other bills totaling eighty thousand dollars for yet another monument. In April, however, Secretary of State James G. Blaine received a message from the American legation in Stockholm informing him that "Sweden would regard with extreme favor Ericsson's body sent home by man-of-war." Blaine passed this request on to the secretary of the navy, who dawdled but eventually responded in June 1890 that the USS *Essex*, an old and inferior vessel, was available to honor the request of the Swedish government. When public sentiment made it clear that this seemed inadequate recompense for the ingenious inventor of the *Monitor*, an impressive cruiser from the "new navy," the USS *Baltimore*, became available.[27]

On August 18 President Benjamin Harrison sent an order to the commandant of the Navy Yard in New York. It read in part:

> Upon the occasion of the embarkation of the remains of Captain Ericsson, it is the desire of the President to give solemn expression to the cordial and fraternal feeling that unites us with a kindred people, the parent source of a large body of our most valued citizens, of whom the late inventor, a Scandinavian by birth, and an American by adoption, was the most illustrious example. In recognition of this feeling and of the debt we owe to Sweden for the gift of Ericsson, whose genius rendered us the highest service in a moment of grave peril and anxiety, it is directed that at this other moment, when we give back his body to his native country, the flag of Sweden shall be saluted by the squadron.[28]

The Navy Department then followed with elaborate instructions for flags to be lowered to half-mast during the embarkation, minute guns to be fired from the monitor *Nantucket* as the body passed from the shore to the *Baltimore*, and then as that vessel passed through the squadron, Swedish ensigns to be displayed and a twenty-one-gun salute to be fired.

When Ericsson's remains were finally removed from the receiving vault at Marble Cemetery (also known as the Second Street cemetery), Swedish singing societies gathered and serenaded their dead countryman with Adolph Fredrik Lindblad's "Stridsbön," the battle prayer of Sweden. The captain of the *Baltimore* had received a message from one of the executors of Ericsson's estate that read in part:

> We send him back crowned with honor; proud of the life of fifty years he devoted to this nation, and with gratitude for the gifts he gave to us. Was he a dreamer? Yes. He dreamed of the practical application of screw propulsion, and the commerce of the world was revolutionized. He dreamed of making naval warfare more terrible, and the *Monitor* was built. . . . He dreamed of hot air, and behold ten thousand caloric engines. He dreamed of the sun's rays in sandy deserts, where water was hard to get, and the solar engine came.[29]

Following a voyage of nineteen days, the *Baltimore* reached Stockholm and transferred its charge to the Swedish government. Three officers of the Swedish navy and four of Ericsson's nephews had been

*Figure 31.* The White Squadron's farewell salute to the body of John Ericsson, New York Bay, August 23, 1890. 1900 engraving based upon the 1898 painting by Edward Moran, located at the U.S. Naval Academy. Division of Prints and Photographs, Library of Congress.

appointed a committee of reception. Sailors from the American man-of-war placed the coffin on a steam barge commanded by a captain of the Swedish navy, and it was followed ashore by a procession of boats with all flags flying at half-mast. At the landing, troops paraded as an escort while American sailors carried the coffin to a pavilion. After a simple service consisting of Swedish hymns and the recitation of a poem, a hearse followed by an escort including representatives of the royal family took the bier to a train waiting at the railway station, bound for Ericsson's final resting place in Filipstad.[30]

When it reached that town in Vermland, the body was borne by twelve miners into a church, where the Lutheran services for the dead were performed. On the morning of September 14, 1890, the coffin went to its ultimate site—a chapel especially prepared for its reception in an adjoining cemetery, said to be "the finest in Sweden." Like John Paul Jones, Ericsson received the ultimate distinction of burial in a brand-new chapel designed to honor him individually.

On November 7, 1884, Ericsson had written an illuminating letter that casts his fame and reputed fortune in an unexpected light. From my perspective, it supplies a most interesting kind of epitaph.

> They imagine in Sweden that I now possess a large fortune, not considering what it has cost me to be useful to my fellow-men, especially my native country, for which I have worked out a complete system of defence. They do not know that for nearly twenty years (during which time I have spent a million crowns), I have not worked for money. They know that during these years I have produced various machines that now pay well, but they do not know that I have resigned these inventions to certain mechanical manufacturers who most liberally consented to construct experimental machines for me at a time when I was not able to pay for the work.[31]

Part of his estate remained uncertain because he still had claims pending against the U.S. government for his investment in a ship called the Destroyer, not to mention partial recompense for his design of the *Princeton* back in 1841–42, which somehow still remained unsettled.

✛

From this story of a suitably honored hero we now shift to that of an infamous outlaw who eventually managed to become a legendary figure of folklore following an early death. Jesse James was born in 1847, the son of a commercial hemp farmer and sometime Baptist minister in Kearney, Missouri. (Hemp is the raw material used in making rope.) Missouri became a bitterly divided border state during the Civil War, and Kearney was situated in the section known as Little Dixie because of its pro-slavery Confederate partisanship. Jesse's older brother, Frank, and later Jesse himself joined a Southern guerrilla band eventually known as Quantrill's Raiders, active in harassing Federal troops in an arc extending from Missouri to Texas. In 1864 they came upon twenty-two unarmed Union soldiers and murdered them all in what came to be known as the Centralia Massacre. The band subsequently encountered another Union company and killed them as well. After the war, when the group was exiled from Missouri by U.S. military authorities, they became bushwhackers determined to attack those responsible for Radical Reconstruction.[32]

Without abandoning their impassioned political views, the alienated group soon turned to more lucrative outlaw activities, committing in 1866 the first armed bank robbery during peacetime in the United States. Others followed, and in 1869 Jesse began to achieve individual notoriety when he robbed a bank in Gallatin, Missouri, and killed a teller. The James gang teamed up with the Cole Younger band and began an astonishing string of armed robberies and murders across a long swath of territory that stretched from Iowa to Texas. In 1873 they turned to train robberies and achieved a kind of Robin Hood reputation because they bypassed individual passengers in favor of looting large commercial funds being transported in the baggage cars. Meanwhile, Jesse had married a woman named Zerelda, called Zee because her mother was also Zerelda.[33]

Tired of the James gang's ruthless depredations—nine consecutive years of successful train robberies—and eager to gain political capital from its demise, Missouri's Governor Thomas T. Crittenden offered a ten-thousand-dollar bounty for the capture of Jesse James. On the eve of a new robbery scheme aimed at Platte City, Missouri, in April 1882, one of the Ford brothers, new members of Jesse's outlaw gang, shot him in the back of the head while he stood on a chair in his St. Joseph house to dust a picture before departing for the impending hold-up. Crittenden denied that he had sanctioned the assassination, but he pardoned the Fords unconditionally following their convictions for murder. James's death and the subsequent trials sparked an immense wave of sensationalistic newspaper coverage that began in Kansas City and Kearney and spread swiftly across the country.[34]

James's body was placed in a casket and taken home to his mother by train in a baggage car carefully guarded by sheriffs. According to press accounts, the body "lay in state" in Kearney, observed by two thousand curiosity seekers along with supporters of the local bandit, who testified that the corpse "looked natural" with hands folded and a peaceful face. Funeral services were held on the afternoon of April 6 at the Kearney Baptist Church, where Jesse had been a boyhood member but later was "excluded" (fig. 32). The pallbearers were five local men and a mysterious stranger who seemed to be in charge. Some whispered that it was his older brother, Frank, who had been sequestered in hiding; but the stranger was stout, unlike the slender Frank, and an enigma remains. Two clergymen officiated, and one read a passage from the book of Job:

*Figure 32.* The home of Frank and Jesse James showing the Baptist Church in Kearney, Missouri, where the funeral of Jesse James took place. Division of Prints and Photographs, Library of Congress.

"Man that is born of woman is of few days and full of trouble." Jesse James was thirty-four years old.[35]

At the close of a standard funeral service in which James was alluded to only once, one of the pastors announced that James's mother had asked him to request that those present refrain from going to her farm, where interment would take place. Because her third husband, Reuben Samuel, was quite ill and the grave site situated close to the house, she feared that crowd noise might affect him adversely. "It is therefore requested that none but friends and relatives go to the grave." When members of the cortège reached the Samuel farmhouse, however, a considerable number of country folk had gathered anyway. They remained quiet and respectful as James was buried in a corner of the yard outside the house where he had been born, and "where his mother could look from her windows upon the mound at the foot of a big coffeebean tree" (fig. 33).[36]

For the next twenty years Mrs. Samuel planted flowers on the grave and tended them with loving care. James had been buried seven feet deep rather than the usual five or six, to forestall any attempt to steal the body. Mrs. Samuel erected a tall white marble monument on which she had an inscription carved which read, in part: "In Loving Remembrance of My Beloved Son . . . Murdered by a Traitor and Coward Whose Name Is Not Worthy to Appear Here."[37] Eventually, desperate for money because she had always depended upon Jesse for financial support, she sold memorabilia from the house to souvenir hunters. Later, the house itself became a tourist attraction where customers could visit the grave and play golf for five dollars.

In 1898 the surviving Quantrill veterans began to hold reunions tinged with romantic nostalgia for the Lost Cause. Sentiment soon swelled to exhume Jesse from inconvenient access at the farmhouse and place his remains in Kearney's Mount Olivet Cemetery, where people like themselves would find it easier to pay their respects to the most famous rebel outlaw of his time—perhaps of the entire nineteenth century.

*Figure 33.* Jesse James's grave at the Samuel farm, Kearney, Missouri. From Frank Triplett, *The Life, Times, and Treacherous Death of Jesse James* (Chicago: Sage Books, Swallow Press, 1970).

The skeleton they disinterred on June 29, 1902, was indeed his—the evidence being Bob Ford's bullet hole in the head and numerous gold-filled teeth, visible to Jesse James the younger, who was familiar with his father's mouth.[38]

Several family members held the skull in their hands and scrutinized it. (It had rolled off the decayed and tipsy coffin-bottom twice and had to be retrieved each time by a gravedigger from the bottom of the deeply dug cavity.) James was reburied as a Confederate hero in a handsome new coffin. The Quantrill troopers then congregated for dinner in town and gathered afterward at the farmhouse to tell stories of their daring misdeeds during the war. His mother was present yet again for the 1902 reburial—a survivor who got her way more than once but not with finality. The younger Jesse James's reassurance about the authentic remains mattered because of several false, folkloric rumors that arose later.[39]

Jesse James's birthplace, boyhood home, and final resting place have since become celebrated, as he continues to be the most famous resident of Kearney and its environs and serves to boost tourism there. Each year during the third week of September a gala event is held at the Jesse James Festival Grounds. Visitors along with locals can experience a parade, carnival, rodeo, historical reenactments, a teen dance, and a barbecue cook-off—all in the name of community solidarity, hospitality, and much-needed commercial sustenance. A good time is had by all.

Yet tales continued to circulate that Jesse really did not die on April 3, 1882, but escaped to Texas, where he lived to be 103. Hence the need to exhume his bones one more time in 1995 for DNA testing and forensic study. This third exhumation required a request from the county coroner and prosecutor and then a court order. The remains found were indeed Jesse's. I'm not quite sure what has replaced the good old stories once told by the good old boys. But the answer would appear to be Hollywood films, the most recent one released in 2008.[40]

✝

There is an oddly parallel yet symptomatic ending to the reburial of a radically different figure than Jesse James: the English novelist, poet, and writer of short stories D. H. Lawrence. Recall the ultimate conflict between the wishes of James's mother and those of his Quantrill pals;

in Lawrence's case we encounter a conflict of wills between his widow and other strong-willed women who idolized him. There are no other parallels.

Born in 1885 to a puritanical schoolteacher and a drunken coal miner, Lawrence would develop an antipathy to industrialization and social convention, an attraction to primitive religions and a mystical philosophy of nature. In addition to his prolific literary output, he is remembered for his avant-garde theories of sex, morals, and society. He also possessed a restless soul that made extensive travel magnetic for his personal compass—one might almost say compulsive movement—perhaps in search of a congenial homeland and associates; and he shared that passion with his wife, Frieda von Richthofen, who was six years his senior. He met her in 1912, when she was married to Ernest Weekley, his former modern languages professor at the University of Nottingham. Following an intense affair, she divorced Weekley and eloped with Lawrence in 1914.[41]

Seven years later Lawrence received a letter from Mabel Dodge, an independently wealthy member of the modernist avant-garde who had been married twice and, between husbands, became the lover of radical writer John Reed before shifting her enthusiasm from running a salon for artists and intellectuals in Greenwich Village to roughing it in the more primitive environment of an artists' colony in Taos, near Santa Fe, New Mexico. There she shed her artist (second) husband in favor of Antonio Luhan, a statuesque and laconic Indian from the Taos Pueblo (who was eventually banned from the pueblo because of his liaison with Dodge). They married soon after he built a tipi for himself in the front yard of her rough-hewn but capacious lodging.

Because Luhan admired Lawrence's work, especially *Sea and Sardinia* (1921) at the time, she urged him to visit Taos and find inspiration in the mountainous desert area; she believed he would encounter like-minded souls as well as a natural setting that would suit him. He responded with strong interest but one concern: "Is there a colony of rather dreadful sub-arty people?" Then he promptly dismissed his own anxiety: "Even if there is, it couldn't be worse than Florence."[42]

Early in 1922 the strong-willed Frieda, who shared his curiosity about America in general and Taos in particular, wrote to Mabel Dodge, "We were coming *straight* to you at Taos but now we are not—L says he cant face America *yet*—He does'nt feel strong enough! So we are first going to the East to Ceylon—We have got friends there, two Americans, 'Mayflowerers,' and Buddhists. Strengthened with Buddha, noisy, rampageous America might be easier to tackle."[43] Eventually, of course, this famously peripatetic pair did reach Taos in September 1922, acquired property (later known as the Kiowa Ranch) in 1924 in exchange for the manuscript of *Sons and Lovers* (1913), and then made trips to Mexico, briefly back to England, then Taos once again. Because of poor health, they finally settled in a villa north of Florence in Italy.

Lawrence published *The Plumed Serpent* in 1926 and then *Lady Chatterley's Lover* in 1928, sparking a great scandal and protracted litigation because the latter was deemed obscene. He continued to write all manner of poetry, fiction, and reviews even as his tuberculosis worsened. Following a stint at a sanatorium, he went to Vence, situated in the hills above Nice, in France, and there endured his final illness in 1930, the year he published his last book, titled *The Virgin and the Gypsy*. After his burial in Vence, Frieda returned to Taos to commiserate with her friend and rival Mabel Dodge Luhan. Frieda was soon joined by her new lover, Angelo Ravagli, an Italian artist and artisan who later became her third husband. (He still had a wife in Italy.)[44]

In March 1935 a small group of admirers gathered at Lawrence's grave in Vence. One participant, a journalist for the London *Daily Express*, seems to have been deeply moved by the experience, and a headline in his paper soon announced that it was "The Last Wish of D. H. Lawrence" to be buried on Kiowa Ranch. The article declared, "An Italian friend was sent here by Mrs. Lawrence to exhume the body." The ashes would be placed "in a little temple which has been built by Mrs. Lawrence, Indians, and others who loved her husband," presumably a reference to Mabel.[45] There is no evidence that Lawrence had ever indicated where he wished his final resting place to be, but it seems clear that his most significant survivors, Frieda and Mabel, felt certain that spiritually he truly belonged somewhere near Taos, situated at seven thousand feet above sea level, a serene and mystical place that matched his temperament very well.

Ravagli had indeed built a small concrete chapel there, on a slope above the ranch, and had placed an agricultural wheel over the door to form a rustic kind of faux rose window. What the chapel lacked, of course, was Lawrence's body, so Frieda asked a friend, Earl Brewster, who was in France for other reasons, to help organize the translation. When Frieda learned the cost of transporting an intact body across the Atlantic, however, she decided that bringing his ashes would do just as well. Brewster agreed to supervise the exhumation and cremation, but when the requisite papers did not arrive in time, he informed Ravagli, who made periodic visits to Italy to see his wife, that *he* would have to go to Vence to deal with the difficult situation.[46]

The task became an unnerving challenge. Ravagli needed to deal with both French and American bureaucrats in order to procure the necessary documents, and his French was not much better than his English. Frieda, meanwhile, contracted double pneumonia and was convalescing with friends in Santa Fe when Ravagli and the ashes boarded the *Conte de Savoia* sailing from Marseilles. When he reached New York, U.S. customs officials were reluctant to admit a funerary urn containing human remains as part of the baggage of a tourist who was not an American citizen. So Alfred Stieglitz, the pioneering photographer, patron of modern art, and husband of Georgia O'Keeffe, who had already established her own presence near Santa Fe, interceded with the authorities. Ravagli and his precious cargo then boarded a series of trains and headed for the Southwest.[47]

When the last train on his segmented journey reached Lamy, New Mexico (still the nearest rail station to Santa Fe), Frieda and some friends were eagerly waiting to greet Ravagli after his six-month absence. Only when they had almost reached Santa Fe did they realize (according to legend, at least) that the precious urn had been left behind at the train station. So they returned to retrieve it. (In a different version of this episode, a friend accidentally overturned the urn and refilled it with ashes from a fireplace.) From Santa Fe the party headed for Taos, and once again, at least according to Ravagli, the ashes were left behind and needed to be fetched a few days later.[48]

A friend then warned Frieda that Mabel and Dorothy Brett, yet another woman devoted to Lawrence and his memory, were planning to steal the ashes and scatter them across the desert. Some such plot does seem to have existed. Brett always denied it, but Mabel never did. Brenda Maddox has summarized the situation well: "Mabel never denied her belief that Lawrence's ashes would have been more appropriately scattered to the desert winds than enshrined in a gimcrack chapel which she dubbed 'the Angelino temple.' The fear in the Taos colony was that Ravagli wanted to turn 'the shrine' into a tourist attraction and charge admission; alarm intensified when the local paper carried a public invitation from Frieda for everybody to come to the dedication ceremony at which a Mexican mariachi band would play."[49]

Mabel and Tony Luhan persuaded a local judge *not* to preside over the dedication ceremony. They asked the Indians not to attend as well, but a few showed up anyway and performed a ritual dance around a bonfire in front of the chapel at sunset. Frieda seemed pleased, and she had dealt (in her way) with the possibility of theft by Lawrence worshipers. While Ravagli mixed concrete for the slab that would become the altar of the chapel, she emptied the ashes into the concrete mix. She wrote to Una Jeffers (the wife of poet Robinson Jeffers) in Carmel: "When I remember how I had stood in front of Lawrence's narrow grave [in Vence] and thought Here lies the only thing that really ever was mine, he gave himself body & soul—And this 'my friends' wanted to steal from me. . . . Now I get over it. . . . I wish you had been at the ceremony, it was simple and beautiful."[50]

Would that the story ended there, but rumors and speculation persisted. Stieglitz wrote to Dorothy Brett that after he had helped Ravagli negotiate the hurdles at U.S. customs, he found the ashes in their urn standing outside the door of his American Place art gallery in Manhattan. "I left [sic] them go their natural way," he added enigmatically. "Someday I'll tell you the story. Nothing like it has ever happened. Angelo really has no idea of what did happen." And neither do we. In 1956, after Frieda's death and when Ravagli was about to return to Italy for good, he confessed that Lawrence's ashes had never left France. Fearing that heavy customs duties might be levied on the importation of human remains, he said, he had scattered the ashes in Vence, crossed the Atlantic with an empty urn, and then refilled it with ersatz ashes in New York. As Maddox observed, "If true, it would explain the irreverence with which Frieda and Ravagli kept giggling over, and losing, the sacred dust."[51]

In contrast, one thinks of Nicolas Poussin's beautiful early landscape painting *The Ashes of Phocion Collected by His Widow* (1648), located at the Walker Art Gallery in Liverpool. Phocion was a great Athenian general and statesman (fourth century BCE) who was accused of treason on false charges and forced to drink hemlock. Poussin purports to witness the genuinely grieving widow gathering his ashes in the foreground of the scene—a far cry from the apparent lightheartedness and exuberant behavior of Frieda Lawrence at Taos in 1935.

✝

After the American novelist F. Scott Fitzgerald died in Hollywood in 1940, his burial took place at the Union Cemetery in Rockville, Maryland, a municipal facility located about eight miles north of Washington, DC. (The Fitzgeralds originated as a Maryland family whose most famous member was Francis Scott Key.) The Catholic Church would not allow the lapsed Fitzgerald to be buried in ground under its jurisdiction because he had not attended a Catholic service for many years. When his wife Zelda was killed in a fire at the sanatorium in Asheville, North Carolina, where she had been institutionalized, her remains were then placed next to his despite his scandalous affair in Hollywood with gossip columnist Sheilah Graham. The Fitzgeralds' grave lay sadly neglected for many years, but in 1975 the Women's Club of Rockville decided to spruce it up as a bicentennial project. Members of the Rockville Civic Improvement Advisory Commission also urged that some appropriate action be taken.[52]

Not coincidentally, by 1975 the Fitzgeralds' daughter, Scottie Fitzgerald Smith, felt very strongly that her parents should be reburied in the family plot at the St. Mary's Roman Catholic Church cemetery, also in Rockville, which she regarded as "a quiet oasis in an otherwise turbulent world." Receiving permission from the church and from local government, the move occurred, and the little graveyard that accommodated the newcomers now overlooks one of the busiest intersections in densely populated Montgomery County.[53]

A Fitzgerald scholar, Russell E. Hamill Jr., helped Scottie obtain the necessary permission for disinterment and felt moved that "a daughter's love for her parents stayed the course, steady and true, throughout her life." Because he viewed Scottie Smith's mission as a family homecoming, he attended the reburial with his wife and children on the last Friday in October. The Prayers for Christian Burial recited at the small service came from the novelist's own missal, handed down from his mother and grandmother; it had been printed in 1806. A priest blessed the grave site as three generations of Fitzgeralds listened, and Hamill read a passage from *The Great Gatsby* (1925). Fitzgerald himself had in fact once written, "I wouldn't mind a bit if in a few years Zelda and I could snuggle up together under a stone in some old graveyard here. That is really a happy thought and not melancholy at all." He ultimately achieved that happy thought, albeit too late to enjoy it.[54]

✠

Gutzon Borglum is the American sculptor best remembered because he loved to work in granite on a gigantic scale. Born in Idaho in 1867, he worshiped Abraham Lincoln, as had his Danish immigrant father, and named his own son for the sixteenth president. His equestrian statue of General Philip Sheridan was so successful that castings were placed in Washington, DC, and then Chicago as well (1923). He moved on to a huge commission that would display heroes of the Confederacy on Stone Mountain, Georgia (nominally "finished" in 1923–25); but when his project did not please the United Daughters of the Confederacy, he left it and shifted to his most famous work, the four presidents on Mount Rushmore (1926–39).

When Borglum died suddenly in 1939 with his masterpiece not quite completed, the secretary to the Mount Rushmore Commission immediately asked Secretary of the Interior Harold Ickes whether he had any objection to the construction of a crypt "of a design approved by the Park Service and the Commission at an unobtrusive spot in the mountain." Although this would have been undertaken entirely with private funds and the park encompassed eighteen hundred acres with plenty of space to accommodate a crypt for the larger-than-life sculptor, Ickes and his staff strongly opposed the suggestion, explaining that burying a private citizen (even with legitimate professional and personal ties to the site) was contrary to established policy and would lead to countless requests for private burials in federal park areas.[55]

Despite National Park Service opposition, a congressman introduced a bill providing for Borglum's interment on the site of his best-known work. It passed, and President Roosevelt signed it. When private funds were not forthcoming, Congress passed a second bill in 1943; but no crypt was ever funded. Meanwhile, well before his death Borglum had extracted a promise from his son, Lincoln, that he would be buried amongst a plenitude of flowers in California. So he was eventually laid to rest in Forest Lawn Memorial Park Cemetery in Glendale, where a court of honor bears an inscription composed by his lifelong friend, Rupert Hughes. Borglum's son, the key survivor in this case, had honored his father's request, but apparently with reluctance. He, too, had wanted that honorific crypt beneath the presidents, facing the brilliant southern sun.[56]

✝

For an intriguing instance of total domination by the survivor who mattered most in terms of willpower, consider the fascinating case of Frank Lloyd Wright, born in April 1869 to a Welsh family in Richland Center, Wisconsin, not far from Madison. He became one of the most celebrated and distinctively American architects, having pioneered the low-lying Prairie Style and then proceeded to design many other types of structures, residential and public, always exploring the newest technologies to reconceive and reshape the built environment. He conceived the affordable Usonian house for ordinary Americans during the Depression, then the spectacular home he called "Fallingwater" near Pittsburgh for the Kaufmann family, later the extraordinary Johnson Wax administration building in Racine, Wisconsin, and finally the Solomon Guggenheim Museum in Manhattan. These all continue to be celebrated among his many masterpieces. Wright also created the Taliesin Fellowship as a community for his family, student-apprentices, and disciples, first in Wisconsin early in the 1930s and then Taliesin West near Scottsdale, Arizona, completed as a winter home seven years later.[57]

When Wright died in his ninetieth year in April 1959, a burial precedent was followed. Just as he had done almost half a century earlier after his mistress, Mamah Borthwick, was killed by a crazed servant, Wright's coffin was placed on a flower-strewn farm wagon drawn by a sturdy pair of horses (fig. 34). With forty-some family members and friends walking behind it, the wagon proceeded to the modest family burying ground at the foot of a hill a few hundred yards from Taliesin East. Under the supervision of his strong-willed third wife, Olgivanna, he was interred not far from the bodies of his mother and Mamah. For the next twenty-six years Olgivanna presided over the ongoing Taliesin Fellowship and studios, but primarily in Arizona, where she reigned like a queen bee.[58]

The writer Brendan Gill knew the Wrights and visited Taliesin West with some frequency. His account of the last Easter party that he

*Figure 34.* The cortége of Frank Lloyd Wright at Taliesin East, April 1959. From Brendan Gill, *Many Masks: A Life of Frank Lloyd Wright* (New York: G. P. Putnam's, 1987), 500. *Milwaukee Journal* photo from 1959.

attended, in 1984, provides a memorable vision of the elaborate festivities and high jinks that went on, but also a vivid portrait of the domineering woman who survived Wright and determined the fate of his earthly remains.

> Although Olgivanna was in her late eighties and almost totally deaf and blind, in her indomitable fashion she pretended to hear and see as well as ever. Under a hat broad-brimmed to ward off the sun and in a garb that may have owed something to Montenegro and certainly owed much to her imagination, she sat with me at lunch, smiling, dark-eyed, and handsome. As we chatted, I sensed her determination to preside with a show of undiminished strength and grace over a springtime ritual that now after almost half a century, was being gently wrested from her grasp. She had served as the priestess of a shrine whose god had steadily gained in puissance over the years; now she was failing, now against her will she was slipping away . . . but the god remained.[59]

She had kept Wright's spell and will alive by dominating the fellowship and the Frank Lloyd Wright Foundation, maintaining the two Taliesins more or less intact both physically and spiritually. Olgivanna had one last card to play, and she took the trick, thereby stunning a great many of her late husband's family, friends, and followers. When she died in Scottsdale on March 1, 1985, the only person with her was

Wright's former physician, who then called a meeting of the fellowship and informed them of her dying wish: that she, her late husband, and her daughter by her first marriage should all be cremated, with Wright himself removed to Taliesin West, where a special garden would be built, dedicated to all three, and their ashes mingled together. The wish did not appear in her will, and many felt that it had been a last-minute whim. But the remaining entourage at Taliesin, which had dwindled, lacked the will to defy Olgivanna's heart's desire—except for the inclusion of her own daughter. That demand was unequivocally set aside.[60]

Anticipating that there would be opposition to the exhumation, foundation officers moved secretly and quickly. They obtained the requisite approval from Iovanna Wright, the only child that Frank and Olgivanna had together, and from a coroner who also pledged his secrecy. Wright's body was exhumed in Wisconsin and cremated on March 25. When a local newspaper editor learned of it in Madison, too late, the hue and cry began. Iovanna remarked to one family member, "Daddy gets cold up there in Wisconsin." The relative added ruefully, "When Olgivanna told you to do something, you did it." Within a week Wright's ashes were taken to Scottsdale. It took several years to complete the memorial garden and surrounding wall overlooking Paradise Valley in which the ashes of FLW and Olgivanna would be "immured" together; but the story and attendant storm broke quickly in early April, on the twenty-sixth anniversary of Wright's death. It prompted an uproar among family members and some former students, associates, and architects around the country. Disbelief and anger were widespread.[61]

A former Wright apprentice who had researched Wright's wills for a book declared that he found no clear indication of where the architect wished to be buried. Yet he proclaimed his disappointment in no uncertain terms. "This is an example of their [the foundation's] insensitivity and of Mrs. Wright's arrogance because what they have done is overrule Mr. Wright's wishes. I feel that it was almost a sacrilegious act. It was an obscene thing to do to any person." Enraged family members agreed because they felt certain that *they* knew what Wright wanted. One of Wright's sons by his first wife, a retired antitrust lawyer in Washington, called the move "an act of vandalism." He insisted that his father *had* indicated that he wanted to be buried in the cemetery outside of Spring Green because that had been the family burying ground since 1886.[62]

A few family members acknowledged that they at least understood why Olgivanna, his soulmate for thirty-four years, had wanted their bodies to be mingled in death. The actress Anne Baxter, one of Wright's granddaughters, called the grave opening "painfully absurd" but added that "he may be laughing for all we know because his spirit is much bigger than his bones." A managing trustee of the Wright Foundation insisted that the request had not been a last-minute whim. "Mrs. Wright had been talking to many people about doing it for quite a few years," he contended. That is certainly possible, but precious few of those "many people" seem to have come forward in support of the statement.[63]

Karl E. Meyer, a historian of art and archaeology and author of *The Plundered Past* (1973), wrote an editorial for the *New York Times* noting that the remains had been "exhumed and stealthily transported to Arizona. To a Wisconsinite, that is equivalent to uprooting Jefferson from Monticello for reburial in Beverly Hills." Meyer acknowledged that while Wright lived his native state gave him no official commissions and that Madison voted down his project for a splendid civic center on Lake Monona (a decision it later reversed).[64] Nonetheless, he continued, "there is something sad and unfair about Wisconsin's losing yet more to the Sun Belt, where much of its industry has already fled. Frank Lloyd Wright belonged to the Middle West, and once wrote of its weather, 'The lightning in this region, always so crushing and severe, crashed and Taliesin smiled.' They will need a strong wall to contain that spirit amid the retirement condominiums in Paradise Valley."[65] Once again a willfully potent survivor had gotten her way, and in her case defied many others in order to do so.

✝

Less sensational (and somewhat less controversial) variations on that saga continue to occur right up to the present, of course. I shall close this chapter with two examples: one involving a noncelebrity family — ordinary folks, to whom these things also happen — and then a quite recent episode concerning a famous artist and his family.

The following was recounted in the *Washington Post* as a human interest story by a survivor with a very different situation and a less domineering temperament than Olgivanna Wright's. In 1989 an elderly woman in West Virginia called her granddaughter living in a New York

City suburb and said, "I want him to come home at last." She plaintively sought family permission to exhume her eldest son's remains from where he had died two decades earlier, of a brain aneurism that burst without warning when he was only thirty-four. The grandmother's voice was soft and trembling because she called from a nursing home where she was recovering from a stroke, and from the exhaustion of caring for her long-ailing husband, who lay in a bed next to her in a room that they shared. "We want to be ready," she said, and the granddaughter had no need to ask, "Ready for what?" Ready for when they died and were laid to rest themselves. "I think for a while after we have hung up. I will do what she asks, but for my reasons. And I have only one. I do not remember the last time I said good night to my father." Having been only five when her father died, she wanted to put some difficult memories that she did not really trust behind her and thereby put the past to rest.[66]

Contacts with her father's parents had diminished over time. There may have been some acrimony between them and her mother—she couldn't quite be sure. "Such an unexpected death either yields closeness or a desperate need to get as far away as possible from reminders of the pain." Her mother had remarried some time ago. Her older brother had recently become a doctor, and her younger brother was studying to be a lawyer. The grandparents had long been very remote, but her father seemed to belong more to them than to her, because her memories of him were so elusive. The ones that she did have she felt she had been told about, so that they were not even really her own memories. They were borrowed, or linked to some photographs that had been explained to her once upon a time, long ago.

So she began the complicated process of gathering and notarizing the necessary documentation to exhume her father's remains from the Cemetery of the Holy Rood in Westbury, New York. There were various forms and affidavits with numerous lines to be signed. Then there was the problematic stone monument atop the grave. It needed to be moved, and the cemetery didn't do that. What about the plot? Did the family want to sell it? The cemetery would pay only the price paid in 1968, even though that space now cost far more. She learned a great deal about disinterment. She was told that the exhumation could not be done in the summer months because of the heat. She discovered how expensive it is to move a body. And then there is the final paper to which every family member must give consent. The grandmother resisted repeatedly and perversely, despite her own initiative in the matter. "Why? Why? Why?" she asked. "It was hard enough to live through it the first time." Finally she relented. "I guess it's time to close that chapter for all of us," she quietly conceded, and signed.[67]

Visits to the nursing home in West Virginia followed, with stories told about her father as a boy, an adolescent, a student, a young man. She came to appreciate the father she never really knew. An unexpected closeness developed as the family history unfolded, sometimes with repetition, sometimes with variations on a theme. Meanwhile they all had to wait until the state regulatory agency "spits out its approval of our wishes. It will be around late fall by the time he's cremated and brought here, to be buried again with the first of his parents to die. That must be comforting to them, I think, that someone will be there when they leave the earth. And I feel more at peace too." The granddaughter still had one more "duty of my own," a visit to view the new cemetery. She did so, saw the lush landscape, the brilliant blue sky above the meadow and the mountain. She felt glad that she had come and had complied with her grandmother's request, despite all the complications. "Soon we will bring him here forever, home at last. I will say goodbye then, and remember it as long as I can."[68]

✠

Mark Rothko, the celebrated abstract expressionist painter, was born in Latvia in 1903 but came to New York at an early age. He endured years of penury but persisted stubbornly until he found his own distinctive style in the 1940s: large horizontal blocks of paint, one layer misting into another so that they must be viewed carefully and closely to appreciate the nuances of color—red melting into orange, for example, or overlapping green and blue tones that are related yet offsetting. By the time Rothko committed suicide in 1970, following years of depression, the value of his art had escalated, and it continues to do so today. A famous trial occurred, prolonged for more than a decade, after his children's guardians accused his three executors of selling works to the Marlborough Gallery in New York for less than market value while collecting exorbitant commissions and dividing the proceeds. In 1975 the executors were found guilty of negligence and conflict of interest, removed from their positions of trust, and fined, along with Marlborough, the sum of $9.2 million.[69]

When Rothko died he had been buried in a plot belonging to Theodore Stamos at East Marion, New York. Stamos was also an abstract expressionist, a close friend, and subsequently one of the three executors. East Marion is a small village nestled between Greenport and Orient Point on the North Fork of Long Island. In 2007 the artist's daughter and son petitioned the Supreme Court of the State of New York to make it possible to have their father's remains disinterred and reburied at a Jewish cemetery in Westchester County. The first request met with resistance from the owner of the initial burial plot, Stamos's sister. It was also upsetting to many of the residents of East Marion. As the secretary-treasurer of the East Marion Cemetery Association acknowledged, "He's our only notable person." She added, "There's quite an artistic community out here. And when this first started, people who knew who he was were quite alarmed that this was being contemplated."[70] Each side could have considered a line from Shakespeare's *Twelfth Night*: "Is there no respect of place, persons, nor time, in you?" (2.3.100).

Nonetheless, in March 2007 the cemetery association's board voted with one dissent to allow the exhumation. To protect itself against community wrath, however, board members decided to require Rothko's daughter to obtain a court order permitting removal of the remains. The two children (long since adults and both professional people) also sought to exhume their mother, estranged from the artist, who had died six months after their father and was buried at Knollwood Cemetery and Mausoleum in Cleveland. Their objective was to reinter her body with Rothko's in Kensico Cemetery in Valhalla, New York. The key document reads: "Petitioners have long wished to reunite their parents in a final resting place consistent with their parents' wishes and Mark Rothko's Jewish faith."[71]

On April 10, 2008, Justice Arthur G. Pitts of the State Supreme Court in Riverhead agreed to the Rothko family request. He noted that even before the petition was filed in 2007, the sister of Theodore Stamos (who died in Greece) had consented in writing to the proposed removal and reinterment. The fact that she wished to reconsider a year later was dismissed as irrelevant. "Although the Court has received numerous letters regarding the instant petition, no party has sought to intervene and the application must be deemed unopposed," the judge ruled. Nancy Poole, secretary-treasurer of the East Marion Cemetery Association, commented in response: "I think we really lost a piece of history here. A lot of people are going to be pretty miserable about it."[72] Those who maintain cemeteries cannot readily tolerate the premature departure of celebrities—even dead ones who never lived nearby.

Once more, the closest survivors eventually won out, even though in this instance, yet again, the wishes of each estranged parent remain unclear. In the absence of successful spiritualism or necromancy, instructions from beyond the grave are difficult to receive—or to decipher when one believes that they have actually been received.

✝

The deaths discussed in this chapter span the years from Boone's demise in 1820 until Rothko's in 1970, and their reburials from 1845 until 2008. Although the conflicts shifted from being highly public and political in Boone's case to far more personal in Rothko's, the pride-of-place issue persisted. The cemetery in East Marion, New York, did not want to give up its one illustrious figure any more than Missouri wanted to lose the luster associated with Boone's appealing legend. Much more than in the episodes in previous chapters, persuasive and immediate survivors of the famous figures here felt fiercely determined to control where the deceased would ultimately repose, fighting off the wishes of admirers in the case of D. H. Lawrence and disciples in that of Frank Lloyd Wright. Uncertainties about finding or possessing the "right" remains continued to be problematic. We have no more assurance that Boone's bones are really buried in Frankfort than we do that Lawrence's ashes actually made it to Taos.

By now the reader will surely have noticed the virtual absence of famous reburied women. For the most part, female reburials occurred when a dead spouse was relocated alongside her husband or else was reunited with a husband in cases where their original graves were sadly situated in different places, as with the wives of Rothko and Poe. There has been an exception, however, in the case of female missionaries, and we consider that situation next in the context of others involving religious figures.

— FIVE —

# Disinterred by Devotion

## RELIGION, RACE, AND SPIRITUAL REPOSE

I would rather sleep in the southern corner of a little country churchyard, than in the tomb of the Capulets. I should like, however, that my dust should mingle with kindred dust. The good old expression, "Family burying-ground," has something pleasing in it, at least to me.

✠ Edmund Burke to Michael Smith, c. 1750

*T*he American past provides numerous instances of reburial for which the word *enshrinement* is appropriate because they actually involved men of the cloth or laypersons deemed inspirational, in some cases missionaries who were not ordained but believed that they were doing the Lord's work. In certain situations the figures involved were entirely secular, yet their devoted followers felt that they deserved the kind of respect, even veneration, due the founder of a cause, or else the deceased was someone who had achieved an unusual "first" that had not been suitably recognized at the time of death, often owing to racial prejudice. Intense feelings about religion and race have sparked some of the most heated disputes about where people should be buried.

There is also the persistent issue of Native American burials as well as Indian remains belonging to museums and other public institutions. In those cases we encounter feelings similar to those aroused by heroes of the Revolutionary generation, but with a spiritual dimension added. Not only had many Indian chiefs not been interred in the most suitable places, but native religion *required* that they be moved to soil where their descendants could perform the requisite tribal rites. Just as we have seen with the founding Anglo-American generation from the later eighteenth century, sometimes two groups of Native Americans could not agree on which venue was the optimal or the most appropriate one. At times these conflicts even prompted attempts to steal the remains—the most famous figure in that regard being the great Sioux chief Sitting Bull.

✝

George Whitefield arrived in America from England in the later 1730s and became a pivotal figure in the Great Awakening, a broadly based religious revival that pulsed vibrantly in the North American colonies for a full generation. Whitefield emerged as the most widely known among all the notable itinerant preachers, and as a member of the Church of England who anticipated Methodism, he offered an ecumenical message that appealed to men and women of many denominations. Late in September 1770 his travels took him to Newburyport, Massachusetts, where ill-health and physical exhaustion caused his sudden death at age fifty-nine. As the news of his demise spread quickly, a spirited controversy arose over the question of where he should be buried. Because of his fame, it mattered very much, especially since he had no special relationship to Newburyport, where fate had left him almost at random. Eminent figures from Boston wanted him buried there because they perceived their city as the capital of American Calvinism. Portsmouth, New Hampshire, hoped that offering a fine new tomb "hew'd out of a rock" might bring him permanently there; even distant Georgia, where Whitefield had established an orphanage, sought his remains, and the colonial legislature appropriated money for that purpose.[1]

A friend of Whitefield for at least a decade, the Reverend Jonathan Parsons of Newburyport, along with his Presbyterian deacons and local residents, categorically refused to relinquish the body. Immediately following Whitefield's death they began to prepare the vault beneath the main level of their meetinghouse. When the offer arrived from Portsmouth, they responded that Whitefield's body was "not fit to be removed," which seemed to imply a rapid decomposition of the corpse, but that turns out not to have been the case at all. There is no indication that the dying man had expressed any desire to be buried at Newburyport, and one account suggests that he clearly did *not* wish to be. Various communities continued to vie with intensity for the honor of his entombment. He was, after all, the most famous evangelist in British North America.[2]

Whitefield's actual funeral, however, sparked much less controversy. The Reverend Parsons sent invitations to several external ministers requesting their participation. On October 2, 1770, six clergymen served as pallbearers for the procession, which stretched one full mile in length, with Parsons and his family walking immediately behind the coffin to make sure that nothing untoward happened. Mourners sang and wept during the hymns. Following the service they watched as the bier descended into the brick-lined vault. A brief prayer there concluded the service. Estimates vary, but as many as ten thousand worshipers attended the funeral in and around the meetinghouse. They came from near and far.[3]

The burial service itself had been similar to that for most clergymen; what made Whitefield's unusual was the amount of ongoing attention that people paid to the body and the tomb *afterward*. The immediate result was an outpouring of elegiac poems and hymns that highlighted themes of death, burial, but above all salvation, the distinctive aspect of such funeral rites at the time. Few of those tracts are at all memorable, but the most popular bore a hymn that Whitefield himself had composed to be sung over his own body. (He had not expected it would be put to use quite so soon.) Printers often decorated the black-bordered sheets on which these funereal poems and hymns were printed with a crude etching that depicted Whitefield lying on top of a coffin. No other preacher of that generation seems to have elicited the same degree of popular reverence, verging upon fetishism.[4]

Because Whitefield had been interred in a vault within the church rather than buried beneath the earth, people could view the body upon request. The first major viewing occurred in 1775, when the invasion force authorized by the Continental Congress to attack Montreal and Quebec headed north on its appointed mission. At the conclusion of a special service held at Newburyport on September 17, several officers, including Benedict Arnold and Daniel Morgan, approached the sexton with a request: they wanted to enter the burial vault and view the remains. When the sexton did not object, a small group descended below the Communion table, opened the door to the vault, and entered the chamber. The sexton pried open the lid of the coffin, and the group gazed at the fully clothed corpse. Bending over the body, officers cut away parts of the preacher's collar and his wristbands, which they snipped into smaller pieces to distribute among themselves as they departed for Canada—ecclesiastical relics for good fortune on the long journey ahead and in battle.[5]

That created a kind of precedent for subsequent and well-documented episodes when ministers and lay folk entered the vault to view the remains. In 1784 a Mr. Brown from England received permission to do so, having heard from friends that the body remained undecayed—a condition often regarded as an indication of sanctity. Brown wrote in the *Christian Magazine* in 1790 that the body was "perfect" aside from its discolored flesh, adding that "the skin immediately rose after I had touched it." If indeed Whitefield had remained in such a prime condition for two decades, it did not endure much longer. In 1796 a New-buryport resident and several companions opened the coffin to find the "flesh totally consumed."[6]

Lurid fascination with and reverence toward the tomb (along with pride of possession) persisted for generations. In 1829 the Reverend Dr. Proudfit received on behalf of the church the gift of a cenotaph from a prominent Newburyport merchant. The monument contained a description of Whitefield's ministry, which of course included information about how well prepared the tomb had been and an account of the rites performed in 1770 (fig. 35). In that same year, 1829, church fathers re-

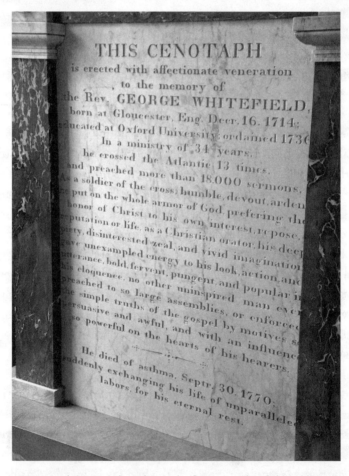

THIS CENOTAPH
is erected with affectionate veneration
, to the memory of
the Rev. GEORGE WHITEFIELD,
born at Gloucester, Eng. Decr. 16. 1714;
educated at Oxford University; ordained 1736
In a ministry of 34 years,
he crossed the Atlantic 13 times,
and preached more than 18,000 sermons.
As a soldier of the cross, humble, devout, ardent,
he put on the whole armor of God, preferring the
honor of Christ to his own interest, repose,
reputation or life, as a Christian orator, his deep
piety, disinterested zeal, and vivid imagination
gave unexampled energy to his look, action, and
utterance, bold, fervent, pungent, and popular in
his eloquence, no other uninspired man ever
preached to so large assemblies, or enforced
the simple truths of the gospel by motives so
persuasive and awful, and with an influence
so powerful on the hearts of his hearers.

He died of asthma, Septr. 30. 1770;
suddenly exchanging his life of unparalleled
labors, for his eternal rest.

*Figure 35.* The cenotaph at the tomb of George Whitefield, Old South Presbyterian Church, Newburyport, Massachusetts. Photograph courtesy of Darryl Dash.

*Figure 36.* The open vault of George Whitefield's tomb, Old South Presbyterian Church, Newburyport, Massachusetts. Photograph courtesy of Robert E. Marshall.

moved the remains from their original coffin and placed them in a new mahogany version within a redone brick-lined vault—all part of a major renovation of the building. Proudfit actually conceived a grandiose plan to construct a "monumental temple" to honor Whitefield, but sufficient encouragement and adequate funds were not forthcoming—foreshadowing the fate of the temple envisioned for Jefferson Davis in New Orleans two generations later. By the close of the nineteenth century, however, visitors to the tomb could view Whitefield's remains in a coffin with a glass lid, as a gas-lit lamp illuminated the chamber. A cast of Whitefield's skull could also be seen in the interior of the vault (fig. 36).[7]

In 1835 a deputation of British Baptists arrived in Newburyport to see "our never to be forgotten evangelist." Once inside the vault, two ministers sat on top of adjacent coffins and peered into the open casket that was the object of their pilgrimage. As others had done and would continue to do, they took Whitefield's skull in their hands and contemplated it as they discussed his inspiring ministry. Another visiting clergyman from England who did exactly the same thing a year earlier had remarked that "more care should be taken to preserve these remains and less freedom used in exhibition of them."[8] As we have already seen, skulls retained their peculiar appeal as cynosures of greatness or notoriety—not to mention a sense of intimate connectedness between the quick and the dead.

Many of Whitefield's English admirers hoped that someday his bones would be brought home for burial in his native land. That would never be possible given the possessiveness and local pride of the church fondly known as Old South in Newburyport. But an English devotee, a Mr. Bolton, hoped for a small memento of the revered minister. In 1829 an unnamed friend of his made the pilgrimage to Massachusetts, gained access to the open casket, and stole Whitefield's right arm bone. According to one account, he had bribed the sexton's son, who permitted him to remove the bone unobserved, and he then shipped it in a tidy parcel to Great Britain. Needless to say, discovery of the missing member shocked the congregation and the town. It is said that Mr. Bolton was horrified when the bone reached his home, calling the robbery a "sacrilegious act." Nevertheless, he chose to keep the relic until 1849, when a new minister at the church received a package containing the missing piece along with a note attesting to the "genuineness of the restoration." The borrowed bone was replaced in the new coffin as part of a solemn ceremony "witnessed" at various removes by two thousand people. Not only did the bone get resituated in its original position, but the "little box" in which the relic had been shipped now adorned the coffin itself as an indication that integrity had triumphed.[9]

Because Methodism was a new denomination at the close of the eighteenth century, and because Whitefield was recognized as a close second to John Wesley, the English founder, Methodists also had special cause to come to Newburyport as pilgrims. Jason Lee, the first Methodist circuit rider in New England and later the founder of a Methodist mission to Oregon, was one of them. (His own reburial account lies just ahead.) After Francis Asbury, the tireless itinerant and founder of American Methodism, died in Spottsylvania, Virginia, in March 1816, his followers disinterred his body from a family cemetery six weeks later and transferred it to the Eutaw Street Church in Baltimore, where a huge public procession, much larger than Whitefield's in 1770, escorted the remains to a new vault beneath the pulpit. In 1854 Methodists removed Asbury yet again, along with two other early leaders, to Mount Olivet Cemetery, a burial ground "exclusively devoted to the Methodists."[10]

By the 1920s and '30s, visitation to Whitefield's tomb had declined; people continued to come, but they now paid a fee for admission to the vault. Commercial tourism and curiosity had caught up with religiosity. By the 1930s guidebooks to Massachusetts and New England barely mentioned the tomb, however, and in 1933 the church covered the coffin with slate tiles. The skeleton that had been so casually displayed for a century and a half was no longer visible. *Sic transit gloria mundi.*[11]

✠

American feelings about the nature and circumstances of physical remains would undergo notable changes during the course of the nineteenth century and into the twentieth. Essentially, the physical condition of a deceased person's body mattered more intensely to people during the first two-thirds of the nineteenth century than later, largely for inconsistently observed religious reasons rooted in traditional Protestantism—though not to the extent we might have expected. At a special moment in time, the second coming of Jesus Christ to earth, corpses (or what was left of them) were to be miraculously reconstituted and reunited with their previously disembodied souls. Gary Laderman explains this doctrine thus: "In spite of natural laws that had ordained bodily disintegration, God had the power to restore life to the dead and 'awaken' the body from its lifeless state."[12]

Nevertheless, the physical condition of a body at the time of burial was believed to matter very much indeed, and that provides one of the reasons that the deceased were normally viewed just prior to interment. Seeing the corpse meant more than extending a mournful farewell. Close inspection was coupled with due respect, and on more than one occasion respect suffered as a consequence of inspection carried to excess. L. M. Sargent, a Boston "sexton of the old school," remarked that the desire to scrutinize bodily decay—he called it a "morbid desire"—was especially prevalent among women; some even wanted to descend into tombs, lift the coffin lid, and "gaze upon the mouldering bones" of their parent or child. Sargent described the poignant intensity of a "female gaze," quite different from what we now mean by the male gaze. According to Laderman, however, this was by no means an exclusively female propensity. The need to contemplate (or even cut) locks of hair, and simply be with the deceased, "to sustain the last look, and to monitor early stages of decomposition—particularly of close relations—expressed a need for maintaining physical proximity and resisting the finality that comes with bodily disintegration."[13]

Gradually, over the course of time, sentiments concerning the *soul* of a loved one became considerably more important than concerns about bodily condition. When the latter came to be deemphasized during the later nineteenth century, decomposition caused less anxiety and watchfulness than before. What mattered most by the later Victorian period was the condition of the spirit at death, rather than the actual body. This shift involved more than changing theological emphases. A growing concern about infectious diseases, and especially about how readily cholera or smallpox might be spread, played a part. When exhumations occurred they prompted unease about the possibility of disease and contagion. For the same reason, burial directly beneath church sanctuaries began to meet with disapproval. Even burial out of doors in vaults became increasingly worrisome to many because of the odors that often emanated from such structures, making memorial visits to churchyards and cemeteries unpleasant. As a growing acceptance of the natural process of decay developed, arguments on behalf of prompt burials beneath the earth became more common. Bodies no longer lingered in open coffins for extended viewing in the parlors of people's homes.[14]

✝

In 1860 some local antiquarians in Providence, Rhode Island, decided that the time had come (actually, was long overdue) to remedy a lamentable oversight in that state's history: locating the burial site of Roger Williams, founder of the colony, precursor of the Baptist denomination in America, "the first theologian on this earth who ever theoretically advocated the separation of 'Church and State,' and the first statesman who practically established religious freedom as the constitutional basis of civil government." Members of the community intended to erect a monument above his "neglected ashes." When Williams died in 1683, however, he was buried on his own "plantation" (meaning home lot) without any marker ("not even a rough stone"), and hence "recourse must now [in 1860] be had to traditionary testimony which is fast disappearing."[15]

In 1771 a special committee had been appointed by the freemen of Providence to ascertain the burial spot and to draft an inscription for a monument that they intended to erect over the grave of the "Founder of this Town and Colony . . . but the troubles of the revolutionary war, which ensued, prevented any active exertions for ascertaining the exact spot, and for erecting thereon the proposed monument." The author of the 1860 narrative of a renewed search was born close to the spring where Williams lived and died. He undertook an extended inquiry into local traditions that might prove helpful. He had called upon Moses Brown prior to the latter's death in 1836 at the age of ninety-eight, and learned that a specific burial lot had always been considered the one used by the Williams family "but that his [actual] grave was unknown."[16]

Acknowledging that the pursuit of his quarry would hinge upon slender evidence, Zachariah Allen examined old newspaper accounts and interviewed various people who had known descendants of Roger Williams and could provide clues based upon family lore. Although acknowledging that Williams's grave had been "leveled many years with the surrounding graveyard," Allen learned from a letter that a woman who died at the age of eighty in 1855 had as a child "often visited the grave" of Roger Williams with her father, who in turn in early boyhood had been put into the grave next to it by his father. How and why? Some unspecified time earlier, in digging another grave for a new interment, "the spade man came upon the bones of Williams, being portions of his lower extremities. Many of the inhabitants gathered to see the bones of the Founder of Rhode Island, and her grandfather among them; who, actuated by a singular whim, lowered, his little son, her father, into the grave, probably thinking that the act would make an indelible impression of the discovery upon his son's memory." I should think that it very well might. Kids just love being lowered into graves![17]

Given such "helpful" clues about the proper site, on the first day of spring in 1860 Allen, with two gentlemen as witnesses and two "experienced superintendents of the public burial grounds," carefully directed excavation research. With no apparent doubt that they were working in just the right spot, they took "the utmost care . . . in scraping away the earth from the grave of Roger Williams. Not a vestige of any bone was discoverable, not even of the lime dust which usually remains after the gelatinous part of the bone is decomposed." Next to Williams's purported grave they found another that they assumed to be his wife's because they found one lock of braided hair, "being the sole remaining human relic."[18]

Then came the most remarkable revelation of all, the discovery of the root structure of an ancient apple tree that had the supernatural prescience to function like a divining rod.

> This tree had pushed downwards one of its main roots in a sloping direction and nearly straight course towards the precise spot that had been occupied by the skull of Roger Williams. There making a turn conforming with its circumference, the root followed the direction of the back bone to the hips, and thence divided into two branches, each one following a leg bone to the heel, where they both turned upwards to the extremities of the toes of the skeleton. One of the roots formed a slight crook at the part occupied by the knee joint, thus producing an increased resemblance to the outlines of the skeleton of Roger Williams, as if, indeed, moulded thereto by the powers of vegetable life.[19]

Mother Nature had provided nothing less than a precise outline of the very spot where Williams had slumbered for 177 years (fig. 37). Instead of lauding the apple tree as a sacred plant that had last touched the founder and guided their quest, however, Allen and his colleagues called it a "thief . . . for it had been caught in the act of robbing a grave and of appropriating its contents to its own use, re-incorporating them into its living trunk and branches." The tree had selfishly garnished Williams's remains for its own nourishment. Quite an unnatural act for a perfectly natural culprit.[20]

What purportedly remained of Williams and his wife was then moved to the tomb of a descendant in the North Burial Ground for interment. Finally, in 1936 those scant seventeenth-century fragments were put in a bronze container and placed beneath the base of a monument in Prospect Terrace Park in Providence. The infamous "Williams root" can now be seen in the collections of the Rhode Island Historical Society, where it is mounted on a panel in the basement of the John Brown House Museum. Family traditions are not always reliable, but sometimes they offer the only clues available. Some people prefer to have venerable memories as guidelines—even ones that defy credibility—than mere guesswork or nothing at all. A Roger Williams National Memorial was established in 1965 at a city park on the southern edge of Providence. His memory and significance live on in historical studies, of course, especially those devoted to works concerned with church-state

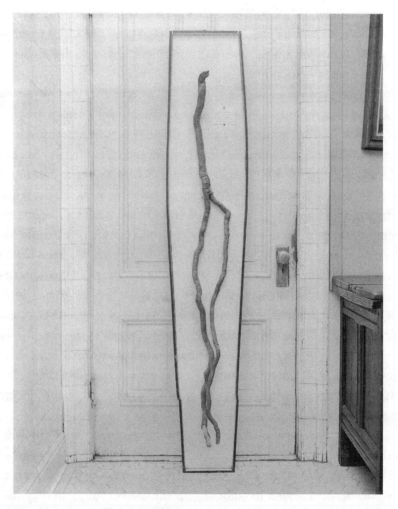

*Figure 37.* Roger Williams's Apple Tree Root. Providence, Rhode Island, March 22, 1860. Wood. Courtesy of the Rhode Island Historical Society (RHi X₃ 2943).

relations in America. One might even say that he enjoys a certain root-edness in the American canon.[21]

✛

Early Protestant missionaries to the Pacific Northwest have also figured prominently in narratives of exhumation and reburial, though in quite different ways from the Williams saga. Although Williams most certainly deserves to be considered a missionary himself, among his other leadership roles, the essence of his life involves a critical chapter in the history of civil religion. Those that follow are dramatic markers in American westward expansion and the belief in divine if not manifest destiny along with the persistent commitment to proselytize on behalf of Protestant Christianity.

Marcus Whitman (1802–47), trained in New York as a physician, applied to the American Board of Commissioners for Foreign Missions to go west in order to educate and Christianize Native Americans in an area still disputed between the United States and Great Britain. Because the board accepted only married couples, Whitman decided in 1835 to join the Ithaca-based missionary Samuel Parker, who raised the requisite funds among Presbyterians, and went to what became northwest Montana and Idaho in order to minister to bands of the Flathead and Nez Percé peoples. Upon his return the following year, Whitman heeded a renewed call from the ABCFM, which required wedded missionaries, and therefore married Narcissa Prentiss of western New York (almost sight unseen), a teacher of physics and chemistry who had been roused by the Second Great Awakening and also felt a call to undertake missionary work. In May 1836 the Whitmans joined a caravan of fur traders and headed west, led by a group of experienced mountain men. Narcissa Whitman and Eliza Spalding became the first European American women to cross the Rocky Mountains.[22]

The Whitmans established several new missions in the Walla Walla valley and settled at Waiilatpu, a word meaning "place of the rye grass" in the Cayuse language. There they farmed, he provided medical care, and she devoted herself to schooling for the native groups. In 1843 Marcus returned east and gathered and then led a large group of wagon trains westward from Fort Hall in eastern Idaho. Later coming to be known as the Great Emigration, this undertaking would establish the viability of the Oregon Trail for subsequent American homesteaders. But the large influx of newcomers brought unwelcome diseases to which the Indians were especially vulnerable, including a severe epidemic of measles in 1847. Indians customarily held medicine men responsible for medical crises. Consequently, on November 29, 1847, Cayuse tribal members murdered the Whitmans in their home along with twelve other whites. Most of the missionary buildings in what would soon become the Oregon Territory were destroyed as well.

By the 1860s, however, Walla Walla began to grow rapidly and money was raised to fulfill Marcus Whitman's dream of establishing a seminary in the vicinity of Waiilatpu. It began in 1866 as a private elementary school, added courses, and a few years later became Whitman Academy. By 1882 it had come under the sponsorship of the Congregational Education Society and was renamed Whitman College on what would have been Whitman's eightieth birthday. Although a modest monument had been put up following the Whitmans' burial early in 1848, a movement got under way late in the 1880s to erect a much grander one. Fundraising based in Portland did not go well at first, but the Whitman Monument Association, formed in March 1897, largely by residents of Walla Walla, fulfilled the dream as the fiftieth anniversary of the Whitmans' death approached.[23]

The Monument Association obtained title to eight acres of land that included the original mission cemetery with the large grave containing all of the massacre victims, as well as a hill more than one hundred feet high that rises adjacent to the cemetery. The total cost of the land and the elaborate memorial stones envisioned by the Association came to about twenty-five hundred dollars. Members erected a granite shaft on top of the hill, eighteen feet high and tapering at the top, square at the base and standing on a pedestal nine feet high with the name Whitman carved boldly on one side (fig. 38). There were also plans to set a memorial slab of Vermont marble over the large grave site. After the granite and marble stones arrived, the remains of all fourteen victims were placed in a large metal casket and reburied on January 29, 1898, basically at the same site where they had been placed by the Oregon militia volunteers half a century before. The names of all fourteen were inscribed on the huge marble slab, which is eleven feet long.[24]

When the remains were exhumed on October 22, 1897, only five skulls and some bones were found beneath the overturned wagon box that the volunteers had used as a temporary covering half a century before. Marcus Whitman's skull was readily identified by the gold filling in a posterior molar tooth. Because there was only one woman's skull among the five, it was presumed to be Narcissa's. To everyone's horror, however, it was discovered that both skulls had been sawed in half, most likely using Dr. Whitman's surgical saw, "the cut commencing at the nasal bones and extending back to the seat of the back wound. . . . The sawing was done unskillfully, probably when the body was lying on the ground face

*Figure 38.* The Whitman Monument (and "Great Grave") at Waiilaptu, Whitman Mission National Historic Site, Walla Walla, Washington. From Clifford M. Drury, *Marcus and Narcissa Whitman* (Glendale, Calif.: Arthur H. Clark, 1973). Courtesy of National Park Service – Whitman Mission National Historic Site.

upward." Various explanations were offered as to what had happened and why. The most plausible is that the deed was done by Joe Lewis, a man of mixed race who was known to have harbored deep grudges against both Whitmans and played a leading role in plotting their deaths.[25]

At the approach of the 1936 centennial of the arrival of the Whitman-Spalding mission in what became Oregon Territory (comprising both the subsequent states of Oregon and Washington), considerable interest was stimulated among church as well as secular groups. The Presbyterian Church U.S.A. became notably active in promoting centennial observances. The denomination's general assembly held a major commemorative service in Syracuse, New York, in May 1936. Communities like Lewiston, Idaho, and Walla Walla, Washington, put on elaborate celebrations lasting several days. The one in Walla Walla highlighted the Whitmans, and the hagiographic status they had already achieved was steadily enhanced during the decades that followed.[26]

The Whitmans were not the earliest missionaries to reach the Pacific Northwest, for there had been a competitive rivalry between ABCFM Presbyterians and Methodists to Christianize the Indians there. Jason Lee was born in 1803 in Stanstead, Quebec. A go-getter, he was self-supporting by the age of thirteen. After undergoing a conversion experience and education at the Wilbraham Academy, he served as a minister in the Stanstead area from 1830 to 1832. One year later he was chosen by the Methodist Episcopal Church to head a mission to the Flathead Indians. Traveling overland with his own party and then joined by another group, he reached Fort Vancouver on the Columbia River in 1834. When the first mission site proved unhealthy, Lee promptly led his people to the Willamette River, where they created a settlement ten miles northwest of the present site of Salem, Oregon. Following some hassles with the Hudson's Bay Company in 1835–36, he helped to draft a petition for the establishment of a territorial government, and in 1838 he made the arduous trip to Washington, DC, to present that petition to Congress, stopping first at the Whitman mission in Walla Walla to visit with Marcus and Narcissa Whitman.[27]

After returning to his own settlement, he continued to found missions and became vigorously active in the territorial organization of Oregon, cementing its ties with the United States even as the American dispute with Great Britain over this area became more heated. Between 1841 and 1843 he was instrumental in the formation of a provisional government for the territory. He also worked actively to promote educational development there and shaped the plan that led to the founding of the Oregon Institute, subsequently Willamette University. Some difficulties at the mission led him to return to New York in 1844. While visiting his sister in Stanstead during March of the following year, his health failed and he died at the age of forty-two. He was buried in the town of his birth.

In 1904 Mrs. Smith French of The Dalles, Oregon, wrote to a Colonel Butterfield of Derby Line, Vermont, suggesting the desirability of moving Lee's remains from Stanstead to the Lee Mission Cemetery in Salem. Butterfield agreed not only to superintend Lee's exhumation but to bear the entire cost of shipping the remains along with his tombstone to Portland and then on to Salem, provided that suitable arrangements could be made to receive and reinter them. When the Columbia River Annual Conference of the Methodist Episcopal Church met at The Dalles later that year, Mrs. French had a resolution ready to present, and the conference appointed a committee of arrangements to provide a program for the reburial. The remains were then expressed from Derby Line to Portland and deposited in the safety vault of the Title Guarantee and Trust Company in the Portland Chamber of Commerce Building. The date chosen for reinterment was June 15, 1906, in conjunction with the sixty-second annual commencement of Willamette University.[28]

An editorial that appeared in the Portland *Oregonian* echoed sentiments expressed in several of the eulogies offered on June 15:

> The return of the dust of Jason Lee to Oregon for final sepulture sixty-one years after his death, the final interment in the cemetery that bears his name, near the site of the old mission that he established away back in the years of a past century, was a grandly significant tribute to the memory of a man who was a moving force in the early settlement of Oregon. The sod in Lee Mission Cemetery has been broken many times since, according to the record, "it was broken to receive the body of Maria Pittman and her child, wife and son of Jason Lee"; but during all the intervening years no form has been more readily consigned to the bosom of our common mother [earth?] than Jason Lee's after all these years.[29]

The Honorable J. C. Moreland, who presided at the services of the Pioneer Association on June 15, recognized that the political importance of filling the newly opened territory with American citizens equaled if not surpassed the importance of Christianizing the Native Americans there. Moreland praised Lee because "he soon saw that when the final settlement of the ownership of this country between this nation and Great Britain then held under treaty of joint occupation should come, that ownership would largely be determined by the citizenship of its settlers." Lee's reburial set a significant precedent: in the years following, many other early missionaries were also exhumed and reburied at the Lee Mission Cemetery.[30]

✝

Father Junípero Serra, born in 1713, received an appointment in 1767 to be the Superior of a band of fifteen Franciscans responsible for the Indian missions of California. Ultimately, twenty-one missions were created by these intrepid proselytizers, and Serra had personal oversight over seven of them. (The chapel at Mission San Juan Capistrano, built in 1782, is believed to be the oldest building still standing in California. Known as Father Serra's Church, it has the distinction of being the only remaining church in which he is known to have officiated.) A man of remarkable energy and administrative ability, Serra died tragically of a snakebite in August 1784 and was initially buried at Mission San Carlos Borromeo de Carmelo (Mission Carmel).[31]

In 1870, when Father Antonio Casanova became the parish priest at Monterey, he made a careful inspection and found the floors of the old church at Mission Carmel buried beneath three feet of debris and covered by grass and weeds. He then determined to rescue the shrine from its ignominious condition. He uncovered four redwood coffins buried below the floor of the sanctuary and in the presence of four hundred faithful worshipers read the original entry in the burial register, including Serra's. Stone slabs were then replaced over the reinterred remains. In so doing, Casanova reawakened interest in the Roman Catholic mission movement and its history.[32] In 1937 the Church introduced the Cause for Serra's beatification, one step from canonization, and in 1988 he was finally beatified by Pope John Paul II, though over the strenuous objection of Native Americans who insisted that their ancestors had been mistreated by Serra.

✝

We even have an intriguing instance of a man who became notorious for his *anti*religious views yet was forgiven and reluctantly reburied thirty-three years following his death. Robert J. Ingersoll was born in 1833, the son of an abolitionist-leaning Presbyterian preacher in upstate New York. After serving in the Civil War, Ingersoll became prominent in the Republican Party and was elected attorney general of the State of Illinois, his home as an adult. Because he was a freethinker—the most notorious of the nineteenth century—he could rise no higher in political circles, but he made a successful career as an immensely popular orator. (His speeches were collected and published in twelve volumes.) Although he spoke on many topics, ranging from Shakespeare to Reconstruction, his best-known and most controversial speeches concerned agnosticism and the sanctity of the family. His radical views about slavery, racial prejudice, and woman suffrage also kept him controversial; but his audiences were never bored, even when he spoke for more than two hours or even three.[33]

After Ingersoll died in 1899, and following his funeral at Dobb's Ferry, New York, where there were readings from his own works and from the New York School of Ethical Culture, the body was taken to Fresh Pond, Long Island, where it was cremated. The noted sculptor George Gray Barnard (who created a controversial statue of young Abraham Lincoln in 1915) selected an urn that had been imported from France. It bore Ingersoll's name and the inscription "L'urne garde la poussière, le coeur, le souvenir" (this urn shelters the ashes, the heart, the memory). Until 1923, when his wife died, the agnostic's urn rested on the mantel of her bedroom. For the next nine years his urn and hers were placed on an altar at the home of their daughter.[34]

On May 4, 1932, both sets of ashes were reinterred at Arlington National Cemetery, on a green knoll across a small declivity from the resting place of the Unknown Soldier. Having been a colonel of the Eleventh Illinois Cavalry and compiled a record for gallantry during the Civil War, he was entitled to burial at Arlington, yet it had been denied at the time of his death because he had so brazenly poked fun at religious belief. He had become an object of pulpit venom all across the country. A few years before she died, however, his widow requested that he be reinterred at Arlington, and the request was honored, albeit reluctantly. Her ashes were placed with his in a grave covered with roses, lilies, and lilacs. Only a few family members and admirers were present for the brief military service.[35]

✠

Reburials involving race and racial issues run a striking gamut of conditions and circumstances, sometimes predictable but quite often not. In what may well be the most notable case, curious and unusual in several respects, there turned out to be a positive culmination in terms of national pride—in this instance Jamaican nationalism. Marcus Garvey, remembered as a journalist, publisher, Black Nationalist orator, and entrepreneur, was born in Jamaica in 1887. From 1912 to 1914 he lived in London, and in the latter year he founded the Universal Negro Improvement Association and African Communities League. During the decade that followed he advocated a pan-African philosophy that aimed to inspire a global mass movement focusing on Africa. Ultimately he created, at the peak of his success during the 1920s, the largest single movement among people of African descent in the black diaspora. His philosophy and charisma would become a source of inspiration for subsequent movements, ranging from the Nation of Islam to Rastafarianism.[36]

After corresponding with Booker T. Washington, Garvey came to the United States in 1916, built his movement from a base in Harlem, where he survived an assassination attempt in 1919, and addressed a throng of twenty-five thousand people at Madison Square Garden in 1925. He hoped to develop Liberia as a genuine and permanent homeland for black people. But he encountered opposition and hostile criticism from prominent figures like W. E. B. Du Bois, who regarded him as a megalomaniac with wildly unrealistic plans. After he worked out a strange entente with the Ku Klux Klan—arguing that its members were less hypocritical than most whites—he became an increasingly divisive figure. In 1935 he left Jamaica permanently for London; but two years later he collaborated with the archracist Senator Theodore Bilbo of Mississippi to promote a repatriation scheme in the U.S. Congress called the Greater Liberia Act.[37]

In 1940 Garvey died in London after suffering two strokes and reading a mistaken and negative obituary of himself in the *Chicago Defender*. Because of trans-Atlantic travel conditions during World War II, Garvey was interred at Kensal Green Cemetery in London. In 1956 what had been the Kingston Race Course in Jamaica, renamed the George VI Park, provided a dramatic scene when a bust of Garvey was unveiled. According to his second wife and widow, Amy Jacques Garvey,

> All classes of the island and foreign invitees were there to take part in the ceremony, which had its inception years before when Kenneth Hill, then mayor, proposed it, and the present mayor and councilors brought it to its climax. Sculptor Alvin Marriott, a Jamaican, had done, not only a good bust, but for years had pressed to have it bronzed and erected. The arrangements for the occasion were carefully and well planned by

the Corporation and representatives from government, military and social services—all willing to help, so that the ceremony would be truly representative of all Jamaica. Invitations had been sent out to persons representative of all walks of life. Thousands assembled.[38]

The entire scene seemed quite grand, and perhaps anticipatory. A military band paraded in the colorful zouave dress uniform of the Old West Indian Regiment. A police guard of honor appeared in formal attire, and there were Girl Guides, Boy Scout troops, and hundreds of children representing different schools. At 4:30 the governor arrived with his aide-de-camp (Jamaica was not yet independent), and there were speeches and eulogies, after which the bust was unveiled. Then came a laying-on of wreaths on behalf of the mayor and council and a eulogy by the president of the UNIA on behalf of the American organization. The bust was later placed on its pedestal near the east gate of the park, facing north, looking up to the hills.[39]

Garvey's last request in 1940 had been that his body be taken back to Jamaica and not left in a "land of Strangers." When Jamaica achieved its independence in 1962, Garvey was named one of the island's national heroes at the ceremonies marking autonomy. Two years later, in August 1964, his remains were disinterred from the catacombs of St. Mary's Catholic Church, to which they had been transferred, and taken to Kingston, where the government had erected a permanent shrine to house the bones of its "first national hero" in King George VI Memorial Park. A crowd of thirty thousand gathered at the rites to hear dignitaries of church and state proclaim their pride in this native son as he was reinterred in an emblematic star-shaped tomb of black marble. It seems fair to say that Garvey himself would have felt extremely gratified.[40]

✛

In 1909 Commander Robert E. Peary allegedly became the first American to reach the North Pole on foot and plant an American flag. But possibly not. A neglected American explorer named Frederick Cook may very well have achieved the same feat one year earlier, but that is a separate and complex story.[41] The highly competitive and self-promoting Peary has received most of the credit, and that is what matters here. He originally hired an African American named Matthew Alexander Henson to be his valet but later came to rely upon him as a navigator and hardy expert on cold-weather trekking. It is not clear which member of the Peary party was actually the very first to place his foot on the North Pole, but it may very well have been Henson who did so and promptly planted the stars and stripes in the ice.

When Peary died in 1920, by then an admiral and recognized worldwide as a great explorer, he was buried at Arlington National Cemetery beneath a globe-shaped monument on the crest of a hill (fig. 39). When Henson died in 1955 at the age of eighty-eight, he was buried in a simple grave at Woodlawn Cemetery in the Bronx, having spent most of his post-Arctic years in obscurity as a clerk in the Customs House of New York City. He was denied burial at Arlington, perhaps because of his race but also because he had never been a member of the U.S. military.[42]

On April 6, 1988, exactly seventy-nine years to the day after Henson and Peary had their historic moment, Henson received a hero's burial close to Peary at Arlington, and his wife, Lucy Ross Henson, was reinterred beside him. She had died in 1968 and had also been buried at Woodlawn. Relatives,

*Figure 39.* Mourners attending the memorial service for Admiral Richard Peary at Arlington National Cemetery (1920). Mourners include President-Elect and Mrs. Harding, Chief Justice and Mrs. Taft, and members of Peary's family. Division of Prints and Photographs, Library of Congress.

friends, and admirers, some of them Inuits from the Arctic, hailed the exhumation and reburial of Matthew Henson as an event that corrected a historic slight and signified a "new day" in race relations. The event also marked the culmination of a long campaign by Henson's family to rectify the "oversight," and he received military honors despite his lack of rank. The black granite marker above Henson's grave includes an inscribed likeness of him in cold-weather gear and several Arctic scenes. The printed inscription actually hails him as "Co-discoverer of the North Pole."[43]

Among those seated at graveside for the ceremony were four Inuits, direct descendants of a son that Henson fathered by a native woman in the Arctic. One of them, Qtdlag Henson, spoke for the Greenland branch of the family: "We are very proud," he said in his native language. "This is a very great day for us." The American branch was represented by a Henson niece, Olive Henson Fulton, who recalled that as a schoolgirl she had been punished by her teacher for insisting that a black man, her own relative, had helped to discover the North Pole. Peary himself had also fathered a son while in the Arctic, and a few years prior to Henson's reburial at Arlington, Kali Peary and Anaukaq Henson had come to the United States for a "North Pole Family Reunion" organized by the same Harvard professor of neurophysiology, S. Allen Counter, who helped lead the drive to recognize Henson's achievements. Dr. Counter, an African American himself, had managed to locate Henson's Inuit offspring.[44]

Speaking at the reinterment, Counter remarked that Henson had been denied his due recognition "because of the racial attitudes of his time." He declared, "We are assembled here today to right a tragic wrong. Welcome home, Matt Henson, to the company of your friend Robert Peary. Welcome home to a new day in America. Welcome home, brother." Along with Henson's relatives and admirers, Counter had to win an order from President Ronald Reagan to have Henson buried at Arlington because he had technically not been enlisted in the military. So recognition and justice were achieved, however belatedly.[45]

✝

An African burial ground (originally known as the Negros [sic] Burial Ground) was created at an unwanted field in lower Manhattan by 1712; it was used exclusively for African American burials until 1790, as blacks had been barred from interment in most New York City churchyards after the 1690s. Owing to rapid growth and new construction, by 1820 builders had deposited vast amounts of fill on top of this site, and it remained largely forgotten until 1991, when excavation for a huge new $276 million federal office building began to reveal unexpected remains. The General Services Administration (GSA) contracted with archaeologists to document and remove them, but when it became clear that significant burials had been unearthed, improper storage had damaged remains, and the archaeological project lacked a proper research design, concerned citizens, especially blacks, protested and pressured politicians to halt excavation. Congress then passed a law in 1992 that stopped excavation on the lot immediately adjacent to the new structure—the primary burial site—and allocated three million dollars for on-site reburial and a memorial.[46]

Ultimately, the remains of more than four hundred individuals were exhumed and examined. When it became apparent that even more might also be disinterred, religious institutions called a halt to the exhumations. The GSA then contracted with a new team of predominantly African American scholars to study the remains, which were transferred to Howard University in Washington, DC, for scientific studies that revealed the West African origins of many of the deceased, most notably from Ghana (based upon patterns of filed teeth, particular kinds of beads surrounding skeletons, etc.).[47]

Nonhuman physical remains from the site were largely kept in New York; these included coins, shells, glass, buttons, beads, clay pipes, coral, and other artifacts that had been found in what survived of wooden coffins. In 1993 the site received National Historic Landmark status, the GSA established an Office of Public Education and Interpretation for the African Burial Ground, and New York City's Landmark Preservation Commission created the African Burial Ground and Commons Historic District, a designation requiring review of any construction or excavation projects proposed for the area. All of the exhumed remains and their associated artifacts were eventually reinterred in 2003, following additional research about the site and the African American community in colonial New York.[48]

✞

The recorded history of Native American remains, burial grounds, and reburials dates back several centuries. During the early American Republic, when white settlers crossed the Appalachians and moved into the Old Northwest, they became fascinated by the great burial mounds made by Indians in long and elaborate configurations, sometimes serpentine in shape. The poet Philip Freneau, author of *The Rising Glory of America* (1771) and decades later the editor of an ardently Jeffersonian newspaper, reflected that interest in 1788 by celebrating Native American practices in a lengthy poem titled "The Indian Burying Ground." Here are just five stanzas.

> In spite of all the learned have said,
> I still my old opinion keep;
> The *posture*, that *we* give the dead,
> Points out the soul's eternal sleep.

> Not so the ancients of these lands—
> The Indian, when from life released,
> Again is seated with his friends,
> And shares again the joyous feast.

> His imaged birds, and painted bowl,
> And venison, for a journey dressed,
> Bespeak the nature of the soul
> ACTIVITY that knows no rest.

> His bow, for action ready bent,
> And arrows, with a head of stone,
> Can only mean that life is spent,
> And not the old ideas gone.

> Thou, stranger, that shalt come this way,
> No fraud upon the dead commit—
> Observe the swelling turf, and say
> They do not *lie*, but here they *sit*.[49]

So long as the romanticized ideal of the Noble Savage persisted, curiosity about the wondrous Indian mounds located in several states prompted positive speculation about their meaning. In 1821 William Cullen Bryant, soon to become the best-known poet in America, wrote "The Ages" (for delivery to the Phi Beta Kappa Society at Harvard), in which he referred wistfully to the "mound-builder" civilization. A decade later Thomas Cole, considered the founder of the Hudson River Valley school of painting, also speculated about their mystery.[50] The mounds subsequently became significant tourist attractions, especially after twentieth-century guidebooks offered explanations and pointed people to the sites.

Within more recent decades, however, the question of repatriation and reburial of Indian remains has become far more complex for a variety of reasons, ranging from the dislocation of burial grounds to make way for "progress" to a resurgence of Native American pride and religious sentiments. White regrets and guilt have also played a part. On Memorial Day in 1979, for example, the skeletal remains of Spokane and Colville Indians unearthed during construction of the Grand Coulee Dam in 1939–40, which had been given to the Eastern Washington State Historical Museum, were reburied "with dignity and respect" at the Colville Indian Reservation in Washington.[51]

The final years of the 1980s turned out to be a pivotal time for widespread changes in attitudes concerning the custody of Indian remains. In 1990 Congress passed legislation called the Native American Graves Protection and Repatriation Act (NAGPRA), which led, to take just one prominent example from April 2006, to the reburial of skeletal remains of 1,590 people within Mesa Verde National Park. The actual burial site was omitted from public announcements in order to deter curiosity seekers and looters. Representatives of the Hopi Nation along with people from the Zuni, Zia, and Acoma pueblos had worked out the details with federal officials.[52]

A major shift in curatorial sentiment had actually preceded the passage of NAGPRA, largely resulting from pressure brought by Native American groups.[53] Early in 1990 the Dickson Mounds Museum in Lewiston, Illinois, decided voluntarily to close an exhibit featuring the exposed graves of 234 prehistoric American Indians because of "heightened sensitivity to display of human remains." The museum director explained that there had not been protests or even complaints but that such a display was a "living-on-borrowed-time sort of thing."[54]

Later that year the remains of sixty-one Native Americans, mostly from a University of Minnesota archaeological collection excavated from mounds throughout the state between the 1930s and 1950s, were reburied in special ceremonies at Indian Mounds Park in St. Paul. That event was only the first in a series of Minnesota reburials planned for an estimated two thousand Indians. The bones buried at Mounds Park in sixty-one swaths of red cloth were estimated to range from three hundred to several thousand years old. According to Paul Little, a spiritual leader of the Devil's Lake Sioux Tribe in North Dakota, "They were kept in boxes and locked up so their spirit didn't go anywhere. When they're released today . . . they'll be free forever."[55]

Episodes involving Indian "celebrities" fit this book's focus more closely, so we turn to a famous failure of long standing and then to the uncertain fate of two great chiefs. When Pocahontas died of smallpox in England in 1617, she was buried at the aptly named Gravesend. The idea of bringing her remains "home" was bruited about from time to time but went nowhere. As the bicentennial of the American Revolution approached in 1975, for example, Representative G. William Whitehurst, Republican of Virginia and formerly a history professor at Norfolk's Old Dominion College for eighteen years, introduced a resolution in Congress to have the American and British governments coordinate arrangements for her return. "It would be a real fine gesture," Whitehurst declared, "if her bones could be returned to the banks of the James [River] where she roamed as a little Indian girl." The resolution died from nonsupport.[56]

In 1947 a state senator from Charleston, South Carolina, proposed moving the grave of Osceola, the famous Seminole chief who died in prison at Fort Moultrie on nearby Sullivan's Island in 1838. His carefully marked grave was situated at the fort, which had been abandoned by the army. Therefore, if the state acquired the military property as it proposed to do, Senator Wallace intended to introduce a bill in the General Assembly to return the body to custody of the Seminole Tribe in Florida. Wallace quite rightly observed that Osceola's capture, "which was under a flag of truce, and his death in prison was a disgrace to the United States, and I want to make amends as far as possible. His body should be somewhere in Florida, near where he lived and ruled over his tribe."[57]

That proposal did not gain any more supporters than Whitehurst's had; but in 1966 a Miami businessman, Otis W. Shriver, claimed that he had dug up Osceola and placed his bones in a bank vault in order to bury them at a tourist destination in Rainbow Springs. Shriver traveled around the state the following year drumming up support for his commercial project, but without success. Subsequently archaeologists proved that what Shriver had were merely animal bones and that what was left of Osceola remained in his coffin. In 1979 the Seminole Nation bought Osceola's bandolier and other items at auction from Sotheby's. But material objects served as inadequate substitutes for his remains, which would have been vastly more meaningful.[58]

The saga of Sitting Bull, the great Sioux chief (1834–90), is even more poignant and complex because he was reburied at least three times, most likely four. In 1889 he retired to the Standing Rock Reservation, which straddles the Dakotas. A revival of the Ghost Dance, in which he placed no faith, brought dancers close to his cabin on Grand River, and fearing that he might decide to lead an uprising, a group of Indian Agency policemen were sent to arrest him. Their charge was merely to "bring him in." When one of them was shot by a follower of Sitting Bull, however, the police returned fire and killed the venerable warrior.

At the post cemetery in Fort Yates, located in what is now North Dakota, three U.S. Army officers stood next to an open grave. In it a rough wooden box contained the canvas-wrapped body of Sitting Bull. As a "pagan" he did not qualify for burial in either the Catholic cemetery or the small frame church of the Congregational mission just south of the Indian Agency. In any case, agency police objected to any sort of service, so a detail of four soldiers, actually prisoners from the guard house, shoveled dirt into the hole and covered the coffin of one of the greatest Native American statesmen—a tragic and undeserved end in the reservation's equivalent of a pauper's grave.[59]

He had been buried less than two months when a North Dakota senator urged the Indian Office to move swiftly to acquire as many of the chief's personal effects as possible. What the state wanted most, and successfully got, was Sitting Bull's cabin to form part of the state's exhibition at the Chicago World's Fair of 1893. With approval from the Interior Department, state agents entered into negotiations with the chief's widow and by the end of 1891 had removed the cabin, log by log, for reconstruction in Chicago. How to present and interpret it became a matter of contention, but the general public simply viewed it as the home of the notorious warrior who had wiped out George Armstrong Custer and his troops at the Little Big Horn in 1876.[60]

Meanwhile, others sought ownership of many of Sitting Bull's personal effects, by hook or by crook, and rumors began to circulate in the press that the coffin placed in the pauper's grave really did not contain

*Figure 40.* Sitting Bull's grave, North Dakota (c. 1906). Photograph by Frank Bennett Fiske. Division of Prints and Photographs, Library of Congress.

Sitting Bull at all. Such gossip may have been prompted because in 1908 the military graves at Fort Yates were disinterred for reburial, most likely including Sitting Bull's; however, the federal government's Indian agent at the reservation had ordered that the Sioux's bones be returned (fig. 40).[61]

The rumors were refuted by the Fort Yates post surgeon and other military officers who had helped to dispose of the body. Yet Hunkpapa tribal leaders (one branch of the Lakota Sioux) who had greatly admired the chief agitated to have his body removed from the military cemetery to his boyhood home thirty miles south on Grand River, where it could be suitably memorialized. White Indian agents and some of their Native allies arduously resisted this request. Clarence Gray Eagle, a son of Sitting Bull's brother-in-law, kept the cause of reburial alive with much passion, but failed. Meanwhile, in 1932 Sitting Bull was reinterred at Fort Yates, once again for logistical reasons.[62]

Problems arose following World War II when construction of the Missouri River dams got under way. Initial plans called for the Fort Yates flatlands to be inundated, prompting Gray Eagle to resume his campaign to remove the chief to Grand River. He pointed out that the great chief's grave had been neglected for years, but state officials of North Dakota swiftly spruced up the grave as a tourist attraction because they did not want to lose their biggest celebrity. The state refused to grant a permit for exhumation. In April 1953 Gray Eagle led an expedition (with an undertaker and diggers) from Mobridge, South Dakota, located in the southeastern corner of the Standing Rock Reservation, that "swooped down on the gravesite in the dark of night and carried off the object of all the controversy." They reburied Sitting Bull on a scenic site overlooking the Missouri a short distance below where the mouth of the Grand River lay beneath a huge reservoir. Twenty tons of steel rails and concrete were placed on top to make sure that he could not be moved again, and a bust sculpted by Korczak Ziolkowski provided memorialization.[63]

But is Sitting Bull really there? Subsequent research by North Dakota historians established a reasonable doubt that Gray Eagle's grave robbers actually removed Sitting Bull or at least obtained *all* of his bones. Dike work in 1962 accidentally exposed other bones that purportedly matched descriptions of Sitting Bull's. The grave was excavated at that time, and a small box with bones was interred once again. In 1984 the curator of collections for the State Historical Society of North Dakota proclaimed that the robbers must have taken the wrong remains—by then a familiar refrain. The North Dakota site, which in the end was not flooded after all, now bears a marker that leaves the issue permanently ambiguous. It simply states that "he was buried here but his grave has been vandalized many times."[64]

Who could possibly have imagined in 1876, when Custer died, or in 1890, when Sitting Bull was killed, that less than a century later North and South Dakota would be battling for possession of these remains, the reasons being partially sentimental and tribal but also touristic and commercial?

✢

We cannot overlook the historical phenomenon of collections of Native American relics, and the current revival of reburial practices among North American Indians, owing partially to the remarkable number of human remains that have been repatriated by anthropological and archaeological museums and major institutions like the Smithsonian Institution in Washington and the American Museum of Natural History in New York. Although much has recently been written about these topics, ranging from Indian religious imperatives to legal issues, this narrative would be incomplete without briefly acknowledging at least two aspects of this complex phenomenon that date back historically further than some might assume. One is the fascination shared by many Americans, especially in the twentieth century, with Native American culture prior to the arrival of Europeans. The other is rather belated respect for the significance of suitable burial in Indian religious beliefs and practices.

Historically many white Americans were fascinated by arrowheads and other items that in the nineteenth century could still be readily spotted on the surface of the ground, especially by observant woodsmen or by people who watched carefully as they made their way by canoe along riverbanks. Henry David Thoreau and his brother John were among these collectors during their youth in the 1820s and '30s. Oddly enough, however, during the depths of the Great Depression in 1933–34, interest in what has been called the Indian curio market notably intensified, perhaps because those who dealt in relics needed pot hunters and grave robbers. Some unemployed people found that they could eke out a living by finding goods for which someone might pay them a pittance, and if they were really enterprising or lucky, more than that. "Pots, pipes, and points" became a kind of shorthand for what diggers hoped to unearth, piece together, and sell.

As the market developed, especially after World War II, but even in the 1930s, the most highly prized artifacts were those produced before the Indians had been relocated on reservations. That meant that excavating and exploring Indian mounds became especially tempting, and in some instances the mounds situated on privately owned land were the most vulnerable to archaeologists as well as unauthorized diggers and grave robbers. To take just one example, a very considerable cluster of Indian mounds existed in eastern Oklahoma just south of the Arkansas River, largely on private farmland. Early in the twentieth century these were simply called the Mound Builders Mounds. Later, as curiosity seekers took note of them, they became the Fort Coffee Mounds because of the proximity of an abandoned fort not far away. By the 1930s they were known as the Spiro Mounds, while several of the larger ones had their own particular names.[65]

A very large main mound came to be called the Craig Mound because the Craig family owned the farm on which it was located, though later—when its extraordinary contents became known—it would be renamed the Great Temple Mound. It stood 33 feet high and ran 180 feet in length and 120 feet wide. Once excavated, it turned out to cover a long-abandoned Indian town complete with all sorts of structures that seem to have been suddenly collapsed by some natural catastrophe, most likely an earthquake but possibly a tornado. Inside, an archaeologist found two sets of burials. The four people situated in one set appear to have died simultaneously, as if their house had been utterly flattened on them in the middle of the night. "Later, the ruins had been burned with the dead inside, and dirt had been piled over it until a small mound resulted. Thirty-two additional skeletons had been inserted into the mound sometime later. Along with the skeletons [Joseph B.] Thoburn found numerous artifacts, including T-shaped pipes, spear points, bowls, and even copper ax-heads."[66]

Relic hunters swiftly formed consortiums to which they gave spurious names, such as the Pocola Mining Company, and the craze to collect grave goods and bones grew in intensity. Not only were valuable grave goods found, but—germane to our focus—crematoriums and charnel houses were also discovered in the ruins. The charnel houses turned out to be especially interesting, as they revealed that distinctions had clearly been made in this prehistoric civilization between commoners and royal families. The bodies of commoners were simply piled into large mortuaries where they might remain for some time, their bones all jumbled together. After months or even years, once this space had been filled it would be cleaned out, and the bones or skeletons would be buried in cemeteries at the very edge of the mounds, or even at the fringe of town, mostly in mass graves. For the nobility, however, burial seems to have been much more elaborate and respectful. The bones of nobles were carefully arranged and eventually placed in a jar or box woven from river cane and then buried. Contemporary grave goods were interred with them.[67]

Although such mounds have surrendered their secrets slowly and much about these civilizations remains altogether mysterious, it is clear from the many levels and layers that have been excavated that burial and reburial practices changed over time.

✛

There is also a contemporary reburial movement among Native peoples in North America, particularly among those that are less fully engaged with the economic and technological complexities of modern life. One representative group whose practices have been carefully examined are called the Lakes' People living at Vallican in south-central British Columbia, between a pair of north-south running ranges, the Monashee Mountains and the Selkirk Mountains. For the Lakes' People, putting exhumed ancestors back into the earth reestablishes a reciprocal relationship between them and their Sinixt tribal members from earlier times, "to bring space and time together," as Paula Pryce has observed, to "reinforce the strength of ethnic longevity, and make the universe function properly once again." Returning bodies to their rightful places becomes a symbolic way of reordering a disruptive and confusing world, of "piecing together the crumbling shards of a precarious existence and making logic out of chaos."[68]

Put differently, reburial for the Sinixt is a "symbolic salve" for the distressing circumstances of contemporary life. By exhuming and reinterring, the Sinixt at Vallican enable their ancestors to fulfill their spiritual commitments of reciprocity by uniting them once again with their land and their descendants. And by placing ancestral remains back into the earth, members of this tribal group believe that they are infusing the land with their own presence, thereby committing themselves and future generations to that land. As Pryce has pointed out, such acts have *political* implications as well, because reburial "asserts their presence in this territory despite the dominant society's view that they do not belong there." So reburial memorializes the longevity of their cultural presence in that region.[69]

The anthropologist Marshall Sahlins has noted that such an ethos and behavior is more than an expression of ethnic identity. Rather, the act of exhumation and reburial reflects and incorporates "the people's attempt to control their relationships with the dominant society, including control of the technical and political means that up to now have been used to victimize them."[70] Considering the discontent and anger of Native Americans prior to 1990 about the "incarceration" of their ancestors in museums controlled by Euro-Americans, one is reminded of two lines from Robert Frost's early poem "The Death of the Hired Man": "And nothing to look backward to with pride / And nothing to look forward to with hope."[71] Happily, that unfortunately hopeless situation is changing.

In June 2008 nearly fifty Native Americans entered the American Museum of Natural History in Manhattan, ahead of the usual throng of visitors. Their cheeks were smeared with rust-colored dye, and red and white woven bands encircled their heads. As one report remarked, "They were at the end of a journey that had, in its way, taken years." Unlike the thousands of schoolchildren who normally fill the museum's halls on a Monday, the forty-six visitors had come to take their ancestors home. "Our people are humans; we aren't tokens," declared Chief Vern Jacks, who heads the Tseycum First Nation, a tiny tribe from northern Vancouver Island in British Columbia. With the museum's complete consent, the Tseycum tribe repatriated the remains of fifty-five of their ancestors.[72]

✦

If only in terms of symbolic gestures, actions, and statements, what has been occurring among North American tribal groups since the late 1980s is not so different from what happened in Eastern Europe, most notably in Hungary, Poland, and Romania following the fall of Communist control in 1989. Both situations had an ideological component, and both arose from feelings of deep resentment and a need to reject persistent domination by others.

A resurgence of religion, the revival of churches, and the resurrection and reburial of political martyrs all reflected an earnest desire to reestablish norms of social and ethical life that had been repressed for decades in Eastern Europe, and in some parts of the Soviet Bloc, for several generations. Therefore we need to conclude by going to such places and noting the disinterment practices that emerged swiftly once the dictators had been displaced and freedom of action and expression became possible.

— SIX —

*Repossessing the*
*Dead Elsewhere*
*in Our Time*

I will talk of things heavenly, or things earthly; things moral, or things evangelical; things sacred, or things profane; things past or things to come; things foreign, or things at home; things more essential, or things circumstantial.

✠ John Bunyan, *Pilgrim's Progress* (1678)

*S*un Yat-sen, leader of the remarkable Chinese Revolution in 1911 and the founder of modern China, died in 1925 in Beijing, where he was attempting to unify his politically unwieldy country. Despite visiting an area controlled by men unsympathetic to him, his body lay in state for two weeks, and massive throngs of supporters appeared with thousands of long funeral scrolls to adorn the route to his burial place at the Azure Cloud Temple. His dying wish, however, was to be buried at Nanjing in a tomb similar to that of Lenin, a man he greatly admired. So late in the spring of 1929 General Chiang Kai-shek orchestrated a spectacular ceremonial reburial in the new capital city as a way of mobilizing support for his Nationalist Party and consolidating its control over the country.[1]

An impressive funeral train reminiscent of Abraham Lincoln's in April 1865 carried the coffin in June to Nanjing, where it lay in state at the central headquarters of Chiang's party. The concept for Sun's enormous mausoleum, located near but even larger than that of the last Ming emperor, derived from the symbolic notions behind Lenin's glorification five years earlier. The architect who chose the design had actually been trained in the United States, and the influence of the Lincoln Memorial is clear, not so much as a stylistic copy as in the way the tomb is situated. Though hard to imagine, the Greek Temple on the Mall in Washington influenced the concept for Sun's final resting place: a temple resembling a bell to remind the masses that Sun had awakened China.[2] It is more than intriguing to consider that a combination of Lincoln and Lenin as heroic national leaders shaped the thinking of those who would memorialize Sun Yat-sen in 1929.

Other ironies abound. When Sun was inaugurated in 1912, the public outpouring of welcome and enthusiasm had been spontaneous, as was the genuine grief when he died in 1925. By contrast, the masses seem to have been rather disinterested in, almost apathetic about, the carefully staged, slow procession of ten thousand marchers (organized by political groups and the military supporting Chiang) that escorted Sun to his mausoleum on July 1, 1929. Those who did not fully support Chiang's party were not included. As Henrietta Harrison has explained very well, the event looked more like an imperial funeral than the burial of an anticolonial and revolutionary modernizer.[3] This very grand interment exercise was highly politicized—its symbolism maximized for the advantage of a new leader still striving to consolidate his power.

On September 30, 1989, an equally massive procession, intended to achieve a comparable outcome, accompanied the remains of Juan Manuel de Rosas (whose death had occurred more than a century before) along a fifty-five-block route to La Recoleta cemetery, the most elite and famous necropolis in Buenos Aires. A military carriage bearing the casket was escorted and accompanied by many dignitaries, including the president of Argentina, his cabinet and government officials, and descendants of the deceased but also of the powerful nineteenth-century generals who had bitterly opposed Rosas during his reign and beyond. Next came grenadiers, and then an escort of federal police arrayed in period uniforms from the middle third of the nineteenth century (actually, the very uniforms of the *mazorca*, Rosas's once widely feared henchmen). Five thousand gauchos from all across Argentina and Uruguay brought up the rear, along with members of the Pro-Repatriation Committee, who had waited nearly four decades for this moment.

Rosas is remembered as the most famous figure in nineteenth-century Argentine history—but also the most notorious. He had been the leader and governor of the Argentine Confederation from 1829 until 1852, when he was defeated in battle and sought exile in England, where he died in 1877 and received burial in a modest Catholic cemetery. Although he had served as a symbol of national unification and a passionate defender of Argentine sovereignty, he was also remembered as a ruthless dictator intolerant of any opposition. Consequently the nation's official historiography had long since developed a strong anti-Rosista tradition.[4]

When Juan Perón returned from *his* exile in 1973, he felt that the time had come for what was left of Rosas to be repatriated, and supporters of that notion even wanted him to be buried in the Cathedral of Buenos Aires, the resting place of José de San Martín, founder of the nation. Rosas remained too controversial to receive that ultimate honor; but after the fiercely anti-Communist rule of military leaders ended and democracy returned to Argentina in 1983, President Carlos

Saúl Menem eventually determined to bring Rosas's remains home as an act of reconciliation between conservatives and liberals. Rosas had wanted to be buried in his native land. The act of reinterment with so much official pomp and vast numbers watching meant different things to different people, yet it did serve Menem's purpose: a moving and highly visible moment of national unification if not instantaneous healing. Rosas found his rest not far from the burial site of Eva Perón, the people's darling. Although it was not the cathedral, he had achieved a place of honor.[5]

An even more sensational and widely noticed reburial involved the revolutionary Che Guevara. He was killed in 1967 by CIA-authorized Bolivian troops and buried with five others in a secret mass grave near an obscure mountain village. In 1995 the Bolivian government, responding to international pressure, reluctantly authorized a search that finally located the site, and the remains were eventually verified. Following agreements with Bolivia and Argentina, countries that had claims to Guevara (the second by birth), he was reburied as a heroic martyr on October 17, 1997, in a specially built mausoleum in the central Cuban city of Santa Clara, the site of his best-known military triumph. Fidel Castro presided over a pomp-filled state funeral with a ringing tribute.[6]

✠

The reasons for exhumations and reburials in modern times range from nationalism in the decade following World War I to the rehabilitation of political reputations as a symptom and symbol of anti-Communist fervor in Eastern Europe following 1989. A desire for national unification has been a prominent motive in recent events as well, not just in China and Argentina but also in Germany after the Berlin Wall came down, not to mention the Balkans following World War II. There are also causes that we have encountered earlier in this book, such as bringing legendary figures home as a gesture of repossession if not always respect.

Religion continues to matter in important ways because individuals seen as saintly often require a more appropriate interment than the one originally received. John Henry Cardinal Newman's burial site is a current case in point, still unresolved as of this writing and posing a dilemma for the Vatican as well as segments of British society. Then there are men like Friedrich Nietzsche, buried in obscure local cemeteries that are threatened either by "progress" (otherwise known as entrepreneurial urban and suburban development) or else by lapses of memory and the physical damage done by time and tourists at grave sites. In some instances, once again for political reasons, issues arise over whether and where to reinter someone whose reputation may have changed or been altered.

To cite a prime American example, when Major Marcus Reno died in disgrace in 1889, he was buried in an unmarked grave at Oak Hill Cemetery in Washington, DC, because he had received a dishonorable discharge from the U.S. Army on grounds of "cowardice" while mobilizing in support of General George A. Custer at the Battle of the Little Big Horn in 1876. Reno had been the highest-ranking officer serving under Custer. Later that year he was also accused of making advances toward the wife of another officer, and in 1880 he received a court-martial for drunkenness. The testimonial record regarding some of these charges is unclear and seems to have been altered by unknown hands; although his decimated company's location was such that he could not have known of Custer's desperate plight, the accusations related to alcohol abuse do seem to have been justified.[7]

In 1967 the Army Board of Corrections cleared Reno of all those unverified charges, and he was reburied in September at what then was still called the Custer Battlefield National Cemetery. (Custer's name has since been removed from the cemetery and national park, which is now simply called the Little Bighorn National Park.) As the mayor of Billings put it in September 1967, the reinterment would be "an occasion of prideful pomp and circumstance" for Reno. And it was.[8]

We might compare that reversal of reputation with an equally remarkable one in France, where late in 2007 the French government requested the return of the remains of its first president and last emperor, Louis Napoleon III. After a number of foreign adventures and misadventures during the 1860s, his forces were defeated in the Franco-Prussian War of 1870, prompting him to flee with his wife, Empress Eugenie, to Chislehurst, Kent, where he remained in exile until his death in 1873. Despite the ignominy of his last years in power, Napoleon III did play a major role in physically reconfiguring Paris into an elegant modern city, replacing those unhealthful medieval streets with wide boulevards. Under his regime major parks were built along with apartment blocks for the middle class and new sewage systems. Hence the request for his ashes (which had lain in a crypt at an English abbey for 120 years) to be repatriated to the French republic over which he presided before proclaiming himself emperor. He is once again home.[9]

It has not been unusual, in America and abroad, for national chauvinism to trump the last wishes of a deceased man who is widely esteemed. Alexandre Dumas *père* (1802–70), a mixed-race novelist best known for such swashbuckling romances as *The Three Musketeers* (1844) and *The Count of Monte Cristo* (also 1844), chose to be buried quite simply and with his parents in his native town of Villers-Cotterets; yet in 2002 his remains were exhumed and reburied with solemnity at the Panthèon in Paris. His central role in the popular national patrimony apparently meant more than respect for his personal preference.

Quite a different saga that also culminated at the Panthèon is intriguing for two reasons: first for what it reveals about French politics under Charles de Gaulle, and second because it has no real counterpart in American annals, unless we make a very approximate comparison with the way that many of those who had opposed Lincoln's presidency later joined in remembering him as a martyr in the cause of preserving the Union.[10] Jean Moulin (1899–1943), founder and leader of the French Resistance during World War II, was arrested in June 1943, was interrogated in Lyon by Klaus Barbie (head of the Gestapo there) but revealed nothing to him about the Resistance's organization, and died the next month on a Paris to Berlin train that was heading to a concentration camp. It is unclear whether he committed suicide or was beaten to death by Barbie.[11]

Following liberation in 1944, Moulin's remains were cremated and his ashes buried at Père Lachaise Cemetery. In 1963, however, the Union des Résistants, Déportés, Internés, et des Familles des Morts proposed that his ashes be exhumed and reinterred at the Panthèon. The leftist opposition took up their cause in Parliament. In 1964, the twentieth anniversary of liberation, as it happened, the French government chose to invent a new historical version of the German occupation so that French chauvinists could claim that France had *always* resisted invaders. Charles de Gaulle, the president, and André Malraux, his esteemed minister of culture, essentially appropriated the compelling idea of reburying Moulin as a way of glorifying de Gaulle, linking him more closely to the Resistance and equating him with the very soul of the French nation. Instead of gaining approval through a legislative vote, the government issued an executive order, thereby making the measure its own.[12]

Reburial of the ashes became an elaborately scripted two-day affair. On December 18 they were removed from Père Lachaise, and the urn was placed in a new container and then in a coffin with a simple inscription: only the hero's name. In the afternoon that casket was taken to the Ile de la Cité, where, to the accompaniment of a funeral march, it was temporarily placed with military honors in the crypt of the Monument to the Martyrs of the Deportation. Much elaborate protocol followed, with an honor guard consisting of 194 members of the Resistance along with leaders from all parties and movements. At ten o'clock that evening a cortège formed, led by the Garde Républicaine of Paris and followed by the flags of various Resistance groups.[13]

This procession carried the remains of Jean Moulin to the Panthèon, where the next day de Gaulle presided over a very formal state ceremony at which his deputy Malraux delivered the eulogy. The casket had been placed at the center of the Panthèon on a temporary altar beneath the cupola, and final interment occurred later in the Panthèon's northern crypt. In a very literal sense, the government in power had co-opted from the Left the ultimate symbol of French Resistance in the name of French political unity following a bitterly divisive war in Algeria. In effect, the glory of Moulin's courageous leadership had to be shared with President de Gaulle. This shabby attempt at political unification following a politically troublesome war was a curious harbinger of the Rosas episode in Argentina twenty-five years later.[14]

✝

Now we turn to a different sort of heroic story of reburial for national pride and honor. Manfred Baron von Richthofen was only twenty-two when World War I broke out in 1914.[15] As a skilled and courageous fighter pilot, he downed many Allied planes in single combat and became the most glamorous hero of the German war effort. Films and postcards were made of the Red Baron preparing for battle, and in 1917 he was awarded the nation's highest military honor. When he was killed in action pursuing an enemy plane over the Somme in April 1918, it seemed not only a national tragedy but a frightful omen for Germany. The British actually buried him with military honors in France, and subsequently the French exhumed and reburied him in a larger cemetery, though still in France. In 1925 the Richthofen family decided that the time had come to bring the body home, and the project swiftly became a momentous national event.[16]

The train from France bearing the Red Baron's remains crossed into Germany on November 17. As it moved through the country toward Berlin, many thousands of people turned out to watch it pass, just as somber Americans had turned out in vast numbers to see Lincoln's funeral train make its circuitous way to Springfield in April 1865. In Frankfurt veterans from the nationalist Stahlhelm, the republican Reichsbanner, and the Jewish Reichsbund Jüdischer Frontsoldaten created an honor guard to meet the train. When it reached Berlin on November 18, a huge crowd was waiting despite the dark and the cold. The following day a continuous stream of people walked past the coffin in the Gnadenkirche. At the funeral two days later, President Paul von Hindenberg led the official delegation. Soldiers beat muffled drums and led a riderless horse in a procession to the Invaliden Cemetery for interment. The grave quickly became a German shrine.[17]

Some years later Manfred's brother Bolko reflected on the symbolic meaning of this powerfully moving funeral: "Not all of the hundreds of thousands who gave their lives for Germany, and who were laid to rest in foreign soil, could be brought home. And so, the thousands of people who streamed to greet our Manfred saw him as the representative of the self-sacrificing German hero, and honored in him the sons and brothers who had given themselves for the fatherland." The event had much to do with a resurgence of German nationalism, of course. But as historian Robert Whalen has observed, "Mass mourning for the Red Baron, then, was more than a reaffirmation of the heroic. Mixed in the mourning was not a little nostalgia for the time when the heroic had meaning, and grief that the heroic was gone. The Red Baron was home, but the Red Baron was dead."[18]

Sixty-six years later Germans would find themselves intensely divided over the decision to disinter King Frederick the Great from what had been West Germany until 1990 and rebury him at Sans Souci, his palace at Potsdam, once the royal suburb of Berlin. The story of Frederick's migratory remains is an intriguing and intensely politicized one. Having somehow claimed the enlightened Prussian king as a forebear of the Nazi movement, Adolf Hitler had his corpse dug up from his original site at a Potsdam garrison church in 1944 and hidden away in a salt mine in order to protect it from seizure by the advancing Red Army. After the war, however, American occupying forces located the royal sarcophagus and gave it a new funeral, after which Frederick's Hohenzollern descendants retrieved the remains and reinterred them at the family castle. In 1991, ten months after the reunification of Germany, Chancellor Helmut Kohl and his conservative Christian Democratic Party decided to celebrate the nation's restored unity by exhuming Frederick yet again for reburial once more at Potsdam in the east on August 17, declaring that the former ruler "should be neither mythologized nor demonized." From Kohl's perspective, the reburial of "Old Fritz" would supply the ideal sign of Germany made whole again, the "crowning moment."[19]

Opposition politicians and historians weighed in critically against Kohl's decision to lend his prestige to the ceremony. Historian Golo Mann called Kohl's role "absolute tastelessness" and remarked that Kohl's blessing of this symbolic gesture "demonstrates the kind of mentality that prompts cheers among the stupid but causes awkward fears in European capitals." Meanwhile, and more important, the opposition party, Social Democrats, also attacked participation by Kohl and the army as a nationalistic display that sent exactly the wrong message about the new Germany. Hadn't Hitler made a dramatic pilgrimage to Frederick's tomb to usher in the Nazis' acquisition of power? Didn't Frederick preside over two of Europe's bloodiest wars: the Seven Years' War and the War of the Austrian Succession? As one Social Democratic party leader said to reporters, "Any historical to-do over Frederick's bones . . . could be understood wrongly."[20] So a gesture conceived as a symbol of reunification instead came to be emblematic of sharp divisiveness over German history and identity. But the enlightened Frederick was now at home once more in Potsdam, and all the intense passion faded away as political discourse moved on to more critical issues.

Much less contested but no less embarrassing in terms of national pride is the bizarre afterlife of Johann Friedrich von Schiller (1759–1805), the great German poet, dramatist, historian, and philosopher of the romantic era, best remembered in the English-speaking world for his play *Maria Stuart*, or *Mary Queen of Scots* (1800). When Schiller died, he was buried in the communal vault at Weimar, not far from Jena in eastern Germany, where he had served as professor of history at the university. According to legend, however, Schiller's skull was entrusted for some months to his close friend, the even more famous writer Johann Wolfgang von Goethe (1749–1832), whose family home (now a fine museum) is in Frankfurt but who, like Schiller, is also associated with the culturally rich and bucolic community of Weimar. A handsome monument to both men stands in front of the German National Theater there.

In the two decades following Schiller's death his reputation grew incrementally, and with it the sentiment that he should not lie in a common grave in Jacob's Cemetery, even though such burial had been standard practice through the eighteenth century, even for many celebrities. So in 1826 the mayor of Weimar entered the communal vault to seek Schiller's remains. He came back with no fewer than twenty-three skulls (and related bones), one of which was determined by two doctors and Schiller's son to belong to the writer, and then a more honorific reburial took place. A debate persisted for generations, however, over whether the designated remains truly belonged to Schiller. In 1911 a prominent anatomist descended into the vault once again and this time emerged with sixty-three additional skulls! He made a new selection with a seemingly matching skeleton, and they were placed in a special coffin in a side room of the ducal vault. Yet questions and doubts understandably persisted.[21]

While the country was politically divided after World War II, with Weimar located in East Germany, a team examined both sets of skeletons in 1959, but inconclusively. Little more than a decade later, in 1970, a group of scientists decided to exhume Goethe's remains in the middle of the night, photographing and treating the bones with chemicals to help preserve them. What remained of the two immortals was then deposited in a pair of matched oak coffins in a place of particular honor at Weimar. In 2007 yet another forensic inquiry was undertaken to determine which bones truly belonged to Schiller, this time using DNA from five members of the Schiller family at a cost of $170,000 to conduct chemical analysis and facial reconstruction—all of which was recorded by a German documentary film company. Ultimately it was decided that *neither* set of Schiller's putative remains was authentic, because the two skeletons included the bones of at least six different people.[22]

The net result of these macabre activities, in what has been aptly described as "a tale more Gothic than Classicist," is that Schiller's coffin is now empty. Hellmut Seemann, president of the Foundation of Weimar Classics, which is responsible for everything from museums and parks in Weimar to the famed Goethe-Schiller Archive, who had cooperated with the German public television station in making the film, declared that the search for Schiller was now finished. His goal would no longer be to find Schiller's true remains but only to settle questions about the ones they had in hand, so to speak. "It is like with a painting," he explained. "Is it by Rembrandt or only a workshop painting? You have also responsibility for the skulls you have." Local officials complained that adverse publicity about an empty Schiller coffin could be very bad for tourism in Weimar, but interviews made with local citizens and tourists at the bronze monument—thus far, at least—have not revealed any great disenchantment, only disappointment and more than a bit of bemusement.[23] As we have seen more than once, decisions made about reinterments in the United States have frequently hinged upon commercial concerns about tourism.

After almost half a century, Germany was still trying to redeem its reputation from the barbarisms committed before and during World War II—the repercussions of that catastrophe, of course continue to be felt to this day. Not long before the Allies liberated northern Holland in the spring of 1945, German military agents had murdered some 422 Dutch nationals and members of the Dutch resistance. Early in May 1945 the remains were found buried in the dunes at Kennemer. Eventually, forty-five separate sites were located, but the task of identifying bodies remained difficult. Most had been robbed of personal belongings and clothing, so that only dentures could reveal who was who. Dentists nationwide participated in the laborious project, and most of the victims were ultimately identified. An imprisoned undertaker had initially been instructed to take those bodies to the sand dunes and leave them "in a tidily orderly manner." His meticulously organized lists and notebooks were very helpful, and by now only two of the 422 people remain unknown.[24]

The first of many reburials at the dunes took place in a new Remembrance Cemetery on November 27, 1945, in the presence of the Dutch royal family. The final reinterment occurred ten years later. Eight large memorial stones serve as reminders of where the bodies were found, and on the stones is inscribed how many murdered members of the resistance are buried there. Victims from other sites have subsequently been added to the Remembrance Cemetery, which now has 373 graves. As with many who died during the American Civil War, some of the 422 victims have since been reburied in family graves, in hometown cemeteries, or even at the place of their execution. Every year on May 4 large numbers of people come from all over the Netherlands to stand in solemn, respectful vigil at this site. It is perhaps the most moving occasion of the Dutch calendar year.[25]

✠

A notable and germane yet little-known work of historical fiction by an Albanian writer provides an interesting parallel with the regional and sectional search for bodies to be brought "home" during and after the American Civil War. Ismail Kadare, born in 1936, was educated in history and philology at the University of Tirana (the capital of Albania). In 1990, immediately before the fall of Communism in Albania, he sought political asylum in France, and since then he has divided his time between Albania and France. In 2005 he won the Inaugural Booker International Prize.

In 1963 Kadare published *The General of the Dead Army*, which was translated into French in 1970 and English in 1991. A kind of summary parable appears as an interlude between chapters two-thirds of the way through the novel.

> Once upon a time a general and a priest [his chaplain] set off on an adventure together. They were going to collect together all the remains of their soldiers who had been killed in a big war. They walked and walked, they crossed lots of mountains and lots of plains, always hunting for those bones and collecting them up. The country was nasty and rough. But they didn't turn back, they kept on further and further. They collected as many bones as they could and then they came back to count them. But they realized that there were still a lot they hadn't found. So they pulled on their boots and their raincoats and they set

off on their search again. . . . They were quite exhausted; they felt they were being crushed into the ground by their task. Neither the wind nor the rain would tell them where to look for the soldiers they were seeking. But they collected as many as they could and came back once again to count them. Many of the ones they had been looking for still hadn't been found.[26]

The novel relates the complex story of an Italian general sent on a mission in 1963 by his government, at the behest of many Italian families, to recover the bodies of an army known as the Blue Battalion that was defeated by Albanian partisans and guerrillas in 1943. The families wanted their husbands and sons brought home for honorable burial. The thankless and exhausting task spans two years, and in the process the general discovers that a one-armed German general and his staff are in Albania for exactly the same reason. (The Germans placed an occupation force there after the Italians defected, but it was driven out by Communist partisans in 1944.) On occasion the Italian general and his chaplain are shocked to find graves that have been opened and the contents removed. At first they assume to their dismay that Albanians have desecrated these graves, but they eventually discover that the rival German team had reached each spot first.[27]

About halfway through the novel a passage printed in italics conveys the interior thoughts of the Italian general when excessive brandy causes him to second-guess his own mission.

> *I don't see why our comrades' remains should be restored to their families. I don't believe that was their last wish, as some people claim. To us, to all old soldiers, such displays of sentimentality seem very puerile. A soldier, living or dead, never feels at ease except among his comrades. So leave them together. Don't split them up. Let the serried graves keep the old warlike spirit of yesterday still alive in us. Don't listen to those chicken-hearted people always ready to yell at the sight of a drop of blood. Listen to us, we fought here and we know.[28]*

Kadare's message would seem to be that military men and civilians think differently about the importance of permanent reburial "at home" as a matter of personal and national honor. It becomes a thankless job to look for the remains of dead souls merely to bring them back for a decent burial. Is it really worth the effort? Does it not involve a misguided sense of national pride?

At the outset, the general had no doubts. "He would do everything in his power to acquit himself worthily of such a sacred task. Not one of his countrymen should be forgotten, not one should be left behind in this foreign land."[29] Two years of frustrating labor prompt a change of heart. It is twenty years too late, and two years of futility are too many. When the general learns that his subordinates have made grievous mistakes in the identification of remains, he is appalled. Attempts at rationalization would be humiliating. "I would be rather more inclined to say that they rebaptized the bones of unknown soldiers with the names of those men they had been particularly requested to look out for. In short, if the story is true, then we are dealing with a gross and appalling fraud. The remains have been sent to families to whom they did not rightfully belong." The disillusioned general concludes: "A nasty business altogether."[30] Sending unknown and unknowable dead men back across the Adriatic had clearly been a colossal blunder.

At the very end, the two generals meet at a hotel in Tirana, the Italian drinking brandy, the German drinking *raki*, the anise-flavored alcoholic beverage beloved in the Balkans, Turkey, and Greece. Because they each have lists of men with particular height specifications whose bodies they were supposed to send back, they cynically contemplate swapping German bodies for Italians so that each one can fulfill his specific mandate. Ultimately they do not, and the one-armed German general philosophizes: "The remains we dig up constitute war's very essence, you might say. What remains when it is all over; the precipitate after a chemical reaction." Mutual recognition of cynical beliefs and behavior thereby gives way to banal sophistries.[31]

A full generation later, however, we discover a distinctive sign of new and changing attitudes toward the ethical imperative of repatriating those who were lost in war. On May 27, 2008, the German press reported that Germany's War Graves Authority had signed an agreement for the remains of some four thousand German soldiers killed in the former Czechoslovakia during World War II to be buried at a special site in the western Czech town of Cheb. In a move hailed by both sides as an act of reconciliation, the Czechs decided to build a military cemetery for the German war dead next to the town graveyard. That felt like a triumph of good faith and reconciliation over cynical recriminations.[32]

✠

The body of Benito Mussolini underwent one of the most intensely politicized migrations of all, from an ad hoc gallows to a blessed sanctuary—all in all, a tortuous rite of passage for his bitterly divided country. After he was captured and killed by anti-Fascist partisans near Lake Como in April 1945, his corpse and those of his mistress and a few associates were taken to Milan, where they were hanged upside down from an elevated pole at a gasoline station, making possible the infamous photos that inspired the Left and enraged the Right for years thereafter. Following autopsies and indecision, in June Mussolini and Clara Petacci were secretly buried in unmarked graves at Musocco Cemetery in Milan. The authorities wanted to keep his resting place from becoming a symbolic marker for the significant number of Il Duce admirers who persisted. The latter had wanted him buried at the Altar of the Nation in Rome's Piazza Venezia, the site of his famous balcony speeches. Although they could not achieve that, on Easter 1946 they did successfully steal the body and took it to a fifteenth-century monastery outside Pavia, where Franciscan monks helped to conceal it. The purpose of this plot was to transform clandestine neo-Fascism into a legitimate political force.[33]

In the process of Mussolini's exhumation and transportation, several of his fingers fell off; they were subsequently fetishized as relics by the Right. Meanwhile the police swung into action and made numerous arrests among known neo-Fascists in the Milan area. Even more momentous, Italians voted in a referendum to abolish the monarchy and establish a republic. After one hundred days of aggressive police work with informers and arrested insiders, police discovered the body sealed in a trunk, wrapped in two rubberized sacks, and hidden in a closet in one of the monk's cells on the monastery's ground floor. Along with Il Duce's remains ("a skeleton falling to pieces") authorities also found a declaration by the Fascist Party that envisioned the day when his body would be buried on Rome's Capitoline Hill. Photos taken of the small trunk at police headquarters became almost as familiar as the grim images photographed at the Milan gas station.[34]

Thereafter Mussolini's remains would be secretly hidden for reasons of state until 1957. On orders from the prime minister and with the agreement of Cardinal Ildefonso Schuster, archbishop of Milan, the government kept Mussolini's remains concealed in the chapel of the convent of Cerro Maggiore, near Milan, thereby honoring a commitment that the police chief had made to a priest to give the dictator a Christian yet secret resting place. For the next eleven years, only a tiny group of politicians, clerics, and civil servants knew the exact location of the "tomb." Given all of that secrecy, of course, by 1950 a Buried in Italy Campaign had begun—rumors spread like wildfire that he was buried here, there, and everywhere. Schemes and searches abounded.[35]

The Italian government resisted requests that he be reinterred in the cemetery at Predappio in Emilia-Romagna, his birthplace, where his grave could easily turn into a pilgrimage site for neo-Fascists or a site of vandalism for his foes. During the summer of 1957, however, the Italian Social Movement newspaper engaged in a forceful campaign to have the remains restored to Predappio. Mussolini's widow, Rachele, negotiated details for the body's return with Prime Minister Adone Zoli, a conservative Christian Democrat. Decoy vehicles were used to deter journalists, and the remains, placed in a wooden box marked "church documents," were accompanied by police and monks from the Lombard convent to the Mussolini family crypt at the San Casciano cemetery on August 31. Neo-Fascist faithful were present for the entombment, and predictably, the site has remained a shrine for political pilgrims ever since.[36]

✛

Joseph Stalin's encounters with death and burial were numerous, fascinating, and virtually without any counterpart in American historical experience. Born in 1878, he married his first wife, called Kato, in 1906. Although he adored her, he also neglected her because of his intense political commitments and ceaseless travel to raise money for Lenin and revolution. On November 22, 1907, Kato died of typhus and dysentery. At her church funeral he declared, "This creature softened my heart of stone. She died and with her died my last warm feelings for humanity." At the burial his composure totally cracked, and he threw himself fully into her grave on top of the coffin. After being hauled out by friends, he spotted members of the czar's secret police entering the graveyard, raced to the back, vaulted the fence, and disappeared for two months.

Eventually he returned to his mother's home in Georgia to grieve. "My personal life is shattered," he sobbed. "Nothing attaches me to life except socialism. I'm going to dedicate my existence to that."[37]

When Stalin died of a cerebral hemorrhage on March 5, 1953, he was elaborately embalmed and placed under glass in the Lenin Mausoleum in Red Square (actually the third one constructed for Lenin). Three years later, however, Nikita Khrushchev addressed the Twentieth Party Congress in a secret session and denounced Stalin's "cult of personality" and his "violation of Leninist norms of legality." Because more than fourteen hundred delegates heard the speech, it did not remain secret for very long. Khrushchev subsequently arranged for his friend Nikolai Podgorny, a future head of state, to propose that the continued presence of Stalin's body next to Lenin's was "no longer appropriate" on account of his "abuse of power, mass repressions against honourable Soviet people, and other activities in the period of the personality cult." At the Twenty-second Party Congress in 1961, Podgorny made that proposal and it carried unanimously.[38]

On the night of October 31, 1961, Stalin's remains were secretly removed from the mausoleum, on which a notice then appeared that it was "closed for repairs." Stalin's name was also removed from the entrance, his body was cremated, and the ashes were buried below the Kremlin wall near those of four former comrades. His new "resting place" was marked by a black granite slab with the simple inscription "J. V. Stalin, 1879–1953." During the winter months of 1961–62, countless statues and portraits of the once-feared dictator were removed throughout the Soviet Union. Resistance was encountered only in Stalin's native Georgia, where a huge statue overlooked the venerable city of Tbilisi. Even that statue eventually disappeared, just before Khrushchev's visit to Georgia with Fidel Castro. In 1970, however, a small bust of Stalin was added to the ultra-brief inscription at his new grave site.[39]

✣

We must turn next to nearby Hungary, where multiple exhumations and reburials since 1988 have been politicized perhaps more intensively than anywhere else. Episodes there are remarkably symptomatic of ideological regime change and a desire to make amends for serious political "sins" of the recent past by honoring as national heroes the martyrs who epitomize integrity, courage, and creativity.[40] It is difficult to identify comparable phenomena in American political culture, because we have not experienced a 180-degree reversal and rebirth comparable to what happened in Hungary beginning in 1988.

The reputations of national heroes wax and wane everywhere. In the United States, for example, esteem for Woodrow Wilson's reputation has gradually declined, whereas Harry S. Truman's aura rose upon reconsideration and because of the political uses to which his persona could be put by subsequent presidents, such as Gerald Ford. But such shifts have depended upon the ebb and flow of historical revisionism and public opinion. In the United States we have not had the kind of overt *manipulation* (as opposed to resuscitation, perhaps) of reputations that has characterized Hungary during the last two decades, and the contrast can be instructive.[41]

As I noted briefly while discussing Rachmaninoff in chapter 1, the composer Bela Bartók died in New York in 1945, somewhat disillusioned with the United States, but having emigrated from Hungary at the beginning of World War II to protest the encroachment of Nazism in Hungarian politics and society. In the spring of 1988 his two sons, one living in the United States and the other in Budapest, decided that their father's remains really should be returned to his homeland. As it happens, the socialist government had been wanting just that for some while, but the timing could not have been more convenient, because nationalist sentiment was then reaching fever pitch.

During the fortnight between his exhumation and reburial, Hungarian newspapers and magazines became obsessed with Bartók. Instead of being flown directly from New York to Budapest, the coffin traveled by ocean liner to England and then by motorcade from France through Germany and Austria, with celebratory concerts held in Southampton, Cherbourg, Paris, Strasbourg, Munich, and Vienna. When the coffin crossed the border into Hungary, people lined the highway to watch the motorcade pass through their villages.[42]

As Susan Gal has observed, it is difficult to imagine a similar welcome, more than four decades following death, for a classical composer, especially an often difficult and musically dissonant one, in the United States or even in Western Europe. Gal believes that Bartók's funeral can best be understood "as a move by intellectuals closely associated with state socialism and the Communist Party to celebrate a national hero who would evoke the sympathy and confidence of a broad internal audience (including opposition intellectuals in both the populist and the urbanist camps) while appealing to an international one as well."[43]

Keep in mind, however, that in his youth Bartók had written a concerto dedicated to Lajos Kossuth, leader of the 1848 Revolution in Hungary, and that Bartók had been inspired by authentic Hungarian folk music. Moreover, he was not a genuine émigré, someone who simply abandoned his country, but had lived in self-imposed exile because he opposed both Fascism and Communism. He also became closely identified with populism when the return of his body was compared with the 1894 return of Kossuth's body and the 1906 return of the remains of Rákóczi, also a leader of Hungarian rebellion against Habsburg rule from Vienna.[44]

In identifying Bartók's reburial with the homecomings of Kossuth and Rákóczi, both of them exiled revolutionaries, the state implicitly offered critical and opposition intellectuals a body they had not even requested while remaining conspicuously silent about the body that the democratic, urbanist opposition had been seeking for years: that of Imre Nagy, leader of the 1956 anti-Soviet uprising who was brutally murdered and placed in an unmarked grave. Because Bartók had opposed Fascism so vehemently, his return meant that symbolically his spirit found Communist Hungary a politically and ethically acceptable place. By that logic, as Gal has remarked, "the return of Bartók's body justified, legitimated, and strengthened the Hungarian government's very weak moral claims on the population."[45]

The composer had actually requested in his will that no great ceremony accompany his funeral. Although it may have turned out to be grander than he envisioned or desired, it actually became a relatively modest skirmish in the discursive battle among Hungarian elites. With the demise of the Hungarian Communist Party the following year, a difficult tension between the desire for distinctive national identity on one hand and pan-European sentiments on the other persisted in the contest between new political parties formed in 1989 in the wake of earlier opposition groups. A certain synthesis of specifically Hungarian qualities along with the broader European culture had been ascribed to Bartók and pleased many Hungarians. It even impressed those who found the funeral rhetoric inappropriate because it stressed a fundamental cultural duality. The idea that Hungarian nationalism could be reconciled with Europeanness became attractive to Hungarians because it helped to resolve a long-standing intellectual and political tension in the Hungarian sense of self.[46]

Hungary may very well have the most notable history of exhuming and reburying political leaders who fell from grace because of revolutionary changes. Count Lajos Batthyány, chosen as prime minister of the 1848 Revolution, was executed on October 6, 1849, but eventually reburied in the renamed Kerepesi Common Cemetery in 1870. During the later nineteenth century this cemetery increasingly became the final resting place for rich or famous Hungarians. A special section was set aside for persons who had committed suicide or been executed and therefore could not receive an ecclesiastical burial. On March 15, 1860, students organized a celebration in front of the cemetery to commemorate the outbreak of the 1848 Revolution. When police shot into the crowd, killing a law student, his funeral turned into the largest anti-Habsburg demonstration the city had seen. The martyr, Géza Forinyák, was buried in the cemetery wall.[47]

The most notorious and carefully studied modern example of political rehabilitation and exhumation, however, involves Imre Nagy, prime minister of Soviet-controlled Hungary in the early 1950s who led the anti-Soviet revolt in 1956. Once that rebellion had been crushed, Nagy and four "coconspirators" were convicted in a closed trial, hanged in 1958, and secretly buried in the courtyard of their prison. Three years later, their pseudonymously identified bodies were moved to an unmarked mass grave in the largest cemetery in Budapest. Rumors emanated from drunken gravediggers that they had been placed in plot 301, situated in an obscure corner of the burial ground. During the early 1980s, on the anniversary of the execution, family members and surviving victims of the abortive revolution began placing flowers on the ground at the presumed resting place. Their guess must have been correct, because in 1982 the police started closing that part of the cemetery on October 23, the anniversary of the day when the 1956 Revolution began.[48]

In July 1988 the last secretary-general of the Hungarian Communist Party announced that the family of Imre Nagy would be allowed to rebury him in private. By then, however, he had already received a symbolic public burial—but elsewhere. On June 16, 1988, the thirtieth anniversary of his death, a commemorative monument to Nagy was erected at Père Lachaise Cemetery in Paris, courtesy of then mayor Jacques Chirac. The monument took the form of a shipwrecked boat—meant to be emblematic of the fate of utopian Communism—designed by László Rajk, son of the executed minister of foreign affairs, the most famous victim of the notorious Hungarian show trials at the end of the 1940s. When the symbolic burial of Nagy occurred in Paris, a demonstration took place in Budapest at the Eternal Sacred Flame honoring Batthyány, the executed and already reburied prime minister of 1848–49. Following the suggestion of one of the organizers of the demonstration, the Eternal Sacred Flame was renamed the Batthyány-Imre Nagy Flame.[49]

The ideological and political transformation of Hungary in 1989 occurred with such nonviolent smoothness that it barely qualified as a revolution. Changes occurred by means of radical reform. The most symbolic and memorable event took place on June 16, when Nagy was reburied on Heroes' Square in front of the Millenary Monument, which had been erected as part of observances of the thousand-year anniversary of the Hungarians' arrival in the Carpathian Basin. As the historian István Rév has written in his thorough account, "The monument links a Magyar past with the Hungarian Holy Crown that represents the country's Christian and European civilizing mission in the Carpathian Basin."[50]

Within a month of his widely noted ceremony, the political rehabilitation of Nagy was complete. This pattern of honorific exhumation, reburial, and restoration would continue for some years and would be replicated with various other heroic figures in Hungary. After János Kádár, the Communist leader for thirty-three years, died in 1989, the son of László Rajk, who had been betrayed by Kádár while he served as foreign minister, decided to remove his father from his ignominious grave so that he would not lie anywhere near his executioner. The son had him reinterred close to the exiled and reburied president Count Károlyi in a *depositio ad sanctos*, a practice carried over from antiquity when Christian noblemen buried their relatives in close proximity to martyrs of the church. (As Rév has noted of these ironic *danses maca-*

*bres*, Kádár died at *exactly* the hour when Nagy received legal rehabilitation from the Supreme Court of Hungary.)[51]

Admiral Miklós Horthy had served as Hungary's interwar regent
and eventually guided Hungary into an alliance with Hitler in return for
the redemption of pieces of Hungarian territory. Horthy died in 1944,
unmourned after the war by Communists. When he was exhumed and
reburied in 1993 at the request of Hungary's first prime minister following the revolution (a former history teacher, as it happens),[52] Horthy's new entombment was deemed the obliteration of Communism
from national memory. But as Rév has written, "Those weeping over
Horthy's new grave mourned the hundreds of thousands of soldiers
who fell along the Don River in the Second World War against the Soviet Union just [even] as they mourned the man who sent them to their
death, and they sought to camouflage their own recent past with the
corpse of the regent. . . . Those who were present at the funeral hoped
that their physical proximity to the regent's remains would prove that
they had always been implacable anti-Communists, the secret oppo-
nents of his enemies."[53]

It's very curious the way complex memories and shadowy reputations change when the political context has been altered. We have already seen that to be true in the case of such Americans as James Wilson
and Jefferson Davis—both men the victims and then the beneficiaries
of shifting political climates.

✢

The outcome and the legacy of most of these European episodes has
been more than national reconciliation and the notable rehabilitation
of selected reputations for leadership and courage. Their heritage has
also involved historical revisionism on a large scale—revisionism that
has not only been accepted but embraced, partially for reasons of partisan satisfaction but mainly in the interest of truth—correcting the
record. Here we must distinguish between two related yet rather different forms of "revisionism." I am profoundly struck by the contrast with
the United States, where we have learned, especially in recent decades,
that what most Americans understand by "revisionist history" is mistrusted. It is not readily acceptable to the lay public and has frequently
been denounced on the floor of Congress by well-educated and well-

meaning senators and representatives, ranging from liberals like Dianne Feinstein of California to conservatives like Alan Simpson of Wyoming, not to mention Lynne Cheney's notorious attack during the 1990s on the new History Standards for secondary schools in the United States.

The frequent refrain of resistance runs along these lines: "Why can't they just leave history alone—the way it really happened and got recorded?" There seems to be an American assumption that the first attempts at historical narration and understanding get it all quite right. Much of the public believes that the books we once read in school were authoritative. More often than not, new information and challenging interpretations seem to be suspect because troublesome: they require the reconsideration of cherished assumptions. "Historical revisionism" has not been well received in America, not ordinarily and certainly not in recent decades.[54]

Revisionism and its potential for conflict take unexpected forms in diverse venues, however, and the varied examples never cease to compel attention. Some are especially awkward in terms of challenges to institutional authority. Still others pose a problem for popular beliefs. Consider several from 2008. A Capuchin monk called Padre Pio died in 1968 at the age of eighty-one in his hometown of San Giovanni Rotondo, located not far from Puglia, on the heel of Italy's boot. In April 2008 his body was exhumed and put on display until the end of the year because he had become the most popular saint in Italy, having been canonized by Pope John Paul II (who canonized more saints than any other pope). Padre Pio's appeal and mystery arose from the fact that he claimed to have stigmata similar to the wounds of Christ, from which he bled and could feel actual pain. Pope John XXIII had considered him a fraud and a womanizer, accusing him of "immense deception."[55]

Nevertheless, he is beloved by the masses. There is no lack of testimony from witnesses. "He was suffering," explained a woman with a German friend who saw him in 1966. "He had blood coming out of his hands. If you saw it, you would believe it." More than 750,000 people made reservations to view the body during the seven-month span while it was displayed in 2008. Padre Pio seems to appeal to something mystically spiritual, which many feel the Vatican does not—at least not sufficiently. Moreover, the hospitality industry in southern Italy promoted the viewing opportunity with all its might because that area receives the least amount of tourism in Italy. The man in charge of tourism for the Puglia region put it quite frankly: "This is an opportunity we have to turn religious tourism into mass tourism." Replicas of Padre Pio's "famous" half-gloves could be purchased for the equivalent of eight dollars; a snow globe of Padre Pio went for for $4.75.[56]

Unfortunately, when Padre Pio's crypt had been opened a few months earlier, in bitter cold, his hands were reported to be in perfect condition with no signs of stigmata at all. The archbishop who presided at the exhumation, Domenico D'Ambrosio, would say only the following: "As soon as we got inside we could clearly make out the beard. The top part of the skull is partly skeletal, but the chin is perfect and the rest of the body is well preserved." According to medical experts who peered at the body, neither the feet nor the hands showed any signs of the wounds expected of someone who supposedly bled spontaneously, on and off, for more than fifty years. Whether Padre Pio was duplicitous remained to be determined during the months of visitation, but the Vatican placed strict limits on the number of people who could be present when the tomb was opened. What the millions would see, and their understanding of what they saw, well, . . . differences persisted, perhaps predictably. The outcome remains inconclusive.[57]

In the summer of 2008 the Vatican requested the exhumation of England's most renowned convert to Roman Catholicism as part of his elevation toward sainthood. When John Henry Cardinal Newman died in August 1890, he was buried in the rustic cemetery at Rednal Hill, Birmingham, at the country house of the Birmingham Oratory. He shares a grave and memorial stone there with his lifelong friend Ambrose St. John, who converted to Catholicism at the same time as Newman. The pall above Newman's coffin bears his motto, "Cor ad Cor Loquitur" (Heart speaks to heart). The Vatican wants Newman's remains to be moved to a marble sarcophagus in the Birmingham Oratory, where people can pay tribute to him more easily because of urban access. It is unclear whether the two beloved friends will now be separated in death if the cardinal achieves sainthood.[58]

✠

For quite a different scenario of potential revisionism, we turn to a contested case where exhumation and reburial elsewhere is demanded because an individual's celebrated reputation has gone from philanthropic benefactor to exploitative racist. Cecil John Rhodes (1853–1902) did much to develop Zimbabwe (formerly Southern Rhodesia) and South Africa by founding the De Beers Company and the Gold Fields of South Africa. When he died a very rich man, he was buried, as he requested, on the massive *dwala* that forms the center of a dramatic site that he named the "View of the World." Although he is best remembered in the Anglo-American sphere as the generous donor of Rhodes scholarships, he is increasingly recalled in Zimbabwe as a man who sequestered land and placed locals in a condition close to slavery as they worked in mines, on farms, and in the industrial and commercial sectors.[59]

A Harare-based pressure group, mainly consisting of highly vocal Shona-speaking activists, insists that the hill where Rhodes is buried is really sacred ground on which indigenous kings were laid to rest. They have campaigned since the 1990s for the removal of the grave and demand that Rhodes's remains be either repatriated to England or else thrown into the Zambezi River. Not everyone in Zimbabwe agrees, however, that "View of the World" truly was a sacred burial site—it is a matter of tradition unsupported by any historical evidence—and because the site is a designated national monument protected by the National Museums and Monuments of Zimbabwe (NMMZ), the site has considerable touristic value. Hence the domestic division over Rhodes's possible reinterment elsewhere.[60]

A compromise solution under consideration is to leave Rhodes where he is but redefine the concept of "national heritage" to include more native sites. Meanwhile, Cecil Rhodes remains in situ despite activists' threats to toss him into the Zambezi.[61] Rhodes's case is intriguing both because of the obvious postcolonial backlash, but also as an example of exhumation being demanded because of a dramatic *decline* in reputation locally, rather than a rediscovery and redemption in historical esteem.

✠

Turning to a totally different type of recent "revisionism," this one resulting from new radiocarbon dating techniques, the English site we know as Stonehenge, located on the Salisbury Plain, has been at least partially demystified—not how it was built but its genesis. Archaeologists based at the University of Sheffield have determined from human cremation burials among and around the massive stones that the site was first used as a cemetery, from about 3,000 BCE until *after* the megaliths were erected sometime around 2,500 BCE. What appeared to be the head of a stone mace, a symbol of authority, was found in one grave, suggesting that this must have been a grave site for the ruling dynasty responsible for erecting Stonehenge. In medieval literature there are stories speaking of Stonehenge as a memorial to the dead—anecdotal evidence, to be sure, but consistent with what the archaeologists are now indicating.[62]

They estimate that as many as 240 people were buried at Stonehenge, all of them as cremation deposits. Evidence from elsewhere in the British Isles indicates that skeletal burials were quite rare at that time and that cremation was the normative custom for the elite. Yet another member of the research team from Sheffield proposes the likelihood that the burials at Stonehenge actually represent generations of a single royal family. Why? The number of burials in the earliest phase (3000 BCE) was relatively small, with larger numbers of burials occurring in the later stages, thereby suggesting a multiplication of offspring. The Stonehenge Riverside Project has been excavating since 2003 with support from the National Geographic Society. Most of the cremated remains were actually uncovered decades ago, but only in recent years have improved methods of radiocarbon dating made it possible to analyze burned bones with reliable accuracy.[63]

✚

When we consider European reburials with an unusually high degree of symbolic content and public performance, such as Jean Moulin's in 1964, two for Imre Nagy in 1988–89 (first in Paris and then in Budapest), or Frederick the Great's political fracas in 1991, American situations come to mind that were similarly high in civic symbolism for contemporaries, albeit much less recent: James Monroe in 1831, Daniel Boone in 1845, Jefferson Davis in 1893, James Wilson and John Paul Jones in 1905–6. During the past century, however, Europe quite clearly exceeds the United States in emblematic exhumations as ideological referenda.

And that raises the question why. As a speculative answer, consider just six lines drawn from W. H. Auden's famous poem about the start of World War II, titled "September 1, 1939":

> Exiled Thucydides knew
> All that a speech can say
> About Democracy,
> And what dictators do,
> The elderly rubbish they talk
> To an apathetic grave.

Nation-states elsewhere have had a marked history of political leaders (and dictators) determined to use exhumation and reburial as a political tool or weapon, which eventually, more often than not, elicits a responsive determination to set the record straight. One thinks of Chiang Kai-shek's exploitation of Sun Yat-sen, Hitler's of Frederick the Great, Juan Perón and Carlos Menem's resuscitation of Juan Manuel de Rosas, and the anti-Communists' resurrection of Imre Nagy. Some Americans have considered Abraham Lincoln's wartime policies as dictatorial yet unavoidable, or similarly regard Franklin Roosevelt's quasi-constitutional measures to fight the Great Depression, but we really have no history of dictatorial leaders who have grievously manipulated death for partisan advantage. John Adams did not do so when Washington died in 1799. Nor was it done by Andrew Johnson in 1865, nor Theodore Roosevelt in 1901, and it was done only minimally by Lyndon B. Johnson after 1963.

Although as we have seen there are many parallels and similarities between celebrity reburials in the Old World and the New, I am ultimately more impressed by several fundamental contrasts. To mention a significant though hardly the most important one first, issues of religious conformity versus heterodoxy in Europe often posed problems largely unknown in the United States. The contested cases of Lajos Kossuth (a Lutheran), Adam Mickiewicz (a lapsed Catholic), William Butler Yeats (a nonobservant Catholic), Vladimir Jabotinsky (a radically revisionist Jew), all discussed in the first chapter, and Padre Pio (a self-dramatizing priest) come promptly to mind. Robert Ingersoll's atheism and F. Scott Fitzgerald's lapsed Catholicism provide rather unusual but minor blips on the American side.

The relationship and connections between exhumation/reburial and nationalism lead us to a much more meaningful basis for comparison.

Issues involving national unity or identity seem to have been more pressing, persistent, impassioned, and politicized in Europe, as we have seen, for example, in the cases of Frederick the Great, Adam Mickiewicz, and Communist Hungary's symbolic need for Bela Bartók's body in 1988.

Amid the sectional tensions that troubled nineteenth-century America, especially in the decades before and following the Civil War, New York nevertheless gave James Monroe back to Virginia very graciously in 1858, and Rhode Island quite reasonably acceded to Georgia's request to keep the remains of Nathanael Greene in 1902. The relocation of Confederate dead from Northern battlegrounds to Southern cemeteries, noted in chapter 3, might be cited, but those partisan and intensely felt issues were resolved fairly promptly because the North felt no great need or desire to keep the remains of vanquished rebels—quite the contrary. And the Northern press covered the reburial of Jefferson Davis with considerable interest but little recrimination. The federal government never even brought Davis to trial for treason, though it very well could have.

✢

In June 2008 the former (and final) Soviet leader, Mikhail Gorbachev, urged that the embalmed body of Vladimir Lenin, leader of the Bolshevik Revolution in 1917, should be moved from its reverential mausoleum in Red Square, where it has rested since his death in 1924, and given a standard burial. Lenin's literal and symbolic presence in the heart of Moscow has provided an ongoing source of controversy since the collapse of the Soviet Union in 1991. Gorbachev explained that, in his view, "we should not be occupied right now with grave-digging. But we will necessarily come to a time when the mausoleum will have lost its meaning and we will bury [Lenin], give him up to the earth as his family had wanted. I think the time will come." Perhaps he is right, but the Communists still remain the second largest political party in Russia. Although the Orthodox Church has also called for Lenin's exhumation and reburial, echoing the suggestion made initially by Boris Yeltsin, the first post-Soviet leader, Communists insist that the founding father of the Soviet Union should stay put. Vladimir Putin acknowledged that the issue is an emotional one and has not committed himself to either side. So the outcome remains unclear. The great irony, of course, though scarcely remembered, is that Lenin and his wife, just like John Calvin and Baron Von Steuben, personally disapproved of visibly memorializing the dead![64]

What also remains unclear is our ability to generalize about the historical "democratization" (a term used advisedly) of burial and reinterment. Those who would prefer to have Lenin receive a much less honorific interment would seem to be tending in that direction—perhaps as an end to Soviet sanctification. As noted in chapter 3, democratization also appears to have been the rationale behind look-alike tombstones in national military cemeteries in the United States and later in Western Europe. Once upon a time, long, long ago, those with high political status received far more elaborate burial in preferred sites, as we know from ancient Egypt, Stonehenge, and the Spiro Mounds in eastern Oklahoma. Ordinary folks were either cremated or interred on the periphery of a special burial ground, often impermanently. Their bones were disposable. No democracy of the dead in those days.[65]

Next consider the transition from the eighteenth to the mid-nineteenth century in the United States. Civil society shifted from comparatively low-key burials with few or modest grave markers in the colonial period to an era when affluent people began to outdo themselves in erecting elaborate vaults and monuments in the "natural paradise" that Mount Auburn and its emulating suburban cemeteries aspired to be. The key distinction to keep in mind, of course, is that government-run cemeteries could be readily democratized after the Civil War, but for those people in the private sector where families owned their own plots, options remained at the discretion of affluent purchasers. In the twentieth century, however, a trend away from grandiosity gradually became apparent, even at private burial grounds. Conspicuous consumption in death diminished somewhat.

Ultimately, European conflicts involving reburial were more likely to become not only intensely politicized—note the fanatical democratization of death that accompanied the French Revolution, yet also the deconsecration of the Panthèon as a site for special reinterments— but often *internationalized*, as we have seen in the episodes concerning Adam Mickiewicz on the Continent, Baron von Richthofen in France and Germany, Lajos Kossuth, and Imre Nagy (keeping in mind the 1988 French embarrassment of Hungary by its honoring of Nagy at Père Lachaise Cemetery, a famous site that also figures in several other episodes that we have considered).[66] The reinterments of John Howard Payne ("Home Sweet Home") and John Paul Jones are rather unusual examples of Americans requiring international action. There is much to be learned from the diverse narratives of American burials, and much more illumination is to be had by observing the contrasts with disputatious stories of contestation that took place in foreign lands.

✠

A major stimulus for this project occurred when I encountered two excellent books dealing with Eastern Europe: anthropologist Katherine Verdery's *The Political Lives of Dead Bodies* (1999) and cultural historian István Rév's *Retroactive Justice* (2005). Although I was already familiar with numerous sagas of exhumation and reburial in the United States, duly noticed out of sheer curiosity and serendipity over a span of several decades, their political resonance and the persistent role of pride were not immediately apparent to me. The recorded narratives of figures like John Paul Jones and Daniel Boone initially seemed rather different from each other and from their European counterparts. In recent years, and with closer scrutiny of many more episodes, although significant contrasts remain, the differences cluster within discernible patterns. Certain similarities have seemed increasingly noteworthy, such as the rehabilitation of individual reputations, pride of possession, devoted adulation of celebrities, and especially the imperatives of commercial tourism. The last is definitely not a distinctively American thing.

Moreover, exhumation and reburial have more often been a tradition-oriented phenomenon with conservative or "preservationist" appeal rather than a cause customarily taken up by progressives, and that is true everywhere. Within the United States I think of the Masonic Dr. Joseph Warren, James Monroe, John Trumbull, and Jefferson Davis as prime examples of tradition-oriented causes. The fates of Robert Ingersoll and Matthew Henson, however, represent progressive outcomes in which invidious distinctions of disbelief and color were overcome. Elsewhere one thinks of Jean Moulin (1964), Juan Manuel de Rosas (1989), and Frederick the Great (1991) as exhumations that served the needs of conciliating nationalists and were stridently opposed by leftist liberals, at least initially.

In contrast, when Karl Marx, who had lived in most of the major European capitals, died in March 1883, he was buried in what is now the rather crowded and funky Highgate Cemetery in North London, joined there fifteen months later by his wife Jenny. No one has proposed relocating them. To the best of my knowledge, his birthplace in Trier (situated in Prussia) has never asked for him.

We must also consider that with each of the striking categories of comparison just mentioned, human agency has been crucial. It matters even more than contingency. Reburials rarely occur by accident or serendipity; they are very carefully planned material events. Recall these four lines penned by Richard Wilbur in 1956:

> What is our praise or pride
> But to imagine excellence, and try to make it.
> What does it say over the door of Heaven
> But *homo fecit*?[67]

The challenging contrast that remains, however, clearly lies in the realm of political sentiment and discourse. Here, perhaps, we find the most important contrasts between the United States and elsewhere. Although many American reburials were quite obviously motivated politically, they mostly seem to have lacked the ongoing ideological edge and intensity of those European reburials where feelings were fiercely fired by anti-Communism (see Nagy) or pro- and anti-Fascism (see Mussolini) or anti-clericalism (see Voltaire).

Revisiting Alexis de Tocqueville's *Democracy in America* brings to mind once again his emphasis upon the American republican consensus and its legacy. A brief passage from each volume of *Democracy* (1835 and 1840) highlights his theme of how very much Americans shared in common compared with Europeans.

> What is meant by a republic in the United States is the slow and quiet action of society upon itself. It is an orderly state founded in reality upon the enlightened will of the nation. It is a conciliatory government where resolutions ripen over time, are discussed slowly and executed only when fully matured. . . . Americans frequently change their laws but the basis of the constitution is respected.[68]

> I have often noticed that theories which are by their nature revolutionary, in that they can be realized only by a complete and sometimes

sudden upheaval in the rights of property or the status of persons, are infinitely less to people's liking in the United States than in the great monarchies of Europe.[69]

Because Americans had less interest in political theory and were less ideological, their society was more stable despite its penchant for perpetual change. Never having had an *ancien régime* or hence a reaction against it, the United States never developed a strong tradition of socialism, a point reiterated and embellished in the twentieth century by the German sociologist Werner Sombart and the American political scientist Louis Hartz. In 1955 Hartz devoted an influential book to a recondite elaboration of Tocqueville and of Lionel Trilling's observation in 1950 that "in the United states at this time liberalism is not only the dominant but even the sole intellectual tradition."[70]

As Tocqueville so astutely noticed, using his innovative approach to the study of politics and society, Americans could very clearly differ among themselves, but not (save for 1861–65) with the enduring and irreconcilable ferocity of monarchists versus republicans, socialists versus capitalists, or Communists versus liberal democrats in Europe. It is not that partisanship has been lacking in America. It began in earnest quite early in George Washington's first administration, when Hamiltonians and Jeffersonians differed on domestic as well as foreign policy. But partisanship here has not, for the most part, had quite the same unbridgeable ideological chasm that has been endemic in European history, and this has had important consequences in contrasting our episodes of exhumation.

Given that long historical context and comparative framework, I believe we are now better situated to comprehend many of the apparent differences between Old and New World experiences with the politics of reburial. While similarities are not unexpected, the differences appear more pronounced. The explanation lies in the contrasts between two kinds of political cultures—one more nearly univocal in terms of basic democratic values, the other with partisans speaking past one another.

# NOTES

## INTRODUCTION

1. Donald E. Collins, *The Death and Resurrection of Jefferson Davis* (Lanham, Md.: Rowman and Littlefield, 2005), 67–88, the quotation at 88.
2. Ibid., 90–94.
3. Ibid., 95–111, the quotation at 103. For an explanation of the etymology of *translation*, see Russell Shorto, *Descartes' Bones: A Skeletal History of the Conflict between Faith and Reason* (New York: Doubleday, 2008), 51–52.
4. Collins, *Death and Resurrection of Jefferson Davis*, 96.
5. Ibid., 110–21; the general is quoted on 154.
6. Ibid., 118, 122–25.
7. *Richmond Dispatch*, September 18, 1892.
8. Collins, *Death and Resurrection of Davis*, 137–47.
9. Ibid., 149–53.
10. Herodotus, *The Persian Wars*, trans. George Rawlinson (New York: Modern Library, 1942), 36–38, the quotation at 37.
11. Plutarch, *The Rise and Fall of Athens: Nine Greek Lives*, trans. Ian Scott-Kilvert (London: Penguin, 1960), 149–50. I am indebted to classicist Hunter R. Rawlings for these citations.

## CHAPTER ONE

1. See George Mosse, *Fallen Soldiers: Reshaping the Memory of the World Wars* (New York: Oxford University Press, 1990), 39–40. William Wordsworth preferred the cypress. See John Morley, *Death, Heaven, and the Victorians* (Pittsburgh: University of Pittsburgh Press, 1971), 49.
2. Mosse, *Fallen Soldiers*, 40–41, 82–84;

Jay Winter, *Sites of Memory, Sites of Mourning: The Great War in European Cultural History* (Cambridge: Cambridge University Press, 1995).
3. See Blanche M. G. Linden, *Silent City on a Hill: Picturesque Landscapes of Memory and Boston's Mount Auburn Cemetery*, 2nd ed. (Amherst: University of Massachusetts Press, 2007), 19–20, 24, 227.
4. See Allan I. Ludwig, *Graven Images: New England Stonecarving and Its Symbols, 1650–1815* (Middletown, Conn.: Wesleyan University Press, 1966); James A. Hijiya, "American Gravestones and Attitudes toward Death: A Brief History," *Proceedings of the American Philosophical Society*, 127, no. 5 (1983), 339–63.
5. Marilyn Yalom, *The American Resting Place: Four Hundred Years of History through Our Cemeteries and Burial Grounds* (Boston: Houghton Mifflin, 2008), 11–12.
6. Joseph B. Doyle, *Frederick William Von Steuben and the American Revolution* (Steubenville, Ohio: H. C. Cook, 1913), 351, 354.
7. Ibid., 376; *New York Times*, October 1, 1872, 1; John McCauley Palmer, *General Von Steuben* (New Haven, Conn.: Yale University Press, 1937), 403–4. In 1936 a replica of Von Steuben's log home was built in the park, based upon a sketch made in 1802 by a traveling clergyman.
8. Linden, *Silent City on a Hill*, 4, 23, 26–27, 86, 163.
9. Mark S. Schantz, *Awaiting the Heavenly Country: The Civil War and America's Culture of Death* (Ithaca, N.Y.: Cornell University Press, 2008), 38, 40, 47, 50. The last quotation (italics mine) is from Rufus W. Clark, *Heaven and Its Scrip-*

*tural Emblems* (Boston: John P. Jewell, 1853), 80.

10. Schantz, *Awaiting the Heavenly Country*, 53, 56.

11. Quoted in Debby Applegate, *The Most Famous Man in America: The Biography of Henry Ward Beecher* (New York: Doubleday, 2006), 36.

12. Linden, *Silent City on a Hill*, 24, 127–28, 137–38.

13. Schantz, *Awaiting the Heavenly Country*, 80–81. The "vile bodies" passage is from Philippians 3:20–21.

14. The "culture of melancholy" seems to be customarily ascribed to the second through the fourth decades of the nineteenth century, demarked especially by William Cullen Bryant's poem "Thanatopsis" (1817) and the "melancholy pleasure" of visiting rural cemeteries during the 1830s and into the 40s.

15. See Gary Laderman, *The Sacred Remains: American Attitudes toward Death, 1799–1883* (New Haven, Conn.: Yale University Press, 1996); James J. Farrell, *Inventing the American Way of Death* (Philadelphia: Temple University Press, 1980).

16. See David Charles Sloane, *The Last Great Necessity: Cemeteries in American History* (Baltimore: Johns Hopkins University Press, 1991), 1–6.

17. See Jessica Mitford, *The American Way of Death* (New York: Simon and Schuster, 1963); Drew Gilpin Faust, *The Republic of Suffering: Death and the American Civil War* (New York: Alfred A. Knopf, 2008).

18. Peter Metcalf and Richard Huntington, *Celebrations of Death: The Anthropology of Mortuary Ritual*, 2nd ed. (New York: Cambridge University Press, 1991); David Stannard, ed., *Death in America* (Philadelphia: University of Pennsylvania Press, 1975); Margaretta J. Darnall, "The American Cemetery as Picturesque Landscape: Bellefontaine Cemetery, St. Louis," *Winterthur Portfolio* 19 (Winter 1983), 249–69.

19. See Annette Becker, "War Memorials: A Legacy of Total War?" in *On the Road to Total War: The American Civil War and the German Wars of Unification, 1861–1871*, ed. Stig Förster and Jörg Nagler, (Washington, D.C.: German Historical Institute, 1997); Sanford Levinson, *Written in Stone: Public Monuments in Changing Societies* (Durham, N.C.: Duke University Press, 1998); Hijiya, "American Gravestones and Attitudes towards Death."

20. For an excellent example of Federalist versus Republican partisanship and conflict in 1813 involving three burials of the first American "martyr" in the War of 1812, see Robert E. Cray Jr., "The Death and Burials of Captain James Lawrence: Wartime Mourning in the Early Republic," *New York History* 83 (Spring 2002): 133–64.

21. See "Bodies of Civil War Dead Moved to Provide New Veteran Graves," *New York Times*, June 29, 1980, 30; Michael C. Kearl and Anoel Rinaldi, "The Political Uses of the Dead as Symbols in Contemporary Civil Religions," *Social Forces* 61 (March 1983): 701.

22. See Annette Gordon-Reed, *Thomas Jefferson and Sally Hemings: An American Controversy* (Charlottesville: University of Virginia Press, 1997); "DNA Tests Confirm the Deaths of the Last Missing Romanovs," *New York Times*, May 1, 2008, A12.

23. Robert Pogue Harrison, *The Dominion of the Dead* (Chicago: University of Chicago Press, 2003), xi.

24. See Cray, "Death and Burials of Captain James Lawrence," 133–64.

25. See http://www.congressionalcemetery.org. I am indebted to Mary Wright, stewardship program director at the Congressional Cemetery, for providing me with an abundant amount of printed information about the cemetery and its history.

26. Peter Andrews, *In Honored Glory: The Story of Arlington* (New York: G. P. Putnam's Sons, 1966), chap. 2.

27. Zora Neale Hurston to W. E. B. Du Bois, June 11, 1945, in *The Correspondence of W. E. B. Du Bois*, ed. Herbert Aptheker (Amherst: University of Massachusetts Press, 1978), 3:41–42. Du Bois replied on July 11, 1945, that the idea "has its attractions but I am afraid that the practical difficulties are too great" (ibid., 43).

28. In March 2008, President Vladimir Putin of Russia launched the creation of a Federal Military Memorial Cemetery, designed to be Russia's counterpart to Arlington National Cemetery, possibly to be located on a wasteland in northern Moscow. Putin hopes to be buried there himself, somewhere close to Stalin, his hero. It is due for completion in 2010.

29. Eric M. Meyers, *Jewish Ossuaries: Reburial and Rebirth, Secondary Burials in Their Near Eastern Setting* (Rome: Biblical Institute Press, 1971), 15–16, 31, 63, 72.

30. G. E. Mylonas, "Homeric and Mycenaean Burial Customs," *American Journal of Archaeology* 52 (January 1948): 56–81. In the Homeric epics the dead are cremated; but we know from archaeological evidence that in Mycenaean times the deceased were inhumed—an interesting discrepancy.

31. Christopher Columbus has two "official" tombs, one in Seville, where he was buried in the cathedral, and another in Santo Domingo.

32. Caroline Walker Bynum, *The Resurrection of the Body in Western Christianity, 200–1336* (New York: Columbia University Press, 1995), 201–3, 212. See also Katharine Park, "The Life of the Corpse: Division and Dissection in Late Medieval Europe," *Journal of the History of Medicine and Allied Sciences* 50 (1995): 111–32.

33. Johan Huizinga, *The Waning of the Middle Ages* (1924, reprint Garden City, N.Y.: Doubleday, 1956), 143–44; Jacob Burckhardt, *The Civilization of the Renaissance in Italy* (1876, reprint New York: Harper and Row, 1958), 2:466; Russell Shorto, *Descartes' Bones: A Skeletal History of the Conflict between Faith and Reason* (New York: Doubleday, 2008), 50–52.

34. See Philippe Ariès, *Images of Man and Death* (Cambridge, Mass.: Harvard University Press, 1985), 14, 19; Peter Brown, *The Cult of the Saints: Its Rise and Function in Late Christianity* (Chicago: University of Chicago Press, 1981).

35. I am indebted for the following to Shorto, *Descartes' Bones*.

36. Ibid., 42, 47–48.

37. Ibid., 69.

38. Ibid., 106, 109–10, 118, 126–29.

39. Ibid., 127, 139, 212, and passim.

40. In 2009 Descartes' skull was relocated to the school in La Fiche where he studied as a boy.

41. See Roger Pearson, *Voltaire Almighty: A Life in Pursuit of Freedom* (New York: Bloomsbury, 2005), 387–91; Haydn Mason, *Voltaire: A Biography* (Baltimore: Johns Hopkins University Press, 1981), 149–51; Craig Nelson, *Thomas Paine: Enlightenment, Revolution, and the Birth of Modern Nations* (New York: Viking, 2006), 329.

42. Gail S. Altman, *Fatal Links: The Curious Deaths of Beethoven and the Two Napoleons* (Tallahassee, Fla.: Anubian, 1999).

43. Michelle Vovelle, "Le Deuil Bourgeois: Du faire-part à la statuaire funéraire," *Le Débat*, no. 12 (May 1981): 60–82; Jean Seznec, "Michelet in Germany: A Journey in Self-Discovery," *History and Theory* 16, no. 1 (1977): 3. For an 1897 image of a man lifting his fiancée from her tomb, see Ariès, *Images of Man and Death*, plate 306. For a nineteenth-century view of Père Lachaise Cemetery, see Ariès, plate 342.

44. Peter Karsten, *Patriot-Heroes in England and America: Political Symbolism and Changing Values over Three Centuries* (Madison: University of Wisconsin Press, 1978), 114, 129, 161; Barbara

Graustark in "Newsmakers," *Newsweek*, March 20, 1978, 67.

45. Martha Lampland, "Death of a Hero: Hungarian National Identity and the Funeral of Lajos Kossuth," *Hungarian Studies* 8, no. 1 (1993): 29–35.

46. Patrice M. Dabrowski, "Eloquent Ashes: The Translation of Adam Mickiewicz's Remains," chapter 3 in *Commemorations and the Shaping of Modern Poland* (Bloomington: Indiana University Press, 2004). I am indebted to this fine book for all that follows.

47. Ibid., 84–86.

48. Ibid., 86–87.

49. Ibid., 88.

50. Ibid., 90.

51. Ibid., 96–99.

52. R. F. Foster, *W. B. Yeats: A Life*, vol. 2, *The Arch-Poet, 1915–1939* (Oxford: Oxford University Press, 2003), 653–55.

53. Ibid., 656–57.

54. Ibid., 657.

55. Alan Cowell, "Ancestors Are Revered and Living Well in Madagascar," *New York Times*, July 26, 1983, A2; the quotation from Katherine Verdery, *The Political Lives of Dead Bodies: Reburial and Postsocialist Change* (New York: Columbia University Press, 1999), 42.

56. Ralph Waldo Emerson, "Works and Days" (1857), in *The Complete Works* (Boston, 1904), 7:177. In the preceding paragraph he insisted that "the use of history is to give value to the present hour and its duty."

57. Wallace Evan Davies, *Patriotism on Parade: The Story of Veterans' and Hereditary Organizations in America, 1783–1900* (Cambridge, Mass.: Harvard University Press, 1955); D. O. S. Lowell, "The Quest of Ancestors," *Munsey's Magazine* 34 (February 1906): 543–48; Florida Pier, "The Power of Ancestors," *Century* 71 (January 1906): 445–47. For an early but significant example of this impulse, see François Weil, "John Farmer and the Making of American Genealogy," *New

England Quarterly* 80 (September 2007): 408–34.

58. See Levinson, *Written in Stone*, 38–68.

59. See David Lowenthal, *The Past Is a Foreign Country* (Cambridge: Cambridge University Press, 1985), 321–24.

60. "Rossini's Remains Exhumed," *Washington Post*, May 3, 1887, 1; "Payne," in *Dictionary of American Biography*.

61. "Rachmaninoff, Buried in New York, May Return to Russia," *New York Times*, April 1, 1992, 31. To view Rachmaninoff's grave, go to the Kensico website, http://kensico.org/historic-scenic-tour .asp, and click on #27.

62. "Reburial of Herzl in Jerusalem Set," *Washington Post*, August 8, 1949, 3.

63. Myron J. Aronoff (Rutgers University), "The Origins of Israeli Political Culture," paper prepared for an international conference, Israeli Democracy under Stress: Cultural and Institutional Perspectives, held at the Hoover Institute, Stanford, June 27–July 1, 1990, 13.

64. Ibid.

65. Louise Hall Tharp, *Saint-Gaudens and the Gilded Era* (Boston: Little, Brown, 1969), 119. It is noteworthy that Polybius reported comparable practices when members of the Roman political and military elite died. See *Polybius on Roman Imperialism: The Histories of Polybius*, ed. Alvin H. Bernstein (South Bend, Ind.: Regnery, 1980), 215–16.

66. *Journals of Ralph Waldo Emerson, 1856–1863*, ed. E. W. Emerson and W. E. Forbes (Boston: Houghton Mifflin, 1913), 9:102–3. It is very odd that this rather curious act by Emerson is not mentioned in the standard biographies.

67. Kenneth A. Lockridge, *The Diary and Early Life of William Byrd II of Virginia, 1674–1744* (Chapel Hill: University of North Carolina Press, 1987), 43; Pierre Marambaud, *William Byrd of Westover, 1674–1744* (Charlottesville: University Press of Virginia, 1971).

68. Quoted in Laderman, *Sacred Remains*, 36.

CHAPTER TWO

1. See John J. Pullen, *Patriotism in America: A Study of Changing Devotions, 1770–1970* (New York: American Heritage, 1971); Cecilia O'Leary, *To Die For: The Paradox of American Patriotism* (Princeton, N.J.: Princeton University Press, 1999); Stuart McConnell, "Nationalism," in *Encyclopedia of the United States in the Twentieth Century*, ed. Stanley Kutler (New York: Charles Scribner's Sons, 1996), 1:251–71.

2. See Hans Kohn, *American Nationalism: An Interpretive Essay* (New York: Macmillan, 1957); John Breuilly, *Nationalism and the State* (Chicago: University of Chicago Press, 1984); Wilbur Zelinsky, *Nation into State: The Shifting Symbolic Foundations of American Nationalism* (Chapel Hill: University of North Carolina Press, 1988); John Pettegrew, " 'The Soldier's Faith': Turn-of-the-Century Memory of the Civil War and the Emergence of Modern American Nationalism," *Journal of Contemporary History* 31 (January 1996): 49–73; Ronald Beiner, ed., *Theorizing Nationalism* (Albany: SUNY Press, 1999); Anatol Lieven, *America Right or Wrong: An Anatomy of American Nationalism* (New York: Oxford University Press, 2004).

3. Robert Cray Jr., "Commemorating the Prison Ship Dead: Revolutionary Memory and the Politics of Sepulture in the Early Republic, 1776–1808," *William and Mary Quarterly*, 3rd ser., 56 (July 1999): 565–90.

4. Ibid., 573, 583–84, 587. See also Matthew Dennis, "Patriotic Remains: Bones of Contention in the Early Republic," in *Mortal Remains: Death in Early America*, ed. Nancy Isenberg and Andrew Burstein (Philadelphia: University of Pennsylvania Press, 2003), 144–47.

5. Walt Whitman, *The Complete Poetry and Prose*, ed. Malcolm Cowley (New York: Pellegrini and Cudahy, 1948), 434–35. Whitman's poem seems to date from

1888. The highly significant tomb of Alexander the Great became obscure and lost in antiquity, despite claims by several Egyptian Ptolemies to know its location and therefore to be Alexander's political heirs.

6. Cray, "Commemorating the Prison Ship Dead," 588–90.

7. John Cary, *Joseph Warren: Physician, Politician, Patriot* (Urbana: University of Illinois Press, 1961), 222–23; Blanche Linden-Ward, *Silent City on a Hill: Landscapes of Memory and Boston's Mount Auburn Cemetery* (Columbus: Ohio State University Press, 1989), 148.

8. A Bostonian, *Biographical Sketch of Gen. Joseph Warren . . . with the Celebrated Eulogy Pronounced by Perez Morton, M.M., on the Re-interment of the Remains by the Masonic Order, at King's Chapel in 1776* (Boston: Shepard, Clark, and Brown, 1857), 67, 73, 75–76, 78, 80–81. For the centrality of antebellum eschatology, see Mark Schantz, *Awaiting the Heavenly Country: The Civil War and America's Culture of Death* (Ithaca, N.Y.: Cornell University Press, 2008), chap. 2.

9. General Hugh Mercer, who may have persuaded George Washington to cross the Delaware River in December 1776, was killed in a skirmish with the British just prior to the Battle of Princeton and died a painful death on January 12, 1777. Originally interred at the Christ Church Burial Ground in Philadelphia, in 1840 he was exhumed and reinterred at Laurel Hill Cemetery. See his Wikipedia entry for excellent recent photographs of his burial site and monument at Laurel Hill. His original gravestone was brought from Christ Church and rests in front of the elaborate 1840s monument.

10. George Vaux, "Settlers in Merion— The Harrison Family and Harriton Plantation," *Pennsylvania Magazine of History and Biography* 13, no. 4 (1889): 453–54. This version of what occurred in 1838, and at whose initiative, has been

contested. Resolution awaits publication of an essay by historian Elliott Shore of Bryn Mawr College, who has been kind enough to share with me his work-in-progress "A Philadelphia Story."

11. Vaux, "Settlers in Merion," 455. Shore is skeptical of Vaux's version that it occurred in the "middle of the night." Nevertheless, he quotes ("A Philadelphia Story," 11) from a contemporary who owned the original burial site and lamented "*the clandestine manner* it was removed to a public cemetery for the purpose of giving éclat to a particular locality."

12. Vaux, "Settlers in Merion," 455–57. For a succinct variant of this scenario that closely follows the Vaux account, see Boyd Stanley Schlenther, *Charles Thomson: A Patriot's Pursuit* (Newark: University of Delaware Press, 1990), 222–23, which properly calls attention to the conflicting property interests among divided descendants of Charles and Hannah Thompson.

13. J. Edwin Hendricks, *Charles Thomson and the Making of a New Nation, 1729–1824* (Rutherford, N.J.: Fairleigh Dickinson University Press, 1979), 190–91, also calls attention to the possibility that the wrong bodies were unearthed because of inadequate markers.

14. Blanche M. G. Linden, *Silent City on a Hill: Picturesque Landscapes of Memory and Boston's Mount Auburn Cemetery*, 2nd ed. (Amherst: University of Massachusetts Press, 2007), 190–91, 195; Marilyn Yalom, *The American Resting Place: Four Hundred Years of History through Our Cemeteries and Burial Grounds* (Boston: Houghton Mifflin, 2008), 102–3.

15. The most complete account, on which I rely here, is by Michael P. Gabriel, *Major General Richard Montgomery: The Making of an American Hero* (Madison, N.J.: Fairleigh Dickinson University Press, 2002), 190–93.

16. Ibid., 193–94. According to one older

but apparently reliable source, the efforts of John Pintard, founder of the New-York Historical Society, were instrumental in having Montgomery's remains buried at St. Paul's. See James Grant Wilson, *The Life and Letters of Fitz-Greene Halleck* (New York: D. Appleton, 1869), 512.

17. Gabriel, *Richard Montgomery*, 194–95.

18. Ibid., 196–97. Italics mine.

19. Ibid., 197–98.

20. Ibid., 199.

21. I have depended most heavily on Paul David Nelson, *Anthony Wayne: Soldier of the Early Republic* (Bloomington: Indiana University Press, 1985).

22. Ibid., 300–301.

23. Ibid., 302.

24. Ibid., 302–3.

25. Kirk Savage, "The Self-Made Monument: George Washington and the Fight to Erect a National Memorial," *Winterthur Portfolio* 22 (Winter 1987): 225–42, esp. 231. In 1930–31, when Washington's birthplace was being excavated and reconstructed in Wakefield, Virginia, remains of his ancestors were disinterred from the family burying ground and reburied in an impressive ceremony, and a new memorial was erected. See Seth C. Bruggeman, *Here George Washington Was Born: Memory, Material Culture, and the Public History of a National Monument* (Athens: University of Georgia Press, 2008), 195.

26. "Washington's Remains," *New York Times*, August 3, 1889, 4. Nevertheless, relics related to Washington were distributed among members of his circle. At the museum home of Elizabeth Powel in Philadelphia there is a kind of relic case containing a lock of Washington's hair and a fragment from his casket, given to Powel as mementoes of her departed friend. I am indebted to David W. Maxey for this information.

27. Theodore Sizer, ed., *The Autobiography of Colonel John Trumbull: Patriot-Artist,*

*1756–1843* (New York: Da Capo, 1970), 378–80 (an appendix reprinted from the Walpole Society *Note Book*, 1948).

28. Ibid., 380–81.
29. Ibid., 381–82.
30. Ibid., 382.
31. See Gerald M. Carbone, *Nathanael Greene: A Biography of the American Revolution* (New York: Palgrave Macmillan, 2008).
32. Terry Golway, *Washington's General: Nathanael Greene and the Triumph of the American Revolution* (New York: Henry Holt, 2005), chaps. 11–12.
33. Russell F. Weigley, "Nathanael Greene," in *Encyclopedia of American Biography*, ed. John A. Garraty (New York: Harper & Row, 1974), 451–53; Carbone, *Nathanael Greene*, chap. 6.
34. *The Remains of Major General Nathanael Greene* (Providence, R.I.: E. L. Freeman and Sons, 1903), 95–96. This very rare book is much more revealing for our purposes than any biography of Greene.
35. Ibid., 105–11, 113, 229.
36. Ibid., 111, 118, 122.
37. Ibid., 135, 140.
38. Ibid., 123, 126–27.
39. Ibid., 128–30. Italics mine.
40. Ibid., 143–44.
41. Ibid., 113, 123, 130, 137. See David W. Blight, *Race and Reunion: The Civil War in American Memory* (Cambridge, Mass.: Harvard University Press, 2001), esp. chaps. 5–7; Paul H. Buck, *The Road to Reunion, 1865–1900* (Boston: Little, Brown, 1937), chaps. 11, 13.
42. Don Higginbotham, *Daniel Morgan: Revolutionary Rifleman* (Chapel Hill: University of North Carolina Press, 1961), 130–55.
43. Quoted in North Callahan, *Daniel Morgan: Ranger of the Revolution* (New York: Holt, Rinehart, and Winston, 1961), 297.
44. William L. Clark, in *Dedication of Mount Hebron Cemetery, in Winchester, Virginia, June 22, 1844* . . . (Winchester, Va.: Republican Office, 1845), 20. My italics.

45. Ibid., 13.
46. Ibid., 6.
47. Callahan, *Daniel Morgan*, 298; Higginbotham, *Daniel Morgan*, 214. For reasons unknown, a Daniel Morgan Monument Association was formed in 1911 in Portland, Maine; but it too did nothing for the new burial site.
48. "Court Gets Reburial Fight," *Washington Post*, August 13, 1951, B1; "Who Gets the General's Body?" *Life* 31 (September 3, 1951): 53–54.
49. Higginbotham, *Daniel Morgan*, 215; Callahan, *Daniel Morgan*, 298.
50. Roger M. Williams, "Who's Got Button's Bones?" *American Heritage* 17 (February 1966): 28–29.
51. Ibid., 30.
52. Ibid., 31.
53. Ibid.
54. Ibid., 31–32.
55. Ibid., 102.
56. Ibid; "Button Gwinnett Is Buried Again," *Washington Post*, October 3, 1964, C31.
57. "Lord Howe's Bones Found," *New York Times*, October 11, 1889, 1.
58. James Austin Holden, "New Historical Light on the Real Burial Place of George Augustus Lord Viscount Howe, 1758," in *Proceedings of the New York Historical Association* 10 (1911): 302. The 1910 meeting of NYSHA was actually held at Fort Ticonderoga, which made the contents of these proceedings especially lively.
59. Ibid., 304–5.
60. Ibid., 306–7.
61. Michael Meranze, "Major André's Exhumation," in *Mortal Remains: Death in Early America*, ed. Nancy Isenberg and Andrew Burstein (Philadelphia: University of Pennsylvania Press, 2003), 124–26, 128–29. Given the bitter feelings about Washington's unyielding treatment of André, it is fascinating that when James Lawrence, captain of the USS *Chesapeake*, was killed in a naval battle off the coast of Massachusetts in 1813, the British victors took his body to

Halifax, Nova Scotia, and buried him with full military honors. See Robert E. Cray Jr., "The Death and Burials of Captain James Lawrence: Wartime Mourning in the Early Republic," *New York History* 83 (Spring 2002): 145–46.

62. Meranze, "Major André's Exhumation," 126–29; James Buchanan, "Narrative of the Exhumation of the Remains of Major André," *United Service Journal and Naval and Military Magazine* (London), pt. 3 (1833), 307–8.

63. *Niles Weekly Register*, August 18, 1821, 386; Buchanan quoted in Meranze, "Major André's Exhumation," 130, italics in the original.

64. Leo A. Bressler, "Peter Porcupine and the Bones of Thomas Paine," *Pennsylvania Magazine of History and Biography* 82 (April 1958): 176–85; Moncure Daniel Conway, *The Life of Thomas Paine . . . To Which Is Added a Sketch of Paine by William Cobbett* (New York: G. P. Putnam's Sons, 1892), 2:451–55; David Hawke, *Paine* (New York: Harper and Row, 1974), 401; Craig Nelson, *Thomas Paine: Enlightenment, Revolution, and the Birth of Modern Nations* (New York: Viking, 2006), 323, 327.

65. Nelson, *Thomas Paine*, 327–28; J. Watson, *A Brief History of the Remains of the Late Thomas Paine from the Time of Their Disinterment in 1819 by the Late William Cobbett, M.P., Down to the Year 1846* (London: J. Watson, 1847).

66. Philadelphia *Public Ledger*, January 6, 1837, 4, and February 11, 1837, 2.

67. Nelson, *Thomas Paine*, 328–30; Conway, *Life of Thomas Paine*, esp. 2:429–59.

68. James Feron, "Paine Tombstone Uncovered Upstate," *New York Times*, July 19, 1976, 31.

69. Thomas Paine, *Collected Writings*, ed. Eric Foner (New York: Library of America, 1995), 152.

70. When Alexander the Great died of a fever in Babylon in 323 BCE, his body was preserved in golden honey, interred in a golden coffin mounted on a golden temple, and hauled westward by sixty-four mules, each one wearing a golden crown. Along the way the conveyance was intercepted by one of his most trusted generals, Ptolemy, who had just become the ruler of Egypt. Ptolemy stole the body and took it back to Egypt, where his descendants showed it to such luminaries as Julius Caesar. When the Ptolemies lost their throne in 30 BCE, the mummified Alexander was lost to history, though scholars have searched for centuries. Heather Pringle, *The Mummy Congress: Science, Obsession, and the Everlasting Dead* (New York: Hyperion, 2001), 134–35.

71. Fergus M. Bordewich, *Washington: The Making of the American Capital* (New York: Amistad, 2008), 12–14, 29–30.

72. Ibid., 73–75; 81–89; Scott W. Berg, *Grand Avenues: The Story of the French Visionary Who Designed Washington, D.C.* (New York: Pantheon, 2007); Saul K. Padover, ed., *Thomas Jefferson and the Nation's Capital . . . 1783–1818* (Washington, D.C.: Government Printing Office, 1946).

73. Berg, *Grand Avenues*, 232–33, 237.

74. Ibid., 233–34, 243–44.

75. Ibid., 272–74.

76. Quoted in ibid., 274.

77. Ibid., 274–75.

78. Ibid., 275–76.

79. Ibid., 276–77.

CHAPTER THREE

1. See William A. Blair, *Cities of the Dead: Contesting the Memory of the Civil War in the South, 1865–1914* (Chapel Hill: University of North Carolina Press, 2004); Caroline E. Janney, *Burying the Dead but Not the Past: Ladies' Memorial Associations and the Lost Cause* (Chapel Hill: University of North Carolina Press, 2008); John R. Neff, *Honoring the*

*Civil War Dead: Commemoration and the Problem of Reconciliation* (Lawrence: University Press of Kansas, 2005).

2. See Caroline E. Janney, "'One of the Best Loved, North and South': The Appropriation of National Reconciliation by LaSalle Corbell Pickett," *Virginia Magazine of History and Biography* 116 (October 2008): 371–406.

3. Mary H. Mitchell, *Hollywood Cemetery: The History of a Southern Shrine* (Richmond: Virginia State Library, 1985), 35–36.

4. Ibid., 36–37.

5. Ibid., 38–39.

6. Ibid., 40.

7. Ibid.

8. Ibid., 41–42.

9. Ibid., 42–43.

10. Ibid., 44–45.

11. Stephen B. Oates, *To Purge This Land with Blood: A Biography of John Brown*, 2nd ed. (Amherst: University of Massachusetts Press, 1984), 351–53.

12. Ibid., 354–56.

13. Ibid., 357–58. Late in August 1899, on the exact anniversary of John Brown's raid at Ossawatomie, Kansas, in 1856, some of his comrades were reburied not far from his grave in North Elba, New York. *New York Times*, August 26, 1899, 6.

14. Gary Laderman, *The Sacred Remains: American Attitudes toward Death, 1799–1883* (New Haven, Conn.: Yale University Press, 1996), 90–91.

15. See Thomas J. Craughwell, *Stealing Lincoln's Body* (Cambridge, Mass.: Harvard University Press, 2007), 1–15; Neff, *Honoring the Civil War Dead*, chap. 2.

16. Lloyd Lewis, *Myths after Lincoln* (New York: Harcourt, Brace, 1929), viii, 260–61. See also Millard Lampell, "The Lonesome Train," a classic cantata about Lincoln's funeral train, first produced in 1944 on the prestigious Columbia Presents Norman Corwin radio series.

17. Lewis, *Myths after Lincoln*, 259.

18. Craughwell, *Stealing Lincoln's Body*, chaps. 2–5.

19. *New York Times*, April 14, 1887, 1; ibid., April 15, 1887, 1.

20. Craughwell, *Stealing Lincoln's Body*, 131, 208.

21. Ibid., 185–86, 193–95; Dorothy Meserve Kunhardt, "Strange History Brought to Light: Rare Photos of Lincoln Exhumation," *Life*, February 15, 1963, 86–88. The photograph on p. 86 shows the exposed coffin in 1901.

22. Craughwell, *Stealing Lincoln's Body*, 198.

23. See Hudson Strode, *Jefferson Davis* (New York: Harcourt, Brace, 1955–56), 3 vols.

24. Donald E. Collins, *The Death and Resurrection of Jefferson Davis* (Lanham, Md.: Rowman and Littlefield, 2005), chaps. 3–4; Robert Penn Warren, *Jefferson Davis Gets His Citizenship Back* (Lexington: University Press of Kentucky, 1980), 107.

25. When Stonewall Jackson was fatally wounded at Chancellorsville on May 3, 1863, his left arm was amputated and buried there with a marker. He died eight days later. In 1929 the arm was exhumed, placed in a steel box, and reburied on a plantation known as Ellwood in the Wilderness Battlefield. The only gravestone there belongs to Jackson's arm and can be visited with National Park Service permission. See http://www.roadsideamerica.com/set/arms.html.

26. Charles P. Roland, *Albert Sidney Johnston: Soldier of Three Republics* (Austin: University of Texas Press, 1964), 352–53.

27. Ibid., 353.

28. Ibid., 353–54; Thomas L. Connelly, *The Marble Man: Robert E. Lee and His Image in American Society* (New York: Alfred A. Knopf, 1977), 25.

29. Neff, *Honoring the Civil War Dead*; Blair, *Cities of the Dead*; Drew Gilpin Faust, *This Republic of Suffering: Death and the American Civil War* (New York: Alfred

A. Knopf, 2008); Janney, *Burying the Dead but Not the Past*; and Mark S. Schantz, *Awaiting the Heavenly Country: The Civil War and America's Culture of Death* (Ithaca, N.Y.: Cornell University Press, 2008).

30. Neff, *Honoring the Civil War Dead*, 108, 126.

31. James McPherson, "Dark Victories," *New York Review of Books*, April 17, 2008, 78–79.

32. Laderman, *Sacred Remains*, 110.

33. Ibid., 111–12.

34. Neff, *Honoring the Civil War Dead*, 111–15, 128.

35. Ibid., 63–64; Walter Muir Whitehill, *Boston and the Civil War* (Boston: Boston Athenaeum, 1963), 10–11.

36. Neff, *Honoring the Civil War Dead*, 56–57, 116–17.

37. Ibid., 3.

38. Janney, *Burying the Dead but Not the Past*, 46, 120–24. See also the insightful essay-review by Joan Marie Johnson, *Reviews in American History* 36 (December 2008): 529–36.

39. Janney, *Burying the Dead but Not the Past*, 9, 49, 119–32, 142–46. See also A. V. Huff Jr., "The Democratization of Art: Memorializing the Confederate Dead in South Carolina, 1866–1914," in *Art in the Lives of South Carolinians*, ed. David Moltke-Hansen (Charleston: Carolina Art Association, 1978), AH 1–8.

40. "Reburial of Confederates," *New York Times*, May 2, 1901, 5.

41. Janney, "One of the Best Loved North and South," 371. When La Salle Pickett died in 1931, Richmond's Hollywood Cemetery refused to bury her beside her husband. Instead her remains were placed in a mausoleum near Arlington National Cemetery. But in 1998 the Virginia Division of the UDC reinterred her remains next to her husband's at Hollywood (ibid., 391).

42. Conrad L. Eckert to Lyndon B. Johnson, April 1, 1964, Papers of the Civil War Centennial Commission, box 99, National Archives, Washington, D.C.

43. Bell Wiley to Edmund C. Gass, April 22, 1964, Papers of the Civil War Centennial Commission, box 99, National Archives, Washington, D.C.

44. "Bodies of Civil War Dead Moved to Provide New Veteran Graves," *New York Times*, June 29, 1980, A30. For the exhumation of the remains of sixty-seven Civil War soldiers, women, and children, mainly African American, from a national cemetery in south-central New Mexico, see "Soldiers' Remains Secretly Exhumed," *New York Times*, April 9, 2008, A19. Exhumation and reburial elsewhere occurred because widespread grave-looting was discovered.

45. "Man on a Mission to Get Recognition for Slaves Who Fought for the Union," MCT News Service, March 4, 2008, History Network News, Breaking News, March 5, 2008.

46. Quoted in Neff, *Honoring the Civil War Dead*, 10–11. See Daniel Aaron, *The Unwritten War: American Writers and the Civil War* (New York: Alfred A. Knopf, 1973), 62–72, in his chapter on Whitman.

47. Neil Harris, "The Battle for Grant's Tomb," *American Heritage* 36 (August 1985): 71–72, 74.

48. Ibid., 75–76.

49. Ibid., 77.

50. Ibid., 78–79.

51. Sumner, *Are We a Nation? Address of Hon. Charles Sumner . . . at the Cooper Institute, November 19, 1867* (New York: Young Men's Republican Union, 1867); my italics.

52. Melville Bell Grosvenor, "How James Smithson Came to Rest in the Institution He Never Knew," *Smithsonian Magazine* 6 ( January 1976): 31–33.

53. Ibid., 34.

54. Ibid., 34–35; S. P. Langley, "The Removal of the Remains of James Smithson," *Smithsonian Miscellaneous Collections* 45 (October 1903): 243–51.

55. Grosvenor, "How James Smithson Came to Rest," 35–36. See also *Proceedings of the Board of Regents for the Year Ending June 30, 1904* (Washington, D.C., 1905), xvi–xxxiv, 7–10; ibid for 1905 (Washington, D.C., 1906), xi–xii, xv, xix, 3, 5–6.

56. See Page Smith, *James Wilson: Founding Father, 1742–1798* (Chapel Hill: University of North Carolina Press, 1956), chap. 25; Geoffrey Seed, *James Wilson* (Millwood, N.Y.: KTO Press, 1978).

57. David W. Maxey, "The Translation of James Wilson," in *Journal of Supreme Court History: 1990 Yearbook of the Supreme Court Historical Society* (Washington, D.C.: [Blackwell], 1991), 29–31.

58. Ibid., 32–33; Smith, *James Wilson*, 390.

59. Maxey, "Translation of James Wilson," 33–34. The opinion written by Wilson argued that federal judicial power could extend to suits against one of the states initiated by citizens of another state or a foreign power. Within less than a generation the nationalistic Marshall Court diminished the force of the Eleventh Amendment, defending state sovereignty, by means of several rulings.

60. Maxey, "Translation of James Wilson," 34.

61. Ibid., 35–36.

62. Ibid., 36.

63. Ibid., 37–38.

64. Ibid., 38–39.

65. Ibid., 40–41.

66. Ibid., 41.

67. James Wilson, "Lectures on Law," in *The Works of James Wilson*, ed. Robert Green McCloskey (Cambridge, Mass.: Harvard University Press, 1967), 1:70–71.

68. H. Marion, *John Paul Jones' Last Cruise and Final Resting Place, the United States Naval Academy* (Washington, D.C.: George E. Howard, 1906), 11–12. This valuable volume includes dozens of photographs, showing scenes ranging from workmen unearthing Jones's coffin through every stage of the many eulogies and ceremonies attendant upon his exhumation, public display in Paris, Franco-American celebrations, and the trip to Cherbourg. Very clearly, an official photographer had been assigned to make a complete visual record of the process. See Charles de Gaulle, *Le fil de l'épée* (Paris: Berger-Levrauit, 1944).

69. Lincoln Lorenz, *John Paul Jones: Fighter for Freedom and Glory* (Annapolis, Md.: U.S. Naval Institute, 1943), 751–52.

70. Ibid., 753–54.

71. Ibid., 756.

72. Ibid., 755–56.

73. Ibid., 757–58.

74. Marion, *John Paul Jones' Last Cruise*, 33, 36.

75. Quoted in ibid., 21.

76. Ibid., 41, 45.

77. Ibid., 53, 56, 74.

78. John Morley, *Death, Heaven, and the Victorians* (Pittsburgh: University of Pittsburgh Press, 1971), 201.

79. Charles W. Stewart and others, *John Paul Jones: Commemoration at Annapolis, April 24, 1906* (Washington, D.C.: Government Printing Office, 1907), 12–13.

80. Ibid., 18–19.

81. Lorenz, *John Paul Jones*, 759, 765.

82. See Schantz, chap. 6, "The Court of Death," in *Awaiting the Heavenly Country*.

83. Alfred Frankenstein, *William Sidney Mount* (New York: Harry N. Abrams, 1975), 11, 260, 285, and the quotation at 248.

84. For a fascinating example of a lifelike painting of two dead children (1865), commissioned by an older sibling and based upon photographs, see Angela Miller, "Death and Resurrection in an Artist's Studio," *American Art* 20 (Spring 2006): 84–95, esp. 92–93. For a study of the residual fascination with images of the dead, especially dead children, during the late Victorian era, see Michael Lesy, *Wisconsin Death Trip* (New York: Pantheon, 1973).

CHAPTER FOUR

1. See John Mack Faragher, *Daniel Boone: The Life and Legend of an American Pioneer* (New York: Holt, 1992); Robert Morgan, *Boone: A Biography* (Chapel Hill, N.C.: Algonquin, 2007).

2. Following a visit by Mr. Peck in 1818, he reported that for "several years he [Boone] had kept his coffin constantly under the bunk in which he slept, and used to sit and regard it with a melancholy satisfaction. . . . And he felt already at rest, in knowing where his body was going to lie when it had finished its earthly service. That ridge overlooking the Missouri was never out of his mind." George Canning Hill, *Daniel Boone: The Pioneer of Kentucky* (New York: Worthington, 1890), 256.

3. Faragher, *Daniel Boone*, 354–55.

4. According to more than one early biographer, however, the men sent from Kentucky to dig up Boone's remains undertook a "holy mission of bearing him back to the land he had loved so well." W. H. Bogart, *Daniel Boone and the Hunters of Kentucky* (Auburn, N.Y.: Miller, Orton, and Mulligan, 1854), 384.

5. Faragher, *Daniel Boone*, 355–56.

6. Ibid., 356.

7. Ibid., 357–58.

8. Ibid., 358.

9. Ibid., 358–59.

10. Ibid., 359.

11. Ibid., 359–60. Two of the most widely read nineteenth-century biographies of Boone acknowledge that his original burial place in Missouri was "the grave he had chosen," yet neither book ever mentions Missouri's dismay and discontent with his removal to Frankfort. The 1890 volume assumes that Kentucky deserved the body even though Boone had made an explicit request on behalf of "the spot his own eyes had selected." See Bogart, *Daniel Boone and the Hunters*, 384–86; Hill, *Daniel Boone*, 259–61.

12. Faragher, *Daniel Boone*, 360–61.

13. Ibid., 361–62; "The Body in Daniel Boone's Grave May Not Be His," *New York Times*, July 21, 1983, C13.

14. See Kenneth Silverman, *Edgar Allan Poe: Mournful and Never Ending Remembrance* (New York: HarperCollins, 1991); Edward Wagenknecht, *Edgar Allan Poe: The Man behind the Legend* (New York: Oxford University Press, 1963).

15. Poe, "The Premature Burial," in *The Complete Works of Edgar Allan Poe*, ed. James A. Harrison (New York: AMS Press, 1965), vol. 5 overall, *Tales* 4:255, 257. For Poe's views concerning death and immortality, see Wagenknecht, *Edgar Allan Poe*, 210–15.

16. John C. Miller, "The Exhumation and Reburials of Edgar and Virginia Poe and Mrs. Clemm," *Poe Studies* 7 (December 1974): 46–47.

17. Ibid., 46.

18. Ibid., 47.

19. Ibid.

20. Ibid. In the late summer of 2008 Poe devotees who insist that he wrote his most important works in Philadelphia began seriously agitating to have his grave removed from Baltimore to Philadelphia. Ian Urbina, "Baltimore Has Poe; Philadelphia Wants Him," *New York Times*, September 6, 2008, A10.

21. Mary Jane Solomon, "Where the Somebodies Are Buried," *Washington Post*, October 25, 1991, 6.

22. "Grave of Miles Standish," *New York Times*, April 20, 1889, 5.

23. Richard W. Leopold, *Robert Dale Owen: A Biography* (Cambridge, Mass.: Harvard University Press, 1940).

24. Ibid.

25. Ibid., 414; Thomas C. Wheeler, ed., *A Vanishing America: The Life and Times of the Small Town* (New York: Holt, Rinehart, and Winston, 1964), 92.

26. William Conant Church, *The Life of John Ericsson* (New York: C. Scribner's Sons, 1907), 2:322–24.

27. Ibid., 325–26.
28. Quoted in ibid., 328.
29. Quoted in ibid., 329.
30. Ibid., 330–31.
31. Quoted in ibid., 332.
32. Ted P. Yeatman, *Frank and Jesse James: The Story behind the Legend* (Nashville: Cumberland House, 2000), 54–58.
33. Robertus Love, *The Rise and Fall of Jesse James* (New York: G. P. Putnam's Sons, 1926), esp. chaps. 6–7, 11–12, 14, 22, 25.
34. Ibid., ch. 26.
35. T .J. Stiles, *Jesse James: Last Rebel of the Civil War* (New York: Alfred A. Knopf, 2002), 377–78; Love, *Rise and Fall of Jesse James*, 366–70.
36. Love, *Rise and Fall*, 370–71.
37. Ibid., 371.
38. "Jesse James's Remains Disinterred and Removed," *New York Times*, June 30, 1902, 1.
39. Love, *Rise and Fall*, 377–81.
40. Yeatman, *Frank and Jesse James*, appendix H, 371–76.
41. Brenda Maddox, *D. H. Lawrence: The Story of a Marriage* (New York: Simon and Schuster, 1994).
42. Ibid., 286.
43. Ibid., 292.
44. Janet Byrne, *A Genius for Living: The Life of Frieda Lawrence* (New York: HarperCollins, 1995), 338–40, 350. Byrne refers to him as Angelino rather than Angelo.
45. Maddox, *D. H. Lawrence*, 499. For much of the saga that follows I am indebted to Brenda Maddox's careful but tongue-in-cheek account.
46. Ibid.
47. Ibid., 499–500. Byrne's narrative in *Genius for Living*, 363, 365–68, basically agrees with Maddox's version and adds some amusing anecdotes.
48. Maddox, *D. H. Lawrence*, 500.
49. Ibid.
50. Ibid., 501. A dancing party followed the dedication, at which a local Mexican orchestra hired by Frieda played and a bonfire was lit. "The guests—some were strangers who had arrived in response to an open notice placed by Frieda in a Santa Fe paper—feasted on hot dogs and red wine." Byrne, *Genius for Living*, 367–68.
51. Maddox, *D. H. Lawrence*, 500–501.
52. Cynthia Gorney, "Fitzgerald Reburied in Simple Ceremony," *Washington Post*, November 8, 1975, A15.
53. Solomon, "Where the Somebodies Are Buried," 7.
54. Ibid.; Gorney, "Fitzgerald Reburied," A15, A28.
55. Gilbert C. Fite, *Mount Rushmore* (Norman: University of Oklahoma Press, 1952), 220.
56. "Authorizing the Construction of a Crypt for the Remains of Gutzon Borglum," April 16, 1941, H.R. 3857, 77th Congress, First Session (Washington, D.C.: Government Printing Office, 1941), 1–12; Robert J. Casey and Mary Borglum, *Give the Man Room: The Story of Gutzon Borglum* (Indianapolis: Bobbs Merrill, 1952), 316–17.
57. Meryle Secrest, *Frank Lloyd Wright* (New York: Alfred A. Knopf, 1992).
58. Brendan Gill, *Many Masks: A Life of Frank Lloyd Wright* (New York: G. P. Putnam's Sons, 1987), 499.
59. Ibid., 514.
60. Secrest, *Frank Lloyd Wright*, 14–15.
61. Ibid., 16–18; Iver Peterson, "Reburial of Frank Lloyd Wright Touches Off Stormy Debate," *New York Times*, April 10, 1985, A14.
62. Peterson, "Reburial of Frank Lloyd Wright."
63. Ibid.
64. The Monona Terrace Convention Center finally got built in the later 1990s on Monona Bay.
65. Karl E. Meyer, "Frank Lloyd Wright Goes West," *New York Times*, April 19, 1985, A30.
66. Kara Swisher, "My Father's Homecoming," *Washington Post*, August 20, 1989, F1.

67. Ibid., F4.

68. Ibid. For a comparable yet different episode, see Amy Dickinson, "Father's Death Leaves Grieving Kin Split over His Final Resting Place," *Ithaca Journal*, March 26, 2008, 2C.

69. Lee Seldes, *The Legacy of Mark Rothko* (New York: Holt, Rinehart, and Winston, 1978).

70. Kathryn Shattuck, "Rothko Kin Sue to Transfer his Remains," *New York Times*, April 8, 2008, E1.

71. Ibid., E5. See Wilbur Zelinsky, "A Toponymic Approach to the Geography of American Cemeteries," *Names* 38 (September 1990): 209–29.

72. Kathryn Shattuck, "38 Years after Artist's Suicide, His Remains Are on the Move," *New York Times*, March 16, 2008, B5.

CHAPTER FIVE

1. Robert E. Cray Jr., "Memorialization and Enshrinement: George Whitefield and Popular Religious Culture, 1770–1850," *Journal of the Early Republic* 10 (Fall 1990): 343–44.

2. Ibid., 344–45. I am indebted to Cray's exhaustive monograph for most of what follows.

3. Ibid., 347.

4. Ibid., 348.

5. Ibid., 349; Alan Heimert, *Religion and the American Mind from the Great Awakening to the Revolution* (Cambridge, Mass.: Harvard University Press, 1966), 483.

6. Cray, "Memorialization and Enshrinement," 350–51.

7. Ibid., 351–52.

8. Ibid., 357.

9. Ibid., 357–58.

10. Herbert Asbury, *A Methodist Saint: The Life of Bishop Asbury* (New York: Alfred A. Knopf, 1927), 305; L. C. Rudolph, *Francis Asbury* (Nashville: Abingdon, 1966), 220.

11. Cray, "Memorialization and Enshrinement," 359–60.

12. Gary Laderman, *The Sacred Remains: American Attitudes toward Death, 1799–1883* (New Haven, Conn.: Yale University Press, 1996), 53–54.

13. Ibid., 76. The decomposition of Abraham Lincoln's corpse, especially his face, when displayed in New York City on April 24–25, 1865, became a major issue, though mainly for aesthetic reasons. See David Herbert Donald and Harold Holzer, eds., *Lincoln in the Times: The Life of Abraham Lincoln as Originally Reported in the New York Times* (New York: St. Martin's, 2005), 330–31.

14. Laderman, *Sacred Remains*, 51, 70–72, 169–70. For parallel sentiments arising slightly earlier in England, see John Morley, *Death, Heaven, and the Victorians* (Pittsburgh: University of Pittsburgh Press, 1971), 34–39.

15. Zachariah Allen, "Memorial of Roger Williams," paper read before the Rhode Island Historical Society, Providence, May 18, 1860, 1.

16. Ibid., 2

17. Ibid., 3–4.

18. Ibid., 6.

19. Ibid., 7.

20. Ibid., 8–9.

21. See Edmund S. Morgan, *Roger Williams: The Church and the State* (New York: Harcourt, Brace, and World, 1967); Edwin S. Gaustad, *Liberty of Conscience: Roger Williams in America* (Grand Rapids, Mich.: Eerdmans, 1991).

22. Julie Roy Jeffrey, *Converting the West: A Biography of Narcissa Whitman* (Norman: University of Oklahoma Press, 1991).

23. Clifford M. Drury, *Marcus and Narcissa Whitman and the Opening of Old Oregon* (Glendale, Calif.: Arthur H. Clark, 1973), 2:341–42.

24. Ibid., 342–43.

25. Ibid., 344.

26. Ibid., 344–45.

27. Robert J. Loewenberg, *Equality on the Oregon Frontier: Jason Lee and the Methodist Mission, 1834–1843* (Seattle: University of Washington Press, 1876).

28. Cornelius Brosnan, *Jason Lee: Prophet of the New Oregon* (New York: Macmillan, 1932), 323.

29. Ibid., appendix 8, "An Echo from the Past."

30. Moreland is quoted in "Memorial Services at Re-interment of Remains of Jason Lee. Salem, Oregon, June 15, 1906" (n.p., n.d.), 9; E. W. Potter, *Idaho: A Bicentennial History* (New York: W. W. Norton, 1977), 105.

31. Maynard J. Geiger, *The Life and Times of Fray Junípero Serra, O.F.M., or The Man Who Never Turned Back, 1713–1784*, 2 vols. (Washington, D.C.: Academy of American Franciscan History, 1959).

32. Kenneth M. King, *Mission to Paradise: The Story of Junípero Serra and the Missions of California* (Chicago: Franciscan Herald, 1975), 182–85.

33. Orvin Larson, *American Infidel: Robert J. Ingersoll* (New York: Citadel, 1962).

34. C. H. Cramer, *Royal Bob: The Life of Robert G. Ingersoll* (Indianapolis: Bobbs-Merrill, 1952), 257, 261–62, 264.

35. "Reburial for Ingersoll," *New York Times*, May 5, 1932, 22.

36. Edmund D. Cronon, *Black Moses: The Story of Marcus Garvey and the Universal Negro Improvement Association* (Madison: University of Wisconsin Press, 1955); Rupert Lewis and Maureen Warner-Lewis, *Garvey: Africa, Europe, the Americas* (Trenton, N.J.: Africa World Press, 1986, 1994).

37. Colin Grant, *Negro with a Hat: The Rise and Fall of Marcus Garvey and His Dream of Mother Africa* (New York: Oxford University Press, 2008).

38. Amy Jacques Garvey, *Garvey and Garveyism* (New York: Collier Macmillan, 1970), 289–90.

39. Ibid., 290–94.

40. John Henrik Clarke, *Marcus Garvey and the Vision of Africa* (New York: Random House, 1974), 344; "Garvey Reburial in Jamaica," *New York Times*, August 14, 1964, 6; Elton C. Fax, *Garvey: The Story of a Pioneer Black Nationalist* (New York: Dodd, Mead, 1972), 278–79.

41. See Bruce Henderson, *True North: Peary, Cook, and the Race to the Pole* (New York: W. W. Norton, 2005).

42. B. Drummond Ayres Jr., "Matt Henson, Aide at Pole, Rejoins Peary," *New York Times*, April 7, 1988, A16.

43. Ibid.

44. See http://www.matthewhenson.com/counter.htm and http://www.people.fas.harvard.edu/~counter/culture.html.

45. Ayres, "Matt Henson, Aide at Pole." For the significant case of Felix Longoria, a Mexican American soldier killed in the Philippines in 1945 who received honorific reburial at Arlington in 1949 through the efforts of Senator Lyndon Johnson, after being denied a place in a Texas cemetery, see http://www.tshaonline.org/handbook/online/articles/FF/vef1.html. I owe this reference to my colleague Maria Cristina Garcia.

46. Andrea E. Frohne, "The African Burial Ground in New York City: Manifesting and Representing Spirituality of Space" (PhD diss., SUNY Binghamton, 2002).

47. Anne-Marie E. Cantwell and Diana di Zerega Wall, *Unearthing Gotham: The Archaeology of New York City* (New Haven, Conn.: Yale University Press, 2001), chap. 16.

48. Cheryl LaRoche and Michael Blakey, "Seizing Intellectual Power: The Dialogue at the New York African Burial Ground," *Historical Archaeology* 31, no. 3 (1997): 84–106; Marilyn Yalom, *The American Resting Place: Four Hundred Years of History through Our Cemeteries and Burial Grounds* (Boston: Houghton Mifflin, 2008), 92.

49. Philip Freneau, *The Poems of Philip Freneau, Poet of the American Revolution*, ed. Fred Lewis Pattee (Princeton, N.J.: Princeton Historical Society, 1903), 2:369.

50. Thomas M. Allen, *A Republic in Time:*

*Temporality and Social Imagination in Nineteenth-Century America* (Chapel Hill: University of North Carolina Press, 2008), 50–52.

51. "Indian Remains from Dam Site to Be Reburied 'with Respect,'" *New York Times*, November 26, 1978, 71.

52. Douglas H. Ubelaker and Lauryn Guttenplan Grant, "Human Skeletal Remains: Preservation or Reburial?" *Yearbook of Physical Anthropology* 32 (1989): 249–87; "Repatriation: An Interdisciplinary Dialogue," special issue of *American Indian Quarterly* 20 (Spring 1996); "NAGPRA: Respectful Reburial Returns Remains to Proper Setting," *Cortez Journal*, April 25, 2006, http://www.cortezjournal.com/asp-bin/article.asp/article.

53. See Devon A. Mihesuah, ed., *Repatriation Reader: Who Owns American Indian Remains* (Lincoln: University of Nebraska Press, 2000), 123–68, 180–210; Robert Layton, ed., *Conflict in the Archaeology of Living Traditions* (London: Unwin Hyman, 1989), chaps. 11, 14, and 16; Jane Hubert, "A Proper Place for the Dead: A Critical Review of the 'Reburial Issue,'" *Journal of Indigenous Studies* 1, no. 1 (1989): 34–45.

54. "Illinois Museum to End Exhibit of Indian Remains," *New York Times*, January 5, 1990, A17; "Illinois to Shut an Exhibit of Indian Skeletons," *New York Times*, November 29, 1991, A30.

55. "Native American Reburials," *Christian Century* 107 (October 17, 1990): 928.

56. This information appeared in a brief list in the *New York Times*, November 5, 1975, 59.

57. "Osceola Reburial Urged," *New York Times*, September 1, 1947, 21. The post surgeon who attended Osceola's death cut off his head and kept it as a souvenir in his own home. He later sent it to another doctor in New York, who is believed to have lost it in a fire in 1866. See Alvin Josephy, *The Patriot Chiefs: A*

*Chronicle of American Indian Leadership* (New York: Viking, 1961), 208; chapter 6 covers the circumstances of Osceola's death.

58. "Osceola," in *Wikipedia*, http://en.wikipedia.org/wiki/Osceola. For the nineteenth-century story of Chief Lone Wolf the Elder (?–1879) and his determination to find and rebury the remains of his son, Tau-ankia, see J. Lee Jones Jr., *Red Raiders Retaliate: The Story of Lone Wolf the Elder (Guipagho), Famous Kiowa Indian Chief* (n.p.: Pioneer Book, 1980).

59. Robert M. Utley, *The Lance and the Shield: The Life and Times of Sitting Bull* (New York: Holt, 1993), 306–7.

60. Ibid., 312.

61. Ibid. Apache Chief Geronimo died a prisoner of war at Fort Sill, Oklahoma, in 1909. It is believed that Prescott S. Bush and some Yale classmates broke into the grave during World War I and made off with the skull, and it has reposed ever since in a glass case at Skull and Bones, a Yale secret society whose house is called The Tomb. Geronimo's heirs have brought suit for the recovery and repatriation of his skull. James C. McKinley Jr., "Geronimo's Heirs Sue Secret Yale Society over His Skull," *New York Times*, February 20, 1909, A13.

62. "Historians Contend Raiders Didn't Get Sitting Bull Bones," *New York Times*, November 11, 1984, 71.

63. Utley, *Lance and the Shield*, 313; "Bones of Sitting Bull Go South from One Dakota to the Other," *New York Times*, April 9, 1953, 29.

64. "Historians Contend Raiders Didn't Get Sitting Bull's Bones," 71.

65. David La Vere, *Looting Spiro Mounds: An American King Tut's Tomb* (Norman: University of Oklahoma Press, 2007).

66. Ibid., 13–14.

67. Ibid., 119–25, esp. 123.

68. Paula Pryce, *"Keeping the Lakes' Way": Reburial and the Re-creation of a*

*Moral World among an Invisible People* (Toronto: University of Toronto Press, 1999), 139.

69. Ibid., 140.

70. Quoted in ibid.

71. From the collection *North of Boston* in *Complete Poems of Robert Frost, 1949* (New York: Henry Holt, 1949), 52.

72. Cara Buckley, "After 100 Years, Tribe's Ancestors Head Home," *New York Times*, June 10, 2008, http://www.nytimes.com/2008/06/10/nyregion/10remains.html.

CHAPTER SIX

1. Henrietta Harrison, *The Making of the Republican Citizen: Political Ceremonies and Symbols in China, 1911–1929* (Oxford: Oxford University Press, 2000), 133–44.

2. Ibid., 207–9.

3. Ibid., 226–30. See also Marie-Claire Bergère, *Sun Yat-sen* (Stanford, Calif.: Stanford University Press, 1998), chap. 11. The whole event was carefully recorded and photographed at the time, and accounts of it appear in numerous memoirs.

4. Jeffrey Shumway, "'Sometimes Knowing How to Forget Is Also Having a Memory': The Repatriation of Juan Manuel de Rosas and the Healing of Argentina," in *Body Politics: Death, Dismemberment, and Memory in Latin America*, ed. Lyman L. Johnson (Albuquerque: University of New Mexico Press, 2004), 105–40, esp. 105, 126–27.

5. Ibid., 119–30. See also Donna J. Guy, "Life and the Commodification of Death in Argentina: Juan and Eva Perón," in *Body Politics*, ed. Johnson, 245–72.

6. Jon Lee Anderson, *Che Guevara: A Revolutionary Life* (New York: Grove, 1997), xv; Richard L. Harris, *Death of a Revolutionary: Che Guevara's Last Mission* (New York: W. W. Norton, 2007), 272–77.

7. See John Upton Terrell and Colonel George Walton, *Faint the Trumpet Sounds: The Life and Trial of Major Reno* (New York: David McKay, 1966).

8. "Major Reno to Be Reburied," *New York Times*, September 6, 1967, 31; Ottie W. Reno, *Reno and Apsaalooka Survive Custer* (New York: Cornwall, 1997), chaps. 39–40, esp. 294–303.

9. London *Telegraph*, December 11, 2007; History Network News, Breaking News, December 11, 2007.

10. See Michael Kammen, "Mourning for a Lost Captain: New York City Comes to Terms with the National Tragedy," in *Lincoln and New York*, ed. Harold Holzer (New York: New-York Historical Society, 2009), 223–57.

11. Patrick Marnham, *Resistance and Betrayal: The Death and Life of the Greatest Hero of the French Resistance* (New York: Random House, 2002); Alan Clinton, *Jean Moulin, 1899–1943: The French Resistance and the Republic* (New York: Palgrave, 2002), 1–2, 196–99.

12. The entire story is told in fascinating detail by Henry Rousso in *The Vichy Syndrome: History and Memory in France since 1944* (Cambridge, Mass.: Harvard University Press, 1991), 81–84.

13. Ibid., 84–86.

14. Ibid., 87–89; Pierre Péan, *Vies et morts de Jean Moulin: Éléments d'une biographie* (Paris: Fayard, 1998), chaps. 33–34, for a detailed French perspective.

15. Von Richthofen was Frieda Lawrence's cousin.

16. Robert Weldon Whalen, *Bitter Wounds: German Victims of the Great War, 1914–1939* (Ithaca, N.Y.: Cornell University Press, 1984), 28–29, 33. For British survivors' pilgrimages to the Western Front during the 1920s to pay homage to their war dead, see Tom Lawson, "'The Free-Masonry of Sorrow'? English National Identities and the Memorialization of the Great War in Britain, 1919–1931," *History and Memory*

20 (Spring 2008): 89–120, esp. 100 and
113. See also Jay Winter, *Sites of Memory:
The Great War in European Cultural History* (Cambridge: Cambridge University
Press, 1995).

17. Whalen, *Bitter Wounds*, 34.

18. Both quoted in ibid., 34–35. For the
many World War I memorials dedicated
by Serbia's King Alexander I during the
1920s and the intensification of Serbian
national sentiment, see Melissa Boko-
voy, "Scattered Graves, Ordered Cemeteries: Commemorating Serbia's Wars
of National Liberation, 1912–1918," in
*Staging the Past: The Politics of Com-
memoration in Habsburg Central Europe,
1848 to the Present*, ed. Nancy Wingfield
and Maria Bucur (West Lafayette, Ind.:
Purdue University Press, 2001), 236–54.
During the war the Serbs were allied
with Britain and France against Germany, the Habsburgs, and the Ottoman
Empire.

19. Marc Fisher, "Frederick: The Grave
Germany Split over Prussian's Reburial,"
*Washington Post*, August 17, 1991, C1.

20. Ibid., C5.

21. Nicholas Kulish, "A Postscript for a
Writer, 200 Years in the Works," *New
York Times*, May 9, 2008, A8.

22. Ibid.; "Where's Schiller?" *New York
Times*, May 5, 2008, E2.

23. Kulish, "Postscript for a Writer," A8;
Nicholas Kulish, "2 More Skulls, but
Still No Schiller," *International Herald
Tribune*, May 9, 2008, 3.

24. Willemien Spook, "In These Ken-
nemerdunes Sleep Our Dead," *Haarlems
Dagblad*, May 4, 1993. Translated by
Donata Trace de Reus of the University
of Northumbria for the Dunes' website.

25. Ibid. I am grateful to Elisabeth Hop-
perus Buma for providing me with the
journalistic account and information
about the ongoing observance.

26. Ismail Kadare, *The General of the Dead
Army* (New York: New Amsterdam
Books, 1991), 181.

27. Ibid., 146.

28. Ibid., 130–31.

29. Ibid., 10.

30. Ibid., 228.

31. Ibid., 235, 249.

32. *Deutsche Welle*, May 27, 2008, posted
on History Network News, Breaking
News, May 29, 2008.

33. Sergio Luzzatto, *The Body of Il Duce:
Mussolini's Corpse and the Fortunes of
Italy* (New York: Metropolitan Books,
2005), 92–112.

34. Ibid., 105–12.

35. Ibid., 117–18.

36. Ibid., 207–11. On p. 210 there is a vivid
photograph of the sarcophagus, a bust
of Mussolini above it, fasces right and
left of the portrait, and a guest book
filled with signatures on a table in
front of the railing. For the ongoing
fetishization of Mussolini's grave by admirers, especially young ones, see Geert
Mak, *In Europe: Travels through the
Twentieth Century* (New York: Vintage,
2008), 297–98.

37. Simon Sebag Montefiore, *Young Stalin*
(New York: Alfred A. Knopf, 2007),
191–94, the quotation at 193.

38. Georges Bortoli, *Death of Stalin* (New
York: Praeger, 1975), 160–63; H. Mont-
gomery Hyde, *Stalin: The History of a
Dictator* (New York: Farrar, Straus, and
Giroux, 1997), 605.

39. Hyde, *Stalin*, 605–6; Bortoli, *Death of
Stalin*, 196.

40. For excellent context, see Alice Freifeld,
"The Cult of March 15: Sustaining
the Hungarian Myth of Revolution,
1849–1999," in *Staging the Past: The Poli-
tics of Commemoration in Habsburg Central
Europe, 1848 to the Present*, ed. Nancy
Wingfield and Maria Bucur (West
Lafayette, Ind.: Purdue University
Press, 2001), esp. 265–69 (for Kossuth),
and 270–73, 276 (for Petőfi).

41. But see James W. Loewen, *Lies across
America: What Our Historic Sites Get
Wrong* (New York: New Press, 1999).

42. Susan Gal, "Bartók's Funeral: Representations of Europe in Hungarian Political Rhetoric," *American Ethnologist* 18 (August 1991): 449.

43. Ibid., 450.

44. Alex Ross, *The Rest Is Noise: Listening to the Twentieth Century* (New York: Farrar, Straus, and Giroux, 2007), 88–90, 94–97, 121–22, 284, 327. For American perceptions, see Tibor Frank, "The Changing Image of Hungary in the United States," *Hungarian Quarterly* 38 (Winter 1997): 116–24.

45. Gal, "Bartók's Funeral," 451–52.

46. Ibid.

47. István Rév, *Retroactive Justice: Prehistory of Post-Communism* (Stanford, Calif.: Stanford University Press, 2005), 103.

48. Ibid., 24–25.

49. Ibid., 25–26.

50. Ibid., 19–21, 24–25.

51. Ibid., 28–29.

52. Freifeld notes that the Hungarian Revolution of 1989 was the most historically minded of all the revolutions that took place in 1989 ("Cult of March 15").

53. Rév, *Retroactive Justice*, 44–45.

54. See Frances FitzGerald, *America Revised: History Schoolbooks in the Twentieth Century* (Boston: Little, Brown, 1979); James W. Loewen, *Lies My Teacher Told Me: Everything Your American History Textbook Got Wrong* (New York: New Press, 1995); Gary B. Nash, Charlotte Crabtree, and Ross E. Dunn, *History on Trial: Culture Wars and the Teaching of the Past* (New York: Alfred A. Knopf, 1997). Even well-educated figures like John and Jacqueline Kennedy preferred to read history that was heroic and inspiring rather than disillusioning. See Sam Tanenhaus, "A Fumbled Handoff of the Torch," *New York Times*, January 25, 2009, Opinion sec., 2.

55. Ian Fisher, "Italian Saint Stirs Up a Mix of Faith and Commerce," *New York Times*, April 25, 2008, A9.

56. Ibid.

57. *The Independent* (UK), March 9, 2008, reported on the History News Network, Breaking News, March 9, 2008. For one of the many Web sites still devoted to his memory in 2009, see http://www.padrepio.com.

58. London *Telegraph*, July 15, 2008, reported in History News Network, Breaking News, July 16, 2008.

59. Svinurayi Joseph Muringaniza, "Heritage That Hurts: The Case of the Grave of Cecil John Rhodes in the Matopos National Park, Zimbabwe," in *The Dead and Their Possessions: Repatriation in Principle, Policy, and Practice*, ed. Cressida Fforde et al. (London: Routledge, 2002), 317–25.

60. Ibid.

61. Ibid.

62. John Noble Wilford, "Stonehenge Began as Cemetery, Data Shows," *New York Times*, May 30, 2008, A11.

63. Ibid.; "For Centuries Stonehenge Was a Burial Site," Associated Press, May 29, 2008, posted on History News Network, Breaking News, May 29, 2008.

64. "Bury Lenin's Body, Says Gorbachev," *The Independent* (UK), June 5, 2008, reported on History News Network, Breaking News, June 6, 2008. See the prescient comment by Ernesto Laclau: "The cycle of events which opened with the Russian Revolution has definitely closed . . . as a force of irradiation in the collective memory of the international left. . . . The corpse of Leninism, stripped of all the trappings of power, now reveals its pathetic and deplorable reality." Laclau, *New Reflections on the Revolution of Our Time* (London: Verso, 1990), ix. See Heather Pringle, *The Mummy Congress: Science, Obsession, and the Everlasting Dead* (New York: Hyperion, 2001), 278–82.

65. With the passage of time, mummification in Egypt became partially "democratized." As the art of embalming became perfected, people other than

kings and queens were increasingly mummified. See Pringle, *Mummy Congress*, 41–42.

66. In a notable coincidence, Père Lachaise was created in 1804 and the Congressional Cemetery in Washington in 1807—both designed to be the new type of garden-style cemetery within city limits, an improvement upon the spatially crowded urban graveyards of the past but not yet the suburban cemeteries portended by Mount Auburn, Massachusetts, in 1831.

67. Richard Wilbur, "For the New Railway Station in Rome," in *Things of This World* (1956), in Wilbur, *New and Collected Poems* (San Diego: Harcourt, Brace, Jovanovich, 1988), 277–78. The poem has eight stanzas. For reasons that remain unclear, the final two are set in quotation marks. This is one.

68. Alexis de Tocqueville, *Democracy in America*, ed. Isaac Kramnick (New York: Penguin, 2003), 464, 468.

69. Ibid., 742.

70. See Jean Heffer and Jeanine Rovet, eds., *Why Is There No Socialism in the United States?* (Paris: École des Hautes Études en Sciences Sociales, 1988), 37–85; Louis Hartz, *The Liberal Tradition in America* (New York: Harcourt, Brace, 1955); Lionel Trilling, *The Liberal Imagination: Essays on Literature and Society* (New York: Viking, 1950), vii.

# INDEX

Page references in italics refer to illustrations.